I0822073

HENRY ADAMS
IN THE SECESSION CRISIS

HENRY ADAMS

IN THE SECESSION CRISIS

DISPATCHES TO THE *Boston Daily Advertiser*, DECEMBER 1860–MARCH 1861

EDITED AND ANNOTATED BY

MARK J. STEGMAIER

Louisiana State University Press *Baton Rouge*

Published by Louisiana State University Press

Manufactured in the United States of America
First printing

DESIGNER: Michelle A. Neustrom
TYPEFACE: Chaparral Pro
PRINTER: McNaughton & Gunn, Inc.
BINDER: Acme Bookbinding

LIBRARY OF CONGRESS CATALOGING-IN-PUBLICATION DATA

Adams, Henry, 1838–1918.
Henry Adams in the secession crisis : dispatches to the Boston daily advertiser, December 1860–March 1861 / edited and annotated by Mark J. Stegmaier.
p. cm.
Includes bibliographical references and index.
ISBN 978-0-8071-4351-3 (cloth : alk. paper) — ISBN 978-0-8071-4352-0 (pdf) — ISBN 978-0-8071-4353-7 (epub) — ISBN 978-0-8071-4354-4 (mobi)
1. Secession—United States—History. 2. Adams, Henry, 1838–1918—Correspondence. 3. United States—Politics and government—1857–1861. 4. United States—History—Civil War, 1861–1865—Causes. 5. Press and politics—History—19th century. 6. Historians—United States—Correspondence. 7. Boston daily advertiser (Boston, Mass. : 1836) I. Stegmaier, Mark Joseph, 1945– II. Title.
E440.5.A235 2012
973.7'13—dc23

2011037856

The paper in this book meets the guidelines for permanence and durability of the Committee on Production Guidelines for Book Longevity of the Council on Library Resources. ♾

for
my grandson, Ryan James Stegmaier
and
my granddaughter, Micaela Grace Stegmaier

CONTENTS

ACKNOWLEDGMENTS

In the preparation of this volume, I am indebted to numerous individuals and institutions for assistance. Foremost among these is my wife, Diane, who has been research assistant, travel arranger, manuscript typist, and my most constructive critic. She not only endured the constant revisions which I regularly foisted upon her but also a computer–word processor–printer system at home which constantly decided to do things its way rather than hers. Dr. Vivian Thomlinson of Cameron University's English Department carefully read through the *Advertiser* letters and provided insights on their stylistic aspects. Cameron University, through its Academic Research Committee and Katherine D. Lacy Endowed Lectureship, provided generous travel and research grants which made the project doable.

The staffs of the Boston Public Library, Massachusetts Historical Society, and Boston Athenaeum contributed generously of their time and resources. The same friendly service was provided by librarians at the Houghton, Widener, and Lamont libraries at Harvard University. I would also like to thank the library staffs of the New York Public Library, the Free Library of Philadelphia, the Collections Deposit Library of the University of Texas at Austin, the Ohio Historical Society, the Cincinnati Public Library, the Historic New Orleans Collection, the University of Michigan Museum of Art, and the Detroit Institute of Art for their valuable assistance.

The staff of the Library of Congress, particularly those in the Manuscripts Division, deserve thanks for facilitating many hours of valuable research there. As on earlier occasions, William H. Davis of the National Archives searched for and provided copies of pertinent documents.

INTRODUCTION

Henry Brooks Adams, not yet 23 years old and just back from a bit of study and a lot of socializing and travel in Europe, served in Washington as private secretary to his father, Rep. Charles Francis Adams (R-MA), during the "Great Secession Winter" of 1860–61 and the second session of the 36th Congress. Henry Adams would write four different accounts of his experiences in those tense and exciting months from December 1860 to March 1861. Historians are familiar with three of the four accounts: the one in his famous autobiographical work *The Education of Henry Adams,* first published in 1907; his essay "The Great Secession Winter of 1860–61," penned immediately after the event and intended to be a magazine article but not actually published until 1910; and the letters which Henry wrote from Washington to his brother Charles Francis Adams, Jr., in those turbulent days, which were published in the J. C. Levenson et al. six-volume edition of Henry Adams's personal correspondence in the 1980s. But there was a fourth account of the secession crisis written by Henry Adams, lengthier and including more information and commentary than the other three, with which modern historians have no familiarity and which few probably even know that Adams wrote. This account, presented in this volume for the first time since its original publication, consists of the twenty-one unsigned letters which Adams wrote from Washington as a correspondent for the *Boston Daily Advertiser.*[1]

J. C. Levenson and the other editors of the Adams correspondence chose not to include Adams's letters to the *Advertiser* in their six-volume edition (or in two supplemental volumes of additional correspondence). In his introduction to the *Letters,* Professor Levenson wrote that the editors decided to exclude the *Advertiser* correspondence because it was "straightforward political journalism"[2] rather than the personal correspondence to which the editors devoted their volumes. Further on in the first volume, at the beginning of the section containing Henry Adams's letters to his brother during the secession crisis, Levenson declared that the account of political affairs in the personal letters of those months was "far more valuable than anything in his newspaper correspondence." Two of Adams's modern biographers, Ernest Samuels (one of the editors of the *Letters* volumes) and Edward Chalfant (editor of a modern edition of *The Education of Henry Adams*), also tended to emphasize the value of Adams's personal letters to his brother rather than his newspaper correspondence for the *Advertiser.*[3]

This judgment, I believe, represents a considerable undervaluation of the importance of Adams's *Advertiser* letters as an account of that momentous Winter session in Washington. I think it is a mistake to dismiss this longest of Adams's four written records of the secession crisis as if it contained a merely colorless record of events written without style or emotion or opinion. Indeed, the *Advertiser* letters depicted events and participants in the crisis with spirit, insight, humor, and, sometimes, strong bias. Overall, Adams's newspaper correspondence is as valuable a tool for the modern researcher studying the Secession Winter as almost any other contemporary source, especially for the study of that group of Republicans who, while wishing to remain steadfastly loyal to the party's platform and doctrines, also sought to find compromise solutions to issues if they possibly could. Adams was a good writer, even at that early stage of his career, and his *Advertiser* letters were both readable and informative. And, unlike many of his fellow Washington correspondents, Adams concentrated his analysis and description entirely on the main events–the fate of the Union and what the Washington politicians and the southern states would do in the wake of Abraham Lincoln's election as president of the United States. Many Washington correspondents attempted to recount everything that went on in Washington, from the significant to the trivial. Adams ignored the trivial, everyday, merely local news; he realized that he was living through and writing about an extraordinary epoch in U.S. history, and he concentrated his correspondence to the *Advertiser* on aspects of the crisis which developed into the Civil War a few months later. His capacity as secretary to an important member of the House provided young Adams with a special vantage point among Washington letter-writers, but it was a privileged position which Adams could not openly acknowledge in his letters nor even allude to in very much detail, for fear of compromising the anonymity he jealously guarded and the important work in which his father was engaged. Henry Adams was not one of the correspondents accredited to sit in the reporters' gallery of either the Senate or the House; he did report on speeches in both chambers, but did so as an observer in the public galleries.[4]

Henry Adams was always conscious of the fact that he had been born into one of the most illustrious families in the history of the early American republic. Great grandfather John Adams had been a major participant in the American Revolutionary era and had become the second president of the United States. Grandfather John Quincy Adams had served as U.S. minister to Russia during the War of 1812, had then achieved greatness as secretary of state, and had become the sixth president of the United States. The tradition of diplomatic brilliance was destined to continue during the Civil War with the distinguished accomplishments of Charles Francis Adams as U.S. minister to Great Britain.

Young Henry Adams grew up in a home environment where notable political and cultural leaders were family acquaintances and frequent visitors. Not blessed with as strong a physical constitution as his two older brothers, Charles Francis, Jr., and John Quincy II, Henry found great satisfaction in reading through the great literary works in his father's and grandfather's libraries. After receiving a classical education at Mr. Dixwell's school in Boston and then matriculating to Harvard, from which he graduated in 1858, the young man decided to study law in Germany. Although law was virtually the Adams family profession, Henry never felt very comfortable in the study of that subject, especially in Berlin where he had difficulty mastering the language. By the spring of 1860 Adams decided to give up his pretensions of interest in the law and he began traveling in Italy and France. He described these journeys and his meeting the great Italian revolutionary Garibaldi in personal letters to his brother Charles, who then decided to publish these reports in the newspapers.

In October 1860 Henry Adams returned to his family in Massachusetts and began studying law again, this time as a clerk under the tutelage of Horace Gray. His father may have recognized his son's lack of enthusiasm for this study and therefore saved him from it by requesting Henry to serve as his private secretary in Washington. Charles Francis

Adams was just finishing his freshman term in the House of Representatives and had been reelected for another term in Congress in the momentous 1860 election. Everyone realized that the short second session of the 36th Congress, from the beginning of December 1860 to March 3, 1861, would play a crucial role in determining whether the nation would remain united until Abraham Lincoln assumed office as president on March 4 or would divide up into separate confederacies of North and South. If the South did secede out of fear of Lincoln and the Republicans in control of the federal government, how many slave states would go with the South or remain aligned with the North? And if secession occurred, would that process be peaceable, or would it result in civil war? These were the questions on almost everyone's minds and lips. The Secession Winter was upon them.

Henry Adams knew that he would be located at the center of developments in Washington, D.C., and he possessed an abiding desire to write a record of his experience there. Already having sent lengthy reports on European affairs to this brother and attracted by the idea of putting into words a record of events which later historians might find useful, Henry told his brother Charles that he would like to try reporting for a newspaper. Charles Jr. had written some letters for the *Boston Daily Advertiser* while in Washington earlier in 1860. The *Advertiser* enjoyed the largest circulation of any newspaper in Massachusetts, and its publisher, Charles Hale, was a friend of the Adams family. Henry and Charles Jr. therefore worked out a deal with Hale whereby Henry Adams, as a fledgling Washington correspondent, would send regular letters to the *Advertiser* as an unpaid volunteer. Unlike many such reporters who signed their correspondence with initials or letters of the alphabet or pseudonyms of various sorts, Adams chose to leave his *Advertiser* letters unsigned. When informed of the arrangement with Hale, Charles Francis Adams did not object to his son's letter-writing, probably with the understanding on Henry's part that he would write nothing which might embarrass or compromise his father's position as a member of Congress.[5]

In editing the letters which Henry Adams wrote for the *Boston Advertiser,* care has been taken to transcribe the letters exactly as they appeared in the newspaper. Unfortunately Adams's original versions of these letters no longer exist, and Adams complained that publisher Hale deleted his spicier criticisms of some individuals. In one case Hale even suppressed one of Adams's letters altogether. The historian has to deal with the evidence which does exist, and that evidence consists of the newspaper copies of Adams's letters. Where obvious errors of spelling or punctuation occurred in the original publication, the errors have been transcribed and corrections provided within brackets.

Henry Adams, of course, wrote his letters to inform an audience generally familiar with the events and persons which were the topics of his Washington correspondence. Modern readers will be less familiar with the material, removed as they are over 150 years from those times. Therefore, I have extensively annotated the letters in order to explain some of Adams's subject matter. In doing so I have utilized information often included in the colorfully detailed accounts written by Adams's fellow Washington correspondents, along with other primary and secondary sources.

Together, the Adams letters, the annotations, and the few essays I have written in order to bridge over certain gaps should assist the reader in gaining a more complete understanding of the Secession Winter Congress, the issues it faced, and the leaders who had to deal with the crisis. The picture of the crisis which emerges here is not a comprehensive one. It is necessarily weighted toward the view of the events held by the more moderate wing of the Republicans who strove for a viable compromise which would at least prevent the secession of the Upper South. Congressman Adams became part of this group, and his son's *Advertiser* letters reflected that emphasis. The letters and annotations portray the leaders and views of the other political factions in the Secession Winter, but the moderate Republicans—a minority of their party bloc in Congress—and their southern Unionist allies occupy the center stage in this volume.

NOTES

1. For the first three accounts, see Henry Adams, *The Education of Henry Adams: A Centennial Version,* ed. by Edward Chalfant and Conrad E. Wright (Boston: Massachusetts Historical Society, 2007), 76–85;

Henry Adams, *The Great Secession Winter of 1860–61, and Other Essays,* ed. by George Hochfield (New York: Sagamore Press, 1958), 1–31 (hereafter cited as H. Adams, "Great Secession Winter"); and J. C. Levenson et al., eds., *The Letters of Henry Adams,* 6 vols. (Cambridge: Belknap Press of Harvard University Press, 1982–1988), 1: 203–234 (hereafter cited as Levenson et al., eds., *Henry Adams Letters*). A slightly abridged edition of these letters earlier appeared in Worthington C. Ford, ed., *Letters of Henry Adams (1858–1891)* (Boston: Houghton Mifflin Co., 1930), 62–89.

2. Levenson et al., eds., *Henry Adams Letters,* 1: xv.

3. Ibid., 203. For the accounts of Adams in the Secession Winter by his modern biographers, see: Ernest Samuels, *The Young Henry Adams* (Cambridge: Belknap Press of Harvard University Press, 1965), 81–90; and Edward Chalfant, *Both Sides of the Ocean: A Biography of Henry Adams: His First Life, 1838–1862* (Hamden, CT: Archon Books, 1982), 188–231.

4. For lists of the correspondents assigned seats in the press galleries of the U.S. Senate and House in this session, see: *Congressional Directory for the Second Session of the Thirty-Sixth Congress of the United States of America* (Washington, 1861), 32–33; and *Department Directory and Register of Officers in the Service of the United States in the City of Washington* (Washington: W H. Moore, Printer, 1861), 46–47. Copies of both of these are in Y4.P93/1: 36–2, box 6072, Record Group 287 (Publications of the U.S. Government), National Archives. For a good introduction to the Washington reporters, see Donald A. Ritchie, *Press Gallery: Congress and the Washington Correspondents* (Cambridge: Harvard University Press, 1991).

5. Levenson et al., eds., *Henry Adams Letters,* 1: 207, n. 10; and Chalfant, *Both Sides of the Ocean,* 143, 190. In his December 9 letter to his brother, Henry actually suggested that he would provide his historic record in private letters to him, but his writing a record for future historical use also applied to his *Advertiser* letters. Levenson et al., eds., *Henry Adams Letters,* 1: 204.

HENRY ADAMS
IN THE SECESSION CRISIS

LETTER 1

Boston Daily Advertiser, December 7, 1860

Letter from Washington
[FROM OUR OWN CORRESPONDENT]

Washington, Dec. 4, 1860

A great crowd assembled at the Capitol Monday morning to see the meeting of what many people think is to be the last session of Congress. But no one would have supposed from the appearance of the House that anything extraordinary was to take place, or that any Cataline [*sic*][1] was plotting treason and war under our very eyes. The organization passed over as easily as in the best days of the republic. The members, even those from South Carolina, selected and took possession of their desks and drew their pay and mileage, or as much of it as they could get,[2] as good-naturedly and as quietly as any one could wish. Perhaps the feeling that the struggle was inevitable made all parties the less ready to hurry it, or perhaps the respite of one day on account of the non-appearance of the President's Message, was a relief, and raised their spirits. At all events there was no fight and the two Houses adjourned quietly to wait twenty-four hours longer.

Today the Message made its appearance punctually. Forney[3] himself read the first part, which relates to the internal affairs, and the House listened with the greatest attention. It was, however, a curious, not a respectful attention, for as soon as the second part, that on foreign affairs, was reached, Forney handed it over to his subordinate, and no one listened to anything further.

The reading over, Mr. Boteler[4] of Virginia, introduced a resolution referring the first part of the message to a committee of one from each State, and after a good deal of scrambling on the democratic side of the House, the ayes and noes were ordered.

It being the settled policy of the republicans now to place themselves simply on the Constitution and ignore the whole secession movement as far as possible, this resolution of Mr. Boteler's seemed rather to puzzle some of them. Its effect would be to take the question for the present out of the House and leave it to a large and cumbrous committee of which the republicans could not have the control. Quite a number of the staunchest men therefore voted against it, preferring, I suppose, to leave the subje[c]t to its natural course through the committee of the whole house, as a matter of which they themselves were not afraid, and knew no reason why any one else should be. The majority, however, voted for the resolution though not precisely liking it, on the ground, I suppose, that it would relieve the House for a time; that as for the committee, it was just as well that the republicans should not control it; and as to the measure itself, as it would probably pass at all events, it would be as great a mistake to oppose it as it would to propose it. They were neither called upon to lead nor to impede here.[5]

So the resolution was adopted and the members from South Carolina and some other States, announced their reasons for not voting.[6] They were very good natured about it, however, and no one seemed to care a great deal. So far as I can learn, the feeling here is that nothing will do any good until secession has been tried. If South Carolina has got this idea so firmly fixed in her head—that free-trade, and the African slave trade, and an independent government will make her prosperous and happy,—no compromise and no kindness will prevent her from trying it. This at least is the impression among the stronger republicans, and so they sat quietly and listened without any display of feeling, to the declaration that South Carolina is out of the Union.[7]

In the middle of the talk, Tom Florence[8] moved to adjourn, and the House was adjourned in spite of itself. Speaker Pennington[9] quietly leaving the chair, as he occasionally likes to do when he thinks business enough has been done, at which every one laughs and acquiesces. So this matter is disposed of for the present, and we must now wait some new excitement.

In the Senate today, Mr. Crittenden punished Mr. Clingman severely,[10] and as in the House, the talking was confined to the Southern side. The wish on the part of the republicans to abstain from any action that shall complicate matters further, is very plain, and is understood to be universal. Of course the rumors about compromises and yielding on their part are mere clap-trap, as far as any one can know. We do not believe a word of it here. So far as the republicans are concerned, the lead is in honest and cautious hands, and among them there is great confidence that all will come out right in the end.[11]

NOTES

1. Adams here misspells the name of the infamous Roman conspirator Lucius Sergius Catilina, or "Catiline," who plotted to grab power in Rome in 63 B.C. However, the great orator and consul Marcus Tullius Cicero rallied leaders and populace against him in four brilliant speeches. Catiline's conspiracy was defeated and he was killed. Young Adams would have studied and translated Cicero's orations against Catiline during his years at Epes S. Dixwell's school prior to Adams's entrance into Harvard. He had mentioned his fondness for Cicero in a letter to his brother Charles while Henry had been in Berlin in April 1859. Levenson et al., eds., *Henry Adams Letters,* 1: 31, 34. Adams referred to Catiline again in Letter 14, below; and in his "Great Secession Winter" essay, 7.

2. Adams refers here to the dire financial straits in which the federal government found itself in the last years under President James Buchanan and Secretary of the Treasury Howell Cobb of Georgia. The Panic of 1857 and reduced federal revenues from the lower Tariff of 1857 had turned a treasury surplus into a deficit of over $50 million by December 1860. The election of Abraham Lincoln to the presidency in early November had added to the economic gloom; fears that the South would repudiate its debts to northern financial institutions caused business interests in New York and elsewhere to lose confidence, and this set off a paralyzing mini-panic after the election. Frederick J. Blue, *Salmon P. Chase: A Life in Politics* (Kent, OH: Kent State University Press, 1987), 143; and Bray Hammond, *Sovereignty and an Empty Purse: Banks and Politics in the Civil War* (Princeton, NJ: Princeton University Press, 1970), 26–32.

Members of Congress experienced the government's economic pinch at the beginning of the 2nd session when they went to draw their pay for the months between the adjournment of the previous session and the beginning of this one. Under ordinary circumstances, each member would have collected $1,300 plus mileage. However, since the U.S. Treasury had allotted only $200,000 for pay and mileage for House members to collect at the start of the 2nd session, this time each House member stood to receive only $600 and no mileage. This situation especially presented a hardship for those who had traveled a long distance, such as the delegate from New Mexico Territory, Miguel Otero; he wrote a letter to a friend in Santa Fe complaining about the financial detriment he suffered because of this. Otero wrote that he had not paid his hotel bill in Washington for three months and saw little prospect of being able to do so anytime soon. See the reports from Washington correspondents in *New York Daily Tribune,* December 5, 1860, and especially the one by "Zed" (George W. Bagby) in Richmond *Daily Dispatch,* December 5, 1860; and Miguel A. Otero to Charles P. Clever, December 10, 1860, William G. Ritch Collection, Henry E. Huntington Library, San Marino, CA.

3. John W. Forney was clerk of the House and the editor and owner of the Philadelphia *Press,* for which he wrote as their Washington correspondent under the pseudonym "Occasional."

4. Rep. Alexander R. Boteler was a member of the American (Know-Nothing) Party and a southern proponent of compromise in the secession crisis. Newspaper correspondents originally reported that Boteler's collegaue Rep. Horace Maynard (A-TN) would move for the Committee of Thirty-three to be appointed. But, since Boteler represented the Virginia district which included Harpers Ferry, the pro-compromise members may have decided that, if Boteler moved for the appointment of the compromise committee, Republicans might favorably react to it as an olive branch offered from the area where abolitionist John Brown had conducted his notorious and fateful raid in October 1859. Boteler stated later in the session that Maynard, Warren Winslow (D-NC), and John Cochrane (D-NY) had each prepared resolutions calling for the appointment of the committee, had he not chosen to do so. The *New York Herald* provided a detailed account of Cochrane's prospective resolution. U.S. Congress, *Congressional Globe,* 36th Congress, 2nd session, 6, 316 (hereafter cited as *Cong. Globe*); *Baltimore Daily Exchange,* December 4, 1860; *Charleston Mercury,* December 3, 1860; *Louisville Daily Journal,* December

7, 1860; *New York Herald*, December 3, 4, 1860; New York *World*, December 3, 1860; and Roy F. Nichols, *The Disruption of American Democracy* (New York: Macmillan Co., 1948), 398.

5. This rationale for Republicans who voted for Boteler's resolution accords with the views of Rep. Charles Francis Adams. C. F. Adams, Diary, December 4, 1860, roll 76, part 1, *Microfilm of the Adams Papers: Owned by the Adams Manuscript Trust and Deposited in the Massachusetts Historical Society* (Boston: Massachusetts Historical Society, 1954–1959). Hereafter cited as *MAP.* In his diary entry, Adams stated his belief that voting for the Boteler resolution would get the volatile issues out of the House and "give leisure for reflection." Since the roll of the House was called alphabetically and Adams's was the first name called, Adams quite naturally believed that his lead in voting for the resolution convinced many of his fellow Republicans to do likewise. The resolution passed by a vote of 145-38; most Republicans did vote for it, but all of the nay votes were also Republicans. The House Republicans who voted against the Boteler resolution may have shared the attitude expressed toward it by Sen. Lyman Trumbull (R-IL) that the resolution was "an admission that to conduct the government on the principles on which we carried the election would be wrong." Lyman Trumbull to Abraham Lincoln, December 4, 1860, Lincoln Papers, Series 1, Manuscripts Division, Library of Congress; and *Cong. Globe*, 36: 2: 6–7.

6. *Cong. Globe*, 36: 2: 7.

7. Stated by Rep. W. Porcher Miles (D-SC). Ibid. Samuels, *Young Henry Adams*, 84, and Chalfant, *Both Sides of the Ocean*, 194, both quote Henry Adams's comment in this paragraph on South Carolina's absolute determination to try secession, while Chalfant on 193 also quotes Adams's observation that the Republican members maintained their silence when Miles made his declaration. Another correspondent, however, noticed that Miles's statement sparked a good deal of laughter and ridicule at the time. This same writer also noticed that border slave state Union men expressed great anger afterwards that South Carolina was trying to drag them into secession. *Cincinnati Daily Commercial*, December 8, 1860.

8. Rep. Thomas B. Florence was a strongly pro-compromise Pennsylvania Democrat; he supported President Buchanan's administration and represented one of the Philadelphia congressional districts.

9. William Pennington, moderate Republican from New Jersey, had been elected speaker in the tumultuous early months of the 1st session of the 36th Congress. The principal Republican candidate for the post, Rep. John Sherman of Ohio, proved too controversial and too unacceptable to southerners after it was shown that he had signed an endorsement of Hinton Rowan Helper's 1857 book *The Impending Crisis of the South: How to Meet It.* Helper's book had urged southern non-slaveholding whites to overthrow the planter elites, free the slaves, and send the blacks back to Africa.

10. Sen. John J. Crittenden of Kentucky occupied the seat once held by the "Great Pacificator" Henry Clay and would author the most prominently debated, most comprehensive compromise plan during this session. Originally a Whig follower of Clay's, Crittenden, after the Whig Party disintegrated in the 1850s, had become a member of the Opposition (Know-Nothing) bloc in Kentucky politics and had supported the Constitutional Union ticket of John Bell of Tennessee for president and Edward Everett of Massachusetts for vice-president (both former Whigs) in the election of 1860. Sen. Thomas L. Clingman, North Carolina Democrat, once had been a Whig but in the early 1850s had switched parties and was a southern states-rights extremist. In the Senate on December 4, following the reading of President Buchanan's annual message, Clingman had moved to print the message and used the occasion to deliver a lengthy and impassioned southern-rights harangue, in which he accused the North of denying southerners their constitutional rights by aiding fugitive slaves to escape. Clingman also portrayed Lincoln and the Republicans as defined by their hostility to slavery in the southern states and their commitment, in southern eyes at least, to its abolition by both subtle and direct means. The southern states, Clingman promised, would secede from the Union to counter this threat, unless the Republicans offered a program of constitutional guarantees to protect slavery, the sort of guarantees Buchanan had recommended in his message.

Crittenden's response was considerably shorter. He declared his regret that Clingman, in the first Senate speech of this critical session, should have resorted to angry denunciations. Instead he believed that everyone there should be striving to find measures of reconciliation to preserve the beloved Union through calm consideration. Sen. Clingman retorted that North Carolina would do what was necessary for her "honor" and safety, even if that meant disunion, and he quoted southern icon and statesman John Calhoun, who had died in 1850, that the Union could not be saved by such eulogies upon it as Crittenden was making. *Cong. Globe,* 36: 2: 3–5; and Albert D. Kirwan, *John J. Crittenden: The Struggle for the Union* (Lexington: University of Kentucky Press, 1962), 373–374.

11. The basic strategy decided upon by virtually all the congressional Republicans at the beginning of the session was one of "masterly inactivity," generally leaving the debate to be conducted by the Democrats and Americans. Republicans believed that they had won the presidential election fairly and constitutionally, and that Lincoln therefore had a right to be inaugurated on March 4, 1861, without the Republicans making any concessions at all, much less anything involving surrender of Republican principles. But the same Republicans had also come to Washington not seriously believing that the southern states would really carry through with their threats of secession, except probably South Carolina. However, the intensity of southern disunionist sentiment in Congress and the scheduling of secession conventions by slave states of the Cotton South woke up Republicans from their presumption that the southerners would accept Lincoln as president once he had won the election. Thus most House Republicans at least were willing to support Boteler's resolution. For a recent analysis of the dilemmas facing Republicans at the start of the session, see Russell McClintock, *Lincoln and the Decision for War: The Northern Response to Secession* (Chapel Hill: University of North Carolina Press, 2008), 71–74.

LETTER 2

Boston Daily Advertiser, December 10, 1860

Letter from Washington
[FROM OUR OWN CORRESPONDENT]

Washington, Dec. 7, 1860

Events move slowly forward here. There is now in point of fact only one issue before the country, and that one is defining itself more sharply every day. It has swallowed up all questions of future Cabinets and appointments and reduces itself to the simple point of secession or Union. Who will go and what will follow?[1]

There can be no doubt that a regular plan has been considered, and probably adopted, by the leading democrats of five Southern States, according to which those States will declare themselves out of the confederacy and will set up a confederacy of their own. We may expect to see the whole process unfold itself within the next two months. Whether the movevement [*sic*] is based on a supposed constitutional right of secession or on that of revolution,[2] is of no great consequence now.

The great matter of debate and anxiety is of course what the States that remain will do. As yet no formal declaration has been made. But of course there are opportunities enough to furnish an idea, until the republican leaders believe that the time has come for a declaration of their policy. It would be an insult to the great leaders of the party to suppose that their ideas on this matter are changed; that they are political gamblers, always on the look-out to hedge or to bluff as the cards turn up.

Their theory has been declared over and over again that disunion is an impossibility. A mere temporary secession is not disunion nor anything approaching to it.[3] Mr. Seward laid this down very clearly in his great speech in the Senate last winter,[4] and he is understood to maintain it now distinctly as ever. Armed coercion has nothing to do with the proposition. His idea goes a great deal deeper than that. He bases it on the ultimate good sense and sure instincts of humanity, on which republicanism itself rests and from which all our institutions get their life. He has faith in human nature as he has in God, and on this he grounds his belief that sooner or later public opinion must recover its true bearings, and the southern magnetic needle must point again to the North,[.]

The deduction from this is easy. He wishes evidently to meet these troubles with patience, kindness and forbearance, perfectly aware that an evil so widely spread and deeply rooted as that of slavery is not to be conquered without spasms and convulsions, but with a religious belief that with gentleness and care the patient must ultimately recover or every known law of human nature be false. As a necessary result of this policy, I take it for granted that he will avoid, so far as possible, every aggressive or irritating measure, and will show every kindness and forbearance to the South, short of a sacrifice of principle. In this policy the republicans in Congress are said to be unanimous and the nation will surely support them cordially.

Suppose, then, that the five southern States declare themselves out of the Union. In the face of a minority even now strong, suppose them to inaugurate an independent government; to declare their ports free; to reopen their African slave trade, and to support an army and a government by direct taxation. Suppose them to seek acknowledgment in England, which is more anti-slavery than we are;[5] in France, which already has all Europe against her,[6] and is too wise to add America to the list of her enemies; in Spain, trembling for Cuba;[7] or in Italy, fresh from Garibaldi;[8] it would not even need the grinding pressure of direct taxation, nor the ever increasing danger of a slave insurrection, nor the active coercion of the northern States, to end their experiment. Unless our whole system of government and religion is false, the moral opposition alone of the whole world would break them down, and before a year was over this whole question would be at rest forever.

This, as I understand it, is the republican theory of secession. This is, I am convinced, the principle on which they are now acting, and with an implicit faith in the honesty and wisdom of Mr. Seward and the other leaders of the party, I consider all the rumors of concession and of aggression as equally false and absurd. Moderation and forbearance are the watch-words now, nothing more and nothing less. No one questions that this is a very critical and dangerous time. Here the responsibility is strongly felt and acknowledged. But the men who have fought this battle so long will be equal to it now, and we feel here especially among the disciples of the Massachusetts school, a firm faith and conviction that

> The clouds we so much dread
> Are big with mercy, and will break
> In blessings on our head.[9]

NOTES

1. Young Adams was quite pleased with his analysis of the crisis in the December 7 letter, as he wrote to his brother on December 13: "My theoretical letter of last Monday was good. Damned if it wasn't. I say it because I have my doubts." Levenson et al., eds., *Henry Adams Letters,* 1: 206. Adams's last sentence in this passage displayed his humility about his new undertaking as a newspaper correspondent and impliedly invited his brother Charles to provide any criticism of the *Advertiser* letter which Charles might wish to give. Charles obliged with frequent and mostly pretty harsh critiques of his younger brother's efforts, and Henry responded in a self-deprecating fashion ordinarily, agreeing with Charles's assessments. While Charles preserved all of Henry's letters to him intact, Henry kept only a few of Charles's and only one involving severe criticism of his *Advertiser* correspondence. In that letter on January 17, 1861, Charles wrote: "Your letters do not contain dash enough for the times;–they should be more dramatic, more artistic, more on the model of the great letter writers of the past." Later in the same letter, he urged Henry to write in the descriptive style of the recently deceased British historian and essayist Thomas Babington Macauley. Letter is on roll 551, part 4, *MAP.* Despite the obvious affection existing between the brothers, the domineering attitude of Charles and the deferential tone of Henry come through in the letters. Later in life Charles's constant criticism would lead the more introverted Henry to become estranged from his older brother. Michael O'Brien, *Henry Adams and the Southern Question* (Athens: University of Georgia Press, 2005), 75–76.

2. Adams here touches upon the two major arguments which disunionist southerners used to defend state secession from the Union. They anchored their constitutional right argument on the reserved rights of states in the 10th Amendment of the Constitution, though the amendment did not specify what those reserved rights included. Southerners argued that the Constitution was a voluntary compact among sovereign states and that, if the North violated the compact, the southern states retained a reserved right to leave such a Union. Republicans, northern Democrats, and some southern Unionists denied that there existed such a right to secede from the Union among the reserved rights of the states. As they pointed out, neither the framers of the U.S. Constitution nor of any other government they knew of ever provided a mechanism for the destruction of that government. As to the right of revolution, not only the disunionists but even the Republicans recognized that the right of people to revolt against tyranny and oppression was legitimate. Southerners loved to recite their litany of wrongs suffered at the hands of northerners, especially Yankee violations of the constitutional requirement that northern states return fugitive slaves to their owners in the South and northern refusal to grant southerners equal rights in national territories, i.e., to recognize and protect slaves as property on the same basis as any other species of property. Union men responded that, even if southerners had legitimate grievances against the North, those complaints did not constitute anything nearly approximating a just cause for the revolutionary device of secession. In fact, northern and southern Unionists declared that southerners were in revolt, not in answer to any oppression from which they already suffered, but against an anticipated, imaginary scenario wherein President Lincoln and the Republicans would use their new power to abolish slavery in the southern states and bring about all the horrors associated with emancipation in the southern white mind. Republicans had repeatedly denied and continued to deny in this session any abolitionist intent toward the southern states, and therefore they argued that any southern invocation of a right of revolution against imagined northern aggression in the future was strictly illegitimate. For some of these arguments on both sides of the secession issue during this session, see *Cong. Globe,* 36: 2: 98–103, 118–119, 212–215, 224–227, 323–326, 367–369, 373–374, 418–419.

3. One Adams biographer quoted this part of the letter as an example of Henry Adams's effort to play down any divisions among the Republicans and to reassure his father's constituents that neither he nor the other Republican members of Congress would desert their principles. Samuels, *Young Henry Adams,* 84.

4. Sen. William H. Seward of New York, considered by many people even after Lincoln's election as president to be the preeminent leader of the Republican Party, had delivered a long speech in the Senate during the 1st session of the 36th Congress on February 29, 1860. Seward had given the speech on the occasion of his introduction of a memorial from the territorial legislature of Kansas requesting Congress to admit Kansas to the Union under its free-state Wyandotte Constitution. In the speech, he had analyzed the issue of slave labor vs. free labor, had ranged over the history of the sectional conflict, had denied that the Republican Party posed any threat to slavery in the southern states themselves, and had condemned John Brown's raid on Harpers Ferry as an act of "sedition and treason." Near the end of his speech, Seward had expressed his belief that, given "the instruments of cohesion"–language, culture, political institutions–binding the people of the Union's separate sections together, decisive popular reaction against disunion attempts would arise everywhere in the country, even among "the cotton and the sugar planters on the Mississippi. . . ." Devoid of the polarizing and inflammatory phrases such as "higher law" and "irrepressible conflict" that Seward had become known for in earlier speeches, his February 1860 address was very mild in tone. He had obviously wanted to sound moderate, national, and presidential, yet loyal to Republican principles, as he prepared for the then-upcoming Republican national convention in Chicago in May. For the February 29, 1860, speech, see *Cong. Globe,* 36: 1: 910–914; and George E. Baker, ed., *The Works of William H. Seward* (Boston: Houghton, Mifflin and Co., 1884), 4: 619–643. The last page of the speech contains the part to which Adams referred in his letter. Henry Adams had already shown his appreciation of this Seward speech in a letter to his brother Charles from Dresden in March 1860. Levenson et al., eds., *Henry Adams Letters,* 1: 105. See also Chalfant, *Both Sides of the Ocean,* 194–195. The admiration of Charles Francis Adams, Jr., for Seward is evident in *Charles Francis Adams, 1835–1915: An Autobiography* (Boston:

Massachusetts Historical Society, 1916), 72–75. A summary of the general public faith in Seward in December 1860 is in Ernest B. Furgurson, *Freedom Rising: Washington in the Civil War* (New York: Alfred A. Knopf, 2004), 33–34.

5. A strong antislavery movement had developed in England and Scotland in the latter part of the eighteenth century under leaders such as Granville Sharpe, William Wilberforce, and others. The movement had first succeeded in effectively eliminating slaves from England itself with Lord Chief Justice Mansfield's decision in the case of *Somerset* v. *Steuart* (1772); then had achieved the legal prohibition of slave importations into the British West Indies (1808); and finally had convinced Parliament in 1833 to pass legislation providing for the gradual emancipation of slaves in those islands. American abolitionists had forged strong ties with their counterparts in England and Scotland and worked closely with them.

6. European nations were very suspicious of and nervous about the imperial ambitions of French Emperor Napoleon III (formerly Louis-Napoleon Bonaparte, nephew of the famous Napoleon I). While over in Europe, young Henry Adams had absorbed that mistrust toward the mercurial French leader, but also found himself grudgingly in favor of Napoleon III's military intervention against the Austrians in northern Italy in tacit support of the movement for Italy's national unification. Levenson et al., eds., *Henry Adams* Letters, 1: 83, 98, 120–121, 124–127; Chalfant and Wright, eds., *Education of Adams,* 65–66, 74; and Chalfant, *Both Sides of the Ocean,* 113, 120, 123, 127.

7. Southern proslavery expansionists had schemed throughout the 1850s to take over more of Mexico, Central America, and Cuba in their desires for slavery extension and as an added bastion of defense for slavery against threatened northern antislavery encroachment on slavery in the southern states. Besides abortive filibuster expeditions against Cuba and an implied threat by several American diplomats (including James Buchanan, then U.S. minister to Great Britain), these efforts also included a bill in Congress in early 1859 to appropriate money for the purchase of Cuba from Spain. The Spanish government, understandably wary of the United States on this issue, had no desire to relinquish their prize colonial possession, and Spain was probably the nation in Europe least likely to recognize an independent southern confederacy. Robert E.

May, *The Southern Dream of a Caribbean Empire, 1854–1861* (Baton Rouge: Louisiana State University Press, 1973), 46–76, 163–189.

8. Giuseppe Garibaldi was an Italian revolutionary and military hero of the campaign in Sicily and southern Italy during the war to unify that nation. Young Adams had traveled to Palermo near the end of his European sojourn and had visited with Garibaldi there. Levenson et al., eds., *Henry Adams Letters,* 1: 146, 153–154, 164–172, 177; and Chalfant and Wright, eds., *Education of Henry Adams,* 73–74.

9. A nearly exact quotation of lines from the hymn "God Moves in a Mysterious Way" by the eighteenth-century English poet and hymnist William Cowper. He was a friend of former-slavetrader-turned-abolitionist John Newton, who himself composed the hymn "Amazing Grace." Newton published Cowper's hymn in his *Twenty-six Letters on Religious Subjects to which are added Hymns &c* (1774).

LETTER 3

Boston Daily Advertiser, December 13, 1860

Letter from Washington
[FROM OUR OWN CORRESPONDENT]

Washington, Dec. 10, 1860

The pressure brought to bear on the North is beginning to produce its results. There is a perfect panic here in all branches of the Executive, Judiciary and Legislative, which may naturally be expected to increase steadily for the next three weeks or more. Every one except the firmer republicans and the extreme secessionists, is considering the terms of a new compromise. Iverson[1] declared in the Senate today that nothing except the complete reversal of the policy of the republicans would satisfy himself and his friends, but that will not prevent an effort of some sort. The pressure on the wavering is intense. What the result will be, a short time will show. My own belief is that this question has got to be tried on the merits of secession and on that alone, and that nothing else can give a final quietus to the dispute, but whether this issue will be made up now or not, seems very doubtful. From the character of the Committee[2] in the House, it is thought that some compromise may be reported and the committee commences its sittings immediately. Still, it is a large body and it must be some time before the report is made.

There are very grave questions going the rounds respecting the President. Every one knows that he has neglected to garrison Fort Moultrie;[3] that Secretary Cobb[4] has so managed the Treasury as to weaken the new administration as far as possible; and that Mr.Floyd[5] has as good as placed large amounts of national arms in the hands of the South Carolinians. It is now said that the South Carolinians have yielded to the President's prayers,[6] and that no act of violence will take place till the 4th of March. But are the Carolinians so tender-hearted as to have yielded this point without an equivalent? What price did they ask? It is thought that Mr. Lincoln will find some curious documents on his inauguration.

It is strange, but even now there is a great deal of scepticism here as to the good faith of many of the loudest talkers, and this not on the republican side of the House only. Clingman of North Carolina is believed generally to want only his reelection to the Senate, and even Mr. Iverson's honesty is doubted. Meanwhile the republicans remain mostly quiet, and not a threat nor a taunt has been uttered. The leaders are not frightened, so far as I know, and, though grave and anxious to prevent explosions, they still persevere in believing that this matter, with proper care, must correct itself. "Quack medicines," as Jefferson Davis[7] calls them, are not to their taste, and they believe that nature, in such difficulties, is best left to her own resources. Socially, the two parties are on excellent terms, much better than last winter, as the secessionists consider themselves now as out of the Union, and before leaving this city forever wish to forget all that is past and bear no ill-will. In this the republicans are not behind them.

But the citizens of Washington are in a most painful position, and the alarm is universal. Property is nowhere. All the slaves in Maryland might be bought out now at half-price with a liberal discount for cash.[8] All this trouble and suffering must be as painful to the republicans as to anyone else, but their belief is unshaken that this present pain must be disregarded, for the sake of future good.

The debate today in the Senate was interesting, but led to nothing in particular. The only new feature in it was the apparent repudiation by the Connecticut Senator[9] of Mr. Seward's lead. His example may and probably will be followed by some others as was to be expected, but the result of this matter will hardly depend on them. Their action may disturb a little the natural course of events, but from the tone of Mr. Brown of Mississippi,[10] Mr. Iverson and Mr. Davis, it seems hardly likely that the South can be appeased by anything but a total, unconditional surrender.[11]

NOTES

1. Sixty-two-year-old Sen. Alfred Iverson (D-GA) was one of the staunchest southern secessionists in the U.S. Senate, and "an oily, fat

little lawyer," according to Republican journalist Benjamin Perley Poore ("Perley"). *Boston Morning Journal,* December 7, 1860. Correspondent L. A. Whiteley ("L. A. W.") described him as being of medium size and stature, with a bald head, rather full red face, and "invariably angry" expression. *Louisville Daily Journal,* December 17, 1860. The *Cincinnati Commercial*'s correspondent reported him a man of little ability or influence who was "wretchedly dissipated" due to fondness for liquor. St. Louis *Daily Missouri Democrat,* December 10, 1860, quoting *Cincinnati Commercial.* But Adams here made a mistake in identifying Iverson as declaring that day his conviction that a complete reversal of Republican policy would satisfy the southerners. For one thing Sen. Iverson made only a few incidental remarks in debate that day. For another, Iverson had no faith that the Republicans could do anything to convince the South of their good will toward the slave states. He believed that the Republican Party had one penultimate goal–the abolition of slavery in the southern states—and they intended to use every newly won federal power at their command, including control of appointments to federal patronage positions in the South, to accomplish that goal by "encouraging incendiarism, John Brown raids, murderings, poisonings, and revolts. . . ." In his view the only recourse for the South, in order to defend slavery, lay in the revolutionary act of secession and the establishment of a separate southern nation from that of the northern states. Iverson had expressed these sentiments in a Senate speech on December 5 and would state his position in greater detail in a speech on December 11. *Cong. Globe,* 36: 2: 10–12, 48–51. The quotation above is from the latter speech, p. 49. The speech on December 10 to which Adams referred in his letter was that of Sen. Jefferson Davis (D-MS), who addressed the Senate during discussion of a resolution (adopted later on December 18) by Sen. Lazarus Powell (D-KY) for appointment of a special compromise Committee of Thirteen in the Senate. Davis was not so despondent of hope for saving the Union as was Iverson, and he initially refused to sign the southern manifesto of December 13 which declared compromise impossible, although he did sign it the next day. He stated that only a wholesale retreat by the North and the Republicans from their hostility to the South and slavery could form the basis for a lasting Union of the two sections. Ibid., 28–30; Washington *Evening Star,* December 15, 1860; *Baltimore American and Commercial Advertiser,* December 17, 1860;

Lynda L. Crist, ed., *The Papers of Jefferson Davis* (Baton Rouge: Louisiana State University Press, 1989), 6: 377–378; William C. Davis, *Jefferson Davis: The Man and His Hour* (New York: Harper Collins, 1991), 289–290; and William J. Cooper, Jr., *Jefferson Davis: American* (New York: Alfred A. Knopf, 2000), 318–319. A hero of the Mexican War and Secretary of War under President Franklin Pierce before becoming U.S. senator from Mississippi, the 52-year-old Davis was only a few months from becoming president of the Confederacy. A man who always cut a dignified and gentlemanly figure in debate or when giving a speech, he was never ranked among the more dynamic or inspiring Senate orators. One reporter referred to him as "monotonously grandiloquent." *Louisville Daily Journal,* January 16, 1861.

2. On December 6 Speaker William Pennington (R-NJ) had appointed one member from each state to the Committee of Thirty-three. They were: Chairman Thomas Corwin (R-OH), John S. Millson (D-VA), Charles Francis Adams (R-MA), Warren Winslow (D-NC), James Humphrey (R-NY), William W. Boyce (D-SC), James H. Campbell (R-PA), Peter E. Love (D-GA), Orris S. Ferry (R-CT), Henry Winter Davis (A-MD), Christopher Robinson (R-RI), William G. Whiteley (D-DE), Mason W. Tappan (R-NH), John L. N. Stratton (R-NJ), Francis N. Bristow (A-KY), Justin S. Morrill (R-VT), Thomas A. R. Nelson (A-TN), William M. Dunn (R-IN), Miles Taylor (D-LA), Reuben Davis (D-MS), William Kellogg (R-IL), George S. Houston (D-AL), Freeman H. Morse (R-ME), John S. Phelps (D-MO), Albert Rust (D-AR), William A. Howard (R-MI), George S. Hawkins (D-FL), Andrew J. Hamilton (D-TX), Cadwallader C. Washburn (R-WI), Samuel R. Curtis (R-IA), John C. Burch (D-CA), William Windom (R-MN), and Lansing Stout (D-OR). Hawkins of Florida and Boyce of South Carolina asked to be excused from serving on the committee because both believed their states would soon secede from the Union, while Morrill of Vermont made the same request because he felt that there were too many members of the Ways and Means Committee also on this one, which would create a conflict if the two committees scheduled meetings at the same time. The House refused to excuse any of the three from service. *Cong. Globe,* 36:2: 22, 36–41, 59–63; *Baltimore American and Commercial Advertiser,* December 7, 1860; and *New York Herald,* December 7, 10, 1860.

3. Fort Moultrie, along with Castle Pinckney, Fort Johnson, and the unfinished Ft. Sumter, were the four U.S. military installations guarding the harbor in Charleston, South Carolina. Fort Moultrie was located at one end of Sullivan's Island and the only one of the forts that was actually garrisoned at the time. Its few officers and sixty-four enlisted men could not have defended this vulnerable position from an attack by land. Allan Nevins, *The Emergence of Lincoln,* vol. 2, *Prologue to Civil War, 1859–1861* (New York: Charles Scribner's Sons, 1950), 348–349; and Maury Klein, *Days of Defiance: Sumter, Secession, and the Coming of the Civil War* (New York: Alfred A. Knopf, 1997), 107–108.

4. Though Republicans, in their partisan attacks on the Buchanan administration, naturally targeted Secretary of the Treasury Howell Cobb of Georgia for mismanagement of his department and federal revenues, Henry Adams also adopted this critical attitude toward Cobb's performance. Actually Cobb had tried his best to deal with a financial collapse not of his making, although as a southern Democrat he could not support the Republican answer to declining federal revenues–a higher tariff on imported goods to replace the low, Democratic-passed Tariff of 1857. As the country still attempted to recover from the financial Panic of 1857, a new economic downturn had struck the nation in 1860 as European investors, fearful of the growing sectional crisis between North and South, had pulled their money out of American markets and banks and had sold their U.S. securities. Lincoln's election in November 1860 only hastened this process further. Specie, i.e., gold and silver money, drained from the U.S., stock prices declined, and banks reduced their loans. Cobb dealt with the crisis in government finances by getting Congress to authorize the issuance of Treasury notes, which added to the already mounting national debt. His efforts were sincere but the problems were beyond his or anyone's abilities to cope with at that time. Nichols, *Disruption of American Democracy,* 193–194; and Margaret G. Myers, *A Financial History of the United States* (New York: Columbia University Press, 1970), 148–149. For Cobb's report on the Treasury's finances, dated December 4, 1860, see *Cong. Globe,* 36: 2: Appendix, 8–10.

5. Secretary of War John B. Floyd of Virginia opposed secession but had been ordering small arms sent to southern arsenals since John Brown's raid in 1859. His most egregious act of this sort, however, would

take place ten days after Henry Adams posted this letter. On December 20, Floyd, from his sickbed, would order the transfer of heavy cannon from a foundry at Pittsburgh to several forts in Texas and Mississippi. News of this created great public outrage and protest at Pittsburgh. The Buchanan administration a few days later countermanded the cannon shipment, and Floyd, also under investigation for a war department financial scandal, soon after resigned from the cabinet. Nichols, *Disruption of American Democracy,* 426–431; McClintock, *Lincoln and Decision for War,* 109–112; and Adams, "Great Secession Winter," 7–8.

6. President Buchanan had received a visit from the South Carolina congressional delegation, Laurence M. Keitt, W. Porcher Miles, and the others, all rabid disunionists, on December 8. The president and the delegation then exchanged written communications. The South Carolinians pledged not to interfere with the Charleston forts and President Buchanan declared that he had no immediate plans to reinforce the forts. Elbert B. Smith, *The Presidency of James Buchanan* (Lawrence: University Press of Kansas, 1975), 172; and Steven A. Channing, *Crisis of Fear: Secession in South Carolina* (New York: Simon and Schuster, 1970), 278.

7. Sen. Jefferson Davis (D-MS) actually used the phrase "quack nostrums" in his December 10 speech to refer to various proposals and statements made that day by other senators: a plan by Sen. James S. Green (D-MO) for a federal border police to guard the South from John Brown type invasions and to prevent fugitive slaves from escaping, which Davis said would give the federal government a military force which could be used against the southern states; an implied threat by Sen. Milton S. Latham (D-CA) that California might secede from the Union unless the federal government financed the building of a transcontinental railroad linking the Pacific Coast states to the rest of the nation; and the partisan accusations by Sen. Lafayette S. Foster (R-CT) which blamed the entire crisis on Democratic politics and policies. Green in particular took umbrage at Davis's characterization of his suggested border police as a "quack nostrum" and spoke in reply. *Cong. Globe,* 36: 2: 25–31. Davis's phrase is on p. 28.

8. Throughout this session of Congress, and especially in the months just after the election, Washington was rife with alarms and rumors, particularly reports that armed groups from nearby Maryland and Vir-

ginia, along with pro-southern sympathizers in the District itself, were going to descend upon and take over what was a very lightly defended capital when the session began. One such version of this plot is in Joseph Medill to Abraham Lincoln, December 26, 1860, Lincoln Papers. Medill, an editor of the *Chicago Tribune*, acted as his newspaper's Washington correspondent under the pseudonym "Chicago" and described the plot in his letter to the *Tribune* on December 12. *Chicago Daily Tribune*, December 17, 1860. These fears exerted a downward pressure on property values for a while. The turmoil and uncertainty about what action the incoming Republican administration might take against slavery in border slave states such as Maryland also caused prices for slaves in Maryland to fall. The prospects for a long continuation of slavery in Maryland looked bleak, given a probably hostile Republican administration in Washington and the nearness of the free state of Pennsylvania to entice runaway Maryland slaves. Sen. Iverson of Georgia addressed the Republican threat to slavery in the border states during his speech on December 11. *Cong. Globe*, 36: 2: 49.

9. This is a reference to Sen. Lafayette Foster's short partisan attack on the Democrats that day (see note 7 above). Seward and most other Republicans in Congress had adopted the strategy of saying little or nothing in those early days of the session and certainly nothing that could be interpreted as provocative to the Democrats or southerners. Foster's remarks are in *Cong. Globe*, 36: 2: 28.

10. Sen. Albert Gallatin Brown of Mississippi was a determined southern secessionist. One Washington reporter described him as a "tall, rather thin, active gentleman, with a full heavy black beard and moustache, and a jaunty, cavalier air." On the day Adams wrote this letter, December 10, Brown had spoken in the Senate against the Powell resolution to establish a Committee of Thirteen. He declared that such a committee would be useless and only serve to give the South false hopes of a fair settlement. The problem was, to Brown, that the Republicans intended to destroy slavery in the southern states, despite their efforts to disguise their agenda. Hopeless that the North would reverse their hostility to slavery or the hatred of the South preached in northern churches and schools, Brown urged a peaceful separation of the Union. However, he acknowledged that war might result. *Cong. Globe*, 36: 2: 33;

Philadelphia Inquirer, December 6, 1860; James B. Ranck, *Albert Gallatin Brown: Radical Southern Nationalist* (New York: Appleton-Century Co., 1937), 202–203.

11. Rep. Charles Francis Adams cynically described what the South wanted: "The true game is to brag us out of all our winnings." Diary, December 9, 1860, roll 76, part 1, *MAP.*

A Supposed Missing Henry Adams Letter to the *Advertiser*

In a letter to his brother Charles on December 20, Henry Adams expressed concern that his letter of the previous Monday had not appeared in the *Boston Advertiser* issues he had seen for that week, saying that he feared that the editor Charles Hale might have suppressed it. He urged his brother to go see Hale "and mark what he says or looks. . . ." Henry said that he was not that sorry his letter had not appeared in the *Advertiser* "as it was written when everything looked fishy." His letter crossed in the mails with a December 18 letter to him from brother Charles wondering why no letter from Henry had appeared in the *Advertiser* on Monday, December 17. Charles also related his own suspicions that Hale might have suppressed that one. Charles said he had seen Hale and that Hale had told him he had not received the letter yet but would publish it when it reached him from Washington. Charles Jr. wrote to his father on the 19th asking about Henry's *Advertiser* letters. The problem, of course, lay in the fact that the mail might take several days to reach Boston. Henry's December 20 letter confused his modern biographer Edward Chalfant into thinking that there was an Adams letter to the *Advertiser* which either Hale did suppress or had gotten lost in the mails. Chalfant mistakenly thought that the missing letter had been dated on December 17. That cannot be correct, for Henry Adams's letter of December 17 was published in the *Advertiser* on December 20. (See letter 4 below).

There actually was no letter written to the *Advertiser* during this period which did not appear. When Adams wrote to his brother on December 20, he was referring to the *Advertiser* letter he had written on Monday, December 10. That was letter 3 above, and it did appear in the *Advertiser* on Thursday, December 13. Henry, for whatever reason, had simply not seen that copy of the *Advertiser* yet. His brother Charles, guessing at the frequency of his brother's *Advertiser* correspondence, had expected another letter to appear on the 17th and had badgered

Hale about it. But that one had not even been posted by Henry until that date, and it did appear in the *Advertiser* on December 20. Although Charles may have expected to see one of Henry's letters in particular issues of the *Advertiser,* Henry was a bit irregular in sending them to Boston. Despite the brothers' suspicions of Hale and despite occasional delays in the mails (Henry's letter of December 22 would not appear in print until the 27th), all of Henry Adams's letters to the *Advertiser* written in December were published.[1]

NOTES

1. Levenson et al., eds., *Henry Adams Letters,* 1: 209; C. F. Adams, Jr., to Henry Adams, December 18, and to C. F. Adams, Sr., December 19, 1860, Letters Received, etc., roll 550, part 4, *MAP;* and Edward Chalfant, *Both Sides of the Ocean,* 201, 416.

LETTER 4

Boston Daily Advertiser, December 20, 1860

Letter from Washington
[FROM OUR OWN CORRESPONDENT]

Washington, Dec. 17, 1860

When I last wrote, there was a good deal of anxiety felt here as to the course things were taking. Not in relation to secession, for if the question were only narrowed down to that, there is great confidence felt here that the troubles would correct themselves; but the fear was of the doctors. So long as the republicans remain united, temperate, and forbearing in tone and manner, it is thought that there is no real danger for the country. If the South seceded, it would soon find out its mistake, and the conservative element would gain strength and bring it back. The danger feared was lest the North at this critical time should split, thus producing a violent contest in the House at the most dangerous time, and with it the danger of universal anarchy. Luckily there has as yet been nothing of this, and as the recess is now near, when they will probably adjourn for a fortnight, there is great hope felt that the worst is over.

Mr. Wade's speech in the Senate today seems to have made a strong impression by its firm and frank declarations.[1] The Western and Southern men now have most of the speaking to themselves as the North and East seem to think themselves less directly implicated in the trouble.

The House amused itself with a sort of child's play today, each party flinging resolutions at the other's head. It was quite lively, and Mr. Morris's resolution[2] especially, declaring that there was no just cause existing for an attempt at dissolution, with a long extract from Washington's Farewell Address, seemed to pinch the southern side very hard. They did all they could to choke him off, but without success. They were noisy enough but quite good-natured, and seemed to feel that the whole thing was of no practical use.

The Union Committee[3] resumed its sittings today, though without any very tangible success. Reuben Davis of Miss., was offended by some action of the majority and seceded.[4] He came into the House and announced his secession, saying that the committee conceded nothing to the South but asked more concessions from them, and he wished to be excused from further service. No doubt the committee would be very glad to have him excused. He has been only a source of trouble apparently.

The committee is working industriously. Its sittings are long and the talking interminable, but they have a very ungrateful piece of work before them. What they are to do is a puzzle to people here, for the ground is already cut from under their feet. Every one must recollect that the democratic party split on the question of protection to slavery in the territories; that Lincoln was elected on that issue, and that a majority in every free State, except two or three, declared themselves for the entire exclusion of slavery from the territories. That was the great issue, and on that issue Breckinridge was beaten out of sight.[5] Yet now the South comes forward and demands of the North as an ultimatum, the absolute protection of slavery in all, or in at least a certain part, of the national territory.[6] This will be the compromise if there is one, and this is the subject that our legislators here in Washington are dodging about, unwilling to attack.

Certainly I cannot undertake to say what course the republicans mean to take about this. They hold no caucuses[7] and have agreed on no united action. From what I hear, however, I believe that even the most decided of them are unwilling to do or say anything that will tend at all towards an increase of the present excitement. If the South want pledges that their constitutional rights will not be attacked the republicans would probably consent. They consented today to recommend the repeal of all unconstitutional personal liberty laws. They voted for the resolutions of Mr. Terry [Ferry][8] and of Mr. Morrill[9] in the Union Committee last Thursday. But when it comes to the direct and active protection of slavery in the territories and an amendment of the Constitution to ensure it, there are eighteen hundred thousand votes behind them and I'm inclined to think that with the best will, they could not yield.

Meanwhile, in order to make the committee wholly useless, the cotton States are not to be held. They are going out and once out, they hope to be able to dictate their own terms. Congress meanwhile is afraid to offer the only concession that would make them hesitate. All parties dodge this question of the territories. The republicans because they see what a storm it would raise behind them if they granted it, and because they know what a storm would rise in Congress if it were proposed. The secessionists because they are committed to secession at all hazards, and don't wish to acknowledge that their object is secession and not compromise. The middle men because they think that it is not yet time.

This I take to be the condition of affairs here at present, and probably Congress will adjourn on Wednesday for a fortnight, leaving the committee to do what they can. Something may turn up to relieve them, but among the republicans there is a strong feeling that the only sure and final settlement of the whole matter is, to try it on the merits of secession, pure and simple. Some of them, no doubt, are willing to give way. It is not strange that the universal fear and distress should move them. The majority, however, see in compromise only a postponement of an inevitable struggle, which every new concession makes more disastrous.

This is the summing-up of the action or inaction of Congress so far. The next stage will be a more advanced one, what with the change in the Cabinet[10] and the action of the seceding States. But sufficient unto the year is the evil thereof.[11]

NOTES

1. Sen. Benjamin Franklin Wade (R-OH), 60 years old, stern, grim-visaged antislavery radical from Ohio's northeast corner, the Western Reserve, descended from Massachusetts Puritan stock. Known affectionately as "Frank" to family and friends and "Bluff Ben" to many outside his intimate circle, Wade had arrived in Washington prepared to do battle. He hated the fact that any Republicans had supported the Boteler resolution in the House, swearing "in good round Anglo Saxon, with characteristic vehemence, rounding off his periods with a ring of tabooed expletives which would startle the piety of old-fashioned Psalm singers." In his opinion the Republicans had won a clear victory, "and d–d if they shall budge an inch." On the "reign of terror" then being conducted

against northern men visiting the slave states, Wade declared that "if the British should hang a Yankee because he is a Yankee, there would be war in two hours; but the South hangs scores of men, and they beg us to conciliate them." *Cincinnati Daily Commercial,* December 6, 1860.

During the first two weeks of the session, he had grown frustrated that only one Republican senator, John P. Hale of New Hampshire on December 5, had so far risen to denounce southern secession and defend the election of Abraham Lincoln (*Cong. Globe,* 36: 2: 9–10). Wade hated sitting in his Senate seat daily listening to southern disunionists attacking the North and defending the South's right to secede or to northern Democrats and southern Unionists urging compromise which would force Republicans to retreat from and surrender the antislavery principles on which the party was based and upon which they had won the election. By December 13 Wade could hardly contain himself, having just listened for two days to a disorganized, vituperative anti-Republican, gesture-filled harangue from the black-bearded Texas secessionist Louis T. Wigfall. Wigfall was a short, thick-set, young-looking man with his black hair stiffly brushed up from his forehead, "where two deep dents" gave him a "vicious daredevil expression . . ."; he was a notorious drunkard and had a record of dueling. As Wigfall concluded, Wade rose at his desk in an obviously angry, wrathful mood, ready to slay Wigfall oratorically. A "nervous fluttering" spread through the galleries and many faces grew pale in anticipation of the imminent fireworks. His fellow Republicans gathered quickly around Wade insisting that he desist from his purpose of replying to Wigfall. He turned towards his adversary and expressed his desire to speak, but finally Wade relented under pressure from his friends. Sen. James Doolittle of Wisconsin persuaded Wade to give way for an adjournment motion, and the Senate quit for that day. *Cong. Globe,* 36: 2: 71–76, 85–87; *Cincinnati Daily Commercial,* December 14, 17, 1860, and February 27, 1861 (description of Wigfall); *New York Herald,* December 14, 15, 1860; Alvy L. King, *Louis T. Wigfall: Southern Fire-Eater* (Baton Rouge: Louisianan State University Press, 1970), 102–103.

Wade wanted no compromise, no prevarication, no kindly words or gestures toward southerners who seemed bent on disunion, and no continued silence from Republicans. The Ohioan let it be known that he would address the Senate on December 17 on the Powell resolution for a special Committee of Thirteen. One report said that on Saturday afternoon, the 15th, three New England Republicans tried to dissuade him from giving a radical speech, to which Wade angrily replied: "Great God! gentlemen, what are you after? I shall give the South the butt end of the poker on Monday!" *National Anti-Slavery Standard* (New York), December 22, 1860. In anticipation of what all expected to be a fiery oration, the Senate galleries were packed that day. Though a man from poor background with little education and not a great speaker, Wade did not disappoint.

Dressed in his black suit and with his characteristic grimness, he reminded one reporter of how one of the Puritan officers in Oliver Cromwell's army during the English Civil War of the 1640s might have looked. Despite a few interruptions for questions interjected by southern senators or for applause from the galleries, Wade spoke for two hours to an audience which listened attentively in "profound silence." Whatever Wade lacked in rhetorical polish, his forcefulness struck one observer as having a blacksmith's "hammer and tongs" style as he conveyed his arguments, another said, with "volume of voice and furiousness of gesticulation, a loud clapping of his hands being a point of emphasis." Wade vehemently argued that the southern states had no just cause for complaint against the North, much less any reason or right to secede from the Union. He denied that the North had violated southern rights and declared that, with a few notorious exceptions, the northern states had largely enforced the evil Fugitive Slave Law of 1850. Wade defended the personal liberty laws of northern states, not as subterfuges for freeing fugitive slaves, but as laws to protect northern free blacks against southern attempts to kidnap these people and sell them into slavery. By contrast with his portrayal of northerners as law-abiding people, Wade attacked the southern states for their "reign of terror" against northern citizens traveling in the slave states and cited numerous incidents of physical violence and even murder against people whose only crime was that they came from a northern state. He also attacked the South's Negro seamen laws which denied northern black sailors who were citizens in New England states their constitutional rights as citizens under the "privileges and immunities" clause of Article 4 when their ships visited southern ports. Wade held that southern fears of Lincoln and the Republicans were grounded in baseless assumptions that the incoming administration would violate southern rights and interfere in the southern states to destroy slavery. While he admitted that Republicans opposed the further spread of the evil of slavery into another inch of territory, Wade unequivocally vowed that neither he nor any other Republican believed they had a right to interfere with slavery in the states where it already existed.

Therefore, given his exoneration of the North from past violations of southern rights or future intent to use federal power to destroy slavery in the South, Wade believed that the real basis of southern complaint and disunionist designs lay in their loss of power, which the Democratic Party and especially that party's dominant southern wing had held in the federal government for most of several decades. Now it had become a simple case of "rule or ruin" for some in the South, and disunionists chose to ruin the greatest government ever created since they would no longer rule it. Under these circumstances, Wade said the Republicans had no compromises to offer. They had won the election fairly and constitutionally and Lincoln had a right to be inaugurated on the coming March 4 without any compromises or concessions. In one of the most powerful passages of the speech, Wade said that "it would be humiliating and dishonorable to us if we were to listen to a compromise by which he who has the verdict of the people in his pocket, should make his way to the presidential chair." He pledged that Lincoln and the Republican party would respect and enforce the South's constitutional rights. Secession, though, was not such a right, Wade argued, and, if the president should attempt to carry out his constitutional duty of enforcing federal law by collecting federal revenues in states which had declared themselves seceded, and if those states resisted that enforcement of law and declared war on the United States, then war it would be against states guilty of treason. In a stirring peroration, Sen. Wade reminded all his listeners that his father had fought in the American Revolution to establish the flag of this grand republic, that he would never allow any star to be torn from it, and that he intended to die under the banner.

When he had finished, the galleries utterly erupted in thunderous ovation. An adoring reporter for the Republican *Cincinnati Commercial* wrote: "Altogether this was the most thrillingly dramatic scene it has been my fortune to witness." Even the *Charleston Courier*'s correspondent grudgingly agreed that it was the strongest speech ever given on the Republican side of the Senate. Most of Wade's Republican congressional colleagues praised the speech and believed that it epitomized Republican thinking on the crisis. Many Republican newspaper commentators followed suit. Some observers said the speech delighted secessionists who heard it as an aid to their cause in the South, while others described southerners as noticeably irritated at Wade's pounding of them. Wigfall of Texas came forth and shook Wade's hand, praising him as a "manly opponent" on the slavery issue. Another southern senator who came up to congratulate Wade after he sat down was Judah P. Benjamin of Louisiana, a states-rights Democrat. He also inquired of the Ohio Republican if he really intended to coerce Louisiana. Wade raised his arm and slammed his desk with it, saying to Benjamin, "Yes, we have purchased your State a desert, and if you secede, we will make it a desert again." St. Louis *Daily Missouri Democrat*, February 12, 1861, quoting *Springfield* (MA) *Daily Republican*. The *Charleston Mercury*'s correspondent called the speech "vulgar fanaticism" while the reporter for the *New Orleans Crescent*, George Bagby, labeled it a "lumbering" failure. While Wade may have reinvigorated some Republicans for the struggle ahead in the next few months, conservatives in both North and South interpreted the speech as a "war" speech which could antagonize already paranoid southerners and possibly destroy any chances for a compromise settlement. For the speech itself, see *Cong. Globe*, 36: 2: 99–104. Good summaries of it are in Hans L. Trefousse, *Benjamin Franklin Wade: Radical Republican from Ohio* (New York: Twayne Publishers, 1963), 133–137; and Shearer D. Bowman, *At the Precipice: Americans North and South during the Secession Crisis* (Chapel Hill: University of North Carolina Press, 2010), 82–84. The most thorough and adulatory newspaper account of the speech is in *Cincinnati Daily Commercial*, December 20, 1860. For various other commentaries and descriptions, see: Lyman Trumbull to Abraham Lincoln, December 14, Joseph Medill to Lincoln, December 18, and George G. Fogg to Lincoln, December 19, 1860, Lincoln Papers, Series 1, Manuscripts Division, Library of Congress; *Baltimore American and Commercial Advertiser*, December 18, 1860; Boston *Daily Atlas and Bee*, December 20, 1860; *Boston Morning Journal*, December 19, 1860;

Boston *Daily Evening Traveller,* December 20, 1860; *Charleston Daily Courier,* December 20, 1860; *Charleston Mercury,* December 20, 1860; *Chicago Daily Tribune,* December 21, 1860; *Cincinnati Daily Enquirer,* December 19, 1860; *New Orleans Daily Crescent,* December 24, 1860; New Orleans *Daily Delta,* December 26, 1860; *New York Commercial Advertiser,* December 18, 1860; *New York Evening Express,* December 18 and 20, 1860; *New York Herald,* December 18, 1860; *New York Times,* December 18, 1860; *New York Daily Tribune,* December 18, 1860; New York *World,* December 19, 1860; *Philadelphia Inquirer,* December 18 and 20, 1860; Richmond *Daily Dispatch,* December 19, 1860; St. Louis *Daily Missouri Republican,* December 22, 1860; and Springfield *Daily Illinois State Journal,* December 20 and 21, 1860.

2. After several congressmen offered plans for compromise proposals in the House on December 17, which were all referred to the Committee of Thirty-three, the House then proceeded to adopt three resolutions. Two of these concerned repeal of personal liberty laws in northern states. The third resolution, as described in Adams's letter, was offered by Rep. Isaac Morris of Illinois, listed as an Anti-Lecompton Democrat because in 1858 he had followed Sen. Stephen Douglas's lead in opposition to the Buchanan administration's support for the admission of Kansas to statehood under the fraudulent, proslavery Lecompton Constitution. Morris's resolution passed the House easily on December 17 by a vote of 116-44. Only three of the negative votes were northern men: Buchanan Democrats Thomas B. Florence of Pennsylvania, Daniel E. Sickles of New York, and Charles L. Scott of California. *Cong. Globe,* 36: 2: 110.

3. The Committee of Thirty-three.

4. Reuben Davis served as a congressman from Mississippi in both the 35th and 36th Congresses. Originally from Tennessee, he was not related to the more famous Jefferson Davis. But like the rest of the Mississippi delegation he was a proslavery radical. Adams in his *Advertiser* letter conveys only a glimpse of what he knew had happened in the committee. If he had dared to write more of what he knew, his dearly guarded anonymity as the *Advertiser*'s Washington correspondent would likely have been compromised; for, if he had given details of the incident, some might have concluded that only someone very close to a committee member, maybe the son of and secretary for Charles Francis Adams,

was the correspondent who divulged the details. Henry Adams's refusal to provide those details was also important to protect his father's role in the special committee, for these proceedings were supposed to be secret at that point. Henry did provide the details in a letter to his brother Charles on December 18 and in his "Great Secession Winter" essay later, while Charles Francis Adams wrote a diary entry of the event. These sources, along with the committee's journal, help the modern researcher to piece together what happened on December 17.

Rep. William R. Dunn (R-IN) moved for the committee to take up for discussion some earlier resolutions and a bill offered in the committee on the 13th by Rep. Henry Winter Davis (A-MD), a southern unconditional Unionist and moderate who was the closest thing to a Republican among slave state members of the House. His resolutions concerned northern states getting rid of laws which interfered with the recovery of fugitive slaves, while the key ingredient of his bill on fugitive slaves would provide a jury trial to anyone accused of being a fugitive slave, even though the jury trial would take place in the claimant's state. Under the stringent Fugitive Slave Law of 1850, all that was necessary was for a master or his agent to locate an alleged fugitive slave in a northern state, use whatever local authority necessary to capture the person, and bring the alleged fugitive before a judge or federal commissioner in a proceeding at which the alleged fugitive could offer no testimony. If the judge or commissioner agreed that the evidence or description provided by the claimant was sufficient to show that the defendant was indeed the slave claimed, then the alleged fugitive was taken to slavery in the South. Northerners bitterly resented this law, and one purpose of personal liberty laws was to protect northern free blacks from being claimed as fugitive slaves. H. W. Davis, desirous of compromise, wanted to get rid of personal liberty laws to satisfy the South on the one hand and to provide a jury trial for alleged fugitive slaves to vitiate some northern objections to the 1850 law on the other. The committee adopted Dunn's motion on the 17th to take up the Davis proposal.

That was too much for southern radicals on the committee, who considered jury trials for alleged fugitive slaves, wherever held, as just another roadblock to their recovery of slave property and caused by northern willingness to harbor these fugitive slaves in the first place. Reuben

Davis declared that the move demonstrated the "unconciliatory temper" of the committee in demanding a concession from the South, and he stalked out of the committee room in a huff, followed by some other southerners from the assembled group. They had not "seceded" very far though, only to the next room. Rep. Albert Rust (D-AR) soon came back into the committee room, read a paper to the members, flung it upon the table, announced that this was the southern ultimatum, and declared that, unless this was immediately taken up by the committee, the rest of the slaveholders would also withdraw. The ultimatum was apparently a proposal to recognize slavery south of 36°30' N.Lat. in any present or future territories as a constitutional amendment. Dunn reacted with "good tempered indignation" to Rust's effrontery, and the committee refused to give in to Rust's demand. So he joined Reuben Davis and a few other "secessionists" in the next room, separated only by a folding door from the committee room. There Davis, Rust, and friends sat smoking and listening closely at the folding doors to the committee discussion. When the discussion of H. W. Davis's fugitive slave bill concluded, Reuben Davis and confreres returned. Davis told the committee that he did not want to be misunderstood and that the group had only meant to withdraw while the other bill was under discussion, not permanently. Davis, though, quickly changed his mind again and at about 4 p.m. went back to the House chamber and requested to be removed from a committee which he said demanded concessions from the South but would grant them none. No one in the House objected and they released this fire-eater from the committee without a roll call vote. The accounts privately written by the Adamses displayed their contemptuous ridicule for what Henry termed the "methodical madness" of the radical southerners. The "ultimatum" they pressed in the committee became the centerpiece of the set of six constitutional amendments offered in the U.S. Senate the following day, December 18, by Sen. Crittenden of Kentucky, which would become popularly known as the Crittenden Compromise. C. F. Adams Diary, December 17, 1860, roll 76, part 1, *MAP;* Henry Adams to C. F. Adams, Jr., December 18, 1860, Levenson et al., eds., *Henry Adams Letters,* 1: 208; Henry Adams, "Great Secession Winter," 13; "Journal of the Committee of Thirty-three," 36th Congress, 2nd session, *House Reports* 31 (Serial 1104): 5–6, 9–10; *Cong. Globe,* 36: 2: 111; and *Baltimore Ameri-*

can and Commercial Advertiser, December 18, 1860. For Reuben Davis's memory of these events nearly thirty years later, see his *Recollections of Mississippi and Mississippians* (Boston: Houghton, Mifflin and Co., 1889), 399–401.

5. In the election of 1860, the Republicans with Lincoln as their candidate campaigned vigorously against any further slavery extension and credited that issue as a major factor in their victory over the northern Democratic candidate Sen. Stephen A. Douglas of Illinois; southern Democratic candidate John C. Breckinridge of Kentucky, Buchanan's vice-president; and Constitutional Union candidate and former senator John Bell of Tennessee.

6. A reference to the ultimatum demanded by Reuben Davis, Albert Rust, and their friends and introduced in the Senate on December 18 by John J. Crittenden. See note 4 above.

7. Adams here refers to the fact that the Republican members of the committee had not yet caucused among themselves. Republicans in Congress as a group and in state delegations had been caucusing since the session had begun.

8. On Thursday, December 13, Rep. Orris S. Ferry of Connecticut, a more hard-line Republican than his moderate reputation would indicate, had proposed a resolution as a substitute for one which emphasized the need to redress southern grievances. Ferry's resolution would remedy grievances from any section of the country. That would force consideration of northern charges that the Negro seamen laws were unconstitutional. This was the favorite tactic of the Republicans in answering the southern mantras that their section alone had been victimized. This became a major theme in Sen. Wade's speech a few days later. Ferry's resolution failed by a vote of 23-8 in the committee, with only Republicans voting for it. "Committee of Thirty-three Journal," 7–8.

On December 17, Ferry would propose a resolution in the committee urging a bill to specifically enforce the "privileges and immunities" clause in Article 4 of the Constitution to protect all citizens. Ibid., 11. Not only did Republicans criticize southern violence against northern citizens there as a violation of Article 4 but also of the 4th Amendment of the Constitution designed to protect citizens against unlawful search and seizure. Rep. John Hutchins (R-OH) on December 12 in *Cong. Globe,* 36: 2: 77.

9. Just after Ferry proposed his resolution, Rep. Justin Morrill of Vermont, another staunch Republican, offered a substitute for a resolution stressing the need to provide remedies to guarantee the "peculiar rights and interests" of the South. Morrill's substitute resolution would water that down by expressing regret that the South felt aggrieved and proposing that any proper and constitutional remedies should be granted "promptly and cheerfully" for the sake of peace and Union. The committee rejected Morrill's more general phrasing 22-9, and then agreed to the version more specifically referring to peculiar southern rights by a vote of 22-8. Ibid.

10. So far in the secession crisis Secretary of the Treasury Howell Cobb of Georgia, an avowed disunionist, had resigned on December 8 and President Buchanan had replaced him with Philip F. Thomas of Maryland. A few days after that, Secretary of State Lewis Cass of Michigan, unhappy with the president's refusal to reinforce the Charleston forts, resigned. Buchanan then shifted Jeremiah S. Black of Pennsylvania from attorney-general to secretary of state and gave his former post to fellow Pennsylvanian Edwin M. Stanton. Later on, Secretary of War John B. Floyd of Virginia, Secretary of the Interior Jacob Thompson of Mississippi, and the recently appointed Secretary of the Treasury Thomas would also resign.

11. "Sufficient unto the day is the evil thereof." 6: 34 Mt (King James Version).

LETTER 5

Boston Daily Advertiser, December 27, 1860

Letter from Washington
[FROM OUR OWN CORRESPONDENT]

Washington, Dec. 22, 1860

In my last letter I said that the only real point in dispute was the territorial question which all parties were afraid of. Things have advanced since then. The Union committee has discussed this question, and we shall soon have their decision.[1]

The course of the thing has been nearly as follows: The committee after referring the question of fugitive slaves to a committee of five from the border States,[2] took up the consideration of what the southern men call their ultimatum. This consists of the reenactment of the Missouri Compromise as an amendment to the Constitution, with the condition that, as North of that line there should be freedom, so South of that line slavery should be acknowledged, protected and perpetuated if necessary by the active interposition of the Federal Government, not only in all territory now belonging to the United States but also in all that may be acquired hereafter.[3]

To this it is of course impossible for the republicans to agree. To offer it, is, as was said by a Senator when Mr. Crittenden proposed it, a direct insult to the North. It is nothing short of calling on the republican party to swallow every profession of principle they ever uttered, and to degrade the whole struggle to a mere contest for office. No real republican would ever consent to listen to it.[4]

On the other hand the South refuse anything less than this. The proposition to leave the territory south of 36°30' to the chances of squatter sovereignty, is scorned by the other side.[5] They will have nothing short of an amendment in the Constitution recognizing and enjoining slavery, and any one who knows anything, knows that the proposition of such a measure to the legislatures of the North, the discussion there and its ultimate infallible rejection, would do five times more harm to the nation than its immediate rejection now.[6]

This is then the issue, clear and plain, and if the South insist on that as their ultimatum, that must end the matter, for the republicans cannot and will not hear of it. But the great leading spirit of the middle men, Winter Davis with his friends, is not willing that the matter should end so, and another proposition has been suggested which obviates the great difficulty.

Let any one glance at the map, and he will see that the territory now open south of 36°30' consists of a district reserved for Indians and called the Indian Territory, and another, stretching from Texas to California, called New Mexico. Under any circumstances the Indians ought to remain undisturbed, so that in point of fact the only open ground is that of New Mexico. This is now slave-territory. It has a violent slave code and is under all the influence of slavery.[7]

Winter Davis[8] comes forward then with the last resort. With a boldness and a vigor that stamp him as one of the strongest men now in public life, he says: Admit New Mexico. Make her a State. Use up this last source of trouble. As for future territory, let it take care of itself when it comes. He says to the South that it is madness to demand of the North such an impossible and exciting measure as a constitutional amendment in favor of slavery. He asks of the republicans to yield to this compromise, which demands no concession of principle on their side, but only a concession of policy. It is not expected that a measure like this would be acceptable to the cotton States. The cotton States want secession and a southern confederacy, and no compromise that a republican could offer would stand a chance of acceptance with them. No compromise that they would accept could be carried at the North, as it must have the form of a constitutional amendment. It is for Maryland and Tennessee and Virginia that this measure is proposed.[9]

Other means of settlement as to the other points in dispute, will be added to whatever will be agreed upon in this territorial matter. The question of fugitive slaves will receive some arrangement. Assurances will be asked for, that the North will not interfere in the internal affairs of the South. The policy of the republicans here has been one of moderation and willingness to accede to any reasonable wish of reasonable men; and the majority of the southern members of the Union Committee are said to be reasonable men. If the repeal of the Personal Liberty laws is asked, it will probably be recommended by a large majority of the republicans, as a matter on which it would be a mistake to quarrel. Indeed it has already been recommended both by the House and the committee.[10] I do not know positively what the position of New England on all these questions has been, but certainly they do not wish to force a quarrel if it can be helped, and from the general harmony of action on the republican side, it is fair to suppose that no very great differences of opinion have arisen.

Today, before taking a vote on any of these matters, the committee has adjourned for a week by general agreement, in order to give time for reflection and consultation. The members will many of them go home to see their constituents, and when they return we shall perhaps get something positive.

NOTES

1. Also on the 22nd, Henry penned a letter to his brother Charles describing this *Advertiser* letter as "important: the most so of any yet, and perhaps a little indiscreet. . . ." Levenson et al., eds., *Henry Adams Letters,* 1: 210; and Chalfant, *Both Sides of the Ocean,* 204. The letter also impressed Henry J. Raymond, editor of the *New York Times,* who reprinted it in his paper on December 31. In a letter to his brother on January 2, Henry Adams expressed his displeasure that the *Times* had reprinted his letter because he feared Raymond or someone connected with the *Times* might have discovered the identity of the *Advertiser*'s Washington correspondent. Levenson et al., eds., *Henry Adams Letters,* 1: 217.

2. The committee agreed on December 18 to refer H. W. Davis's and other remaining proposals relative to fugitive slaves to a special subcommittee of five, to which chairman Thomas Corwin (R-OH) appointed H. W. Davis (A-MD), J. S. Millson (D-VA), F. N. Bristow (A-KY), William Kellogg (R-IL), and T. A. R. Nelson (A-TN). Davis's resolution to recommend that states get rid of any laws obstructing enforcement of the Fugitive

Slave Law had passed the committee on that day just prior to the decision to refer other proposals on the same subject to a committee of five. "Committee of Thirty-three Journal," 11–12.

3. Territorial proposals on slavery by southerners on the committee had resolved themselves into one on December 17, devised originally as a constitutional amendment by Rep. Thomas Nelson (A-TN) and amended by Rep. Albert Rust (D-AR) to explicitly protect slavery in any present territory or future acquisitions south of 36°30' N. Lat., the old Missouri Compromise line which would now be resurrected via constitutional amendment. The Kansas Nebraska Act of 1854 had essentially repealed it and the *Dred Scott* decision of the U.S. Supreme Court in 1857 had declared it to have been unconstitutional. Ibid., 3, 10, 12–14; and Letter 4, note 4 above.

4. On December 18 in the U.S. Senate, 74-year-old John J. Crittenden (A-KY) offered what was to become the most discussed and most comprehensive compromise plan of the session, a set of six constitutional amendments designed to protect slavery from any possible attempts to interfere with it by anyone, including the incoming Republican administration under Lincoln. The centerpiece of the Crittenden Compromise, and the part which dominated subsequent congressional debate on his propositions, was his first segment concerning the territories: he basically adopted the Nelson-Rust proposal offered the previous day in the House committee (see note 3 above), i.e., apply the old Missouri Compromise formula to any territories "now held or hereafter acquired." Other amendments would protect slavery in federal installations in the slave states, secure slavery in the District of Columbia as long as Virginia and Maryland continued it and the District inhabitants wanted to keep it, forbid Congress from interfering with the interstate slave trade, and provide federal payment for any unrecoverable fugitive slaves. Crittenden's final amendment would render the five preceding amendments and the three-fifths clause and the fugitive slave clause of the U.S. Constitution unamendable in future and prohibit Congress from ever abolishing or interfering with slavery in the states. The fact that he extended his territorial provision to include land "hereafter acquired" but spoke in his introduction of the plan as if those crucial words had not originally been part of it may indicate that Crittenden had only added the "here-

after acquired" clause after the southerners on the House Committee of Thirty-three had incorporated the concept of future territories into their Nelson-Rust proposal. In addition to his constitutional amendments, Crittenden also tacked on several resolutions in relation to fugitive slaves, personal liberty laws, and the African slave trade.

Henry Adams's *Advertiser* commentary on the Crittenden Compromise perfectly reflected the feeling of virtually all Republicans that this plan of settlement was impossible because it would force the party to repudiate every principle they had stood for. Republicans respected old Crittenden's effort to save the Union, but, as Henry Adams would write in his essay after the session ended, Republicans believed that his southern colleagues had cornered Crittenden into offering a proposal no Republican could vote for and thus had virtually transformed the venerable Kentucky moderate into an unwitting instrument of the secessionists. *Cong. Globe,* 36: 2: 112–114; Henry Adams, "Great Secession Winter," 10–11; Kirwan, *Crittenden,* 374–377; Klein, *Days of Defiance,* 124, 158; David M. Potter, *The Impending Crisis, 1848–1861* (New York: Harper & Row, 1976), 531–532; Daniel W. Crofts, *Reluctant Confederates: Upper South Unionists in the Secession Crisis* (Chapel Hill: University of North Carolina Press, 1989), 196–200; and Michael Burlingame, *Abraham Lincoln: A Life* (Baltimore: Johns Hopkins University Press, 2008), 1: 679–698.

5. "Squatter sovereignty" was more commonly known as "popular sovereignty." The concept had been around since the late 1840s as a moderate solution to the nagging question of whether to allow slaveholders to take their slave property into national territories of the West or to ban slave property from the territories by federal law. Southerners had insisted that they had nothing less than a constitutional right to have their slaves recognized as a species of property and protected as such in western territories just like any other form of property. Antislavery men, however, had countered that slave property was not recognized by the Constitution, that slaves were deemed property only by local law in certain states. Slaves therefore, the antislavery northerners said, were not to have legal recognition as property outside those states, and they believed that Congress had the authority to ban slavery from national territories by federal law. This doctrine had been the basis for the Wilmot Proviso to ban slavery from the Mexican Cession in the late 1840s, and

in response southerners went so far as to threaten secession from the Union if they were denied what they held to be nothing less than a constitutional right and thus denied access with their slaves to national territories which they too had fought to acquire. As a moderate position in between these irreconcilable extremes, many northern Democrats and some southern Whigs suggested the idea of popular sovereignty, which entailed leaving the issue of slavery in the territories to be decided in a truly democratic fashion by the people who migrated to the territories. This formula, beginning in 1850, had been written into several territorial organization bills, taking the form of a clause in those bills stating that said territory would be received into the Union as a state "with or without slavery" according to the new state's constitution at the time of admission. Proponents of this doctrine saw as one advantage to it that it would remove the volatile issue of territorial slavery from the halls of Congress and away from ambitious agitators northern and southern.

This panacea for the territorial slavery issue suffered, however, from a major division of opinion as to its proper interpretation among its northern and southern supporters. Just when could the territorial populace choose whether to have slavery or to prohibit it? Most northern advocates of popular sovereignty interpreted it to mean that the people of a territory could make their choice in the territorial legislature prior to statehood. Southerners, though, had a distinct southern rights interpretation of the issue, arguing that their constitutional right to hold slaves throughout the territorial stage was inviolable and that a territory could make its choice on slavery only when writing a constitution prior to statehood. Northern and southern proponents of the doctrine of popular sovereignty worked together despite their divergent interpretations down into the mid-1850s.

In 1854 Sen. Stephen A. Douglas (D-IL) had become most identified with the formula when he manipulated the famous Kansas-Nebraska Act to substitute popular sovereignty in those two territories for the prohibition against slavery in that region north of 36°30' N. Lat., which had been in place since the Missouri Compromise of 1820. Douglas's maneuver proved disastrous as northerners reacted extremely negatively to what they believed was a southern plot to spread slavery into territories from which it would have earlier been banned by the Missouri Compromise restriction. Northerners soon created the Republican Party in opposition to what they termed the "Slave Power." Ultimately "Bleeding Kansas" had become a free territory despite attempts by Missourians to protect slavery there, and in the Secession Winter session Kansas was at the doors of Congress with its Wyandotte Constitution asking for admission to the Union as a free state.

Several proposals in 1860–61 for a compromise settlement involved both northern and southern versions of popular sovereignty. The northern ones simply provided that territories would be admitted "with or without slavery," according to their constitutions, while the southern plans stipulated explicit protection for slave property in the territorial stage before admission of the territory to statehood "with or without slavery." After having lost the race to control Kansas for slavery, southerners in the secession crisis wanted no popular sovereignty formula which did not explicitly recognize and protect slaves as property, at least below the old 36°30′ N. Lat. line. Among compromise plans introduced in the House on December 12, 1860, northern versions of popular sovereignty in the territories were part of proposed settlements offered by John Cochrane (D-NY), Garnett B. Adrain (D-NJ), and William H. English (D-IN). Southern versions of the popular sovereignty formula were offered by Robert Mallory (A-KY) and Thomas C. Hindman (D-AR). Sen. Crittenden's compromise of December 18 included the southern interpretation of popular sovereignty in his territories amendment. The various House plans are in *Cong. Globe*, 36: 2: 77–78. For an overall treatment of the territorial slavery issue, see Michael A. Morrison, *Slavery and the American West: The Eclipse of Manifest Destiny and the Coming of the Civil War* (Chapel Hill: University of North Carolina Press, 1997).

6. Adams here states essentially why Republicans saw the Crittenden Compromise, well intended as it might have been, as mischievous and impossible for them to support.

7. New Mexico Territory's legislature enacted a slave code consisting of thirty-one sections in February 1859, despite the fact that the only slaves there were a handful of domestic servants brought into the territory by army officers and territorial government officials. For the code see *Laws of the Territory of New Mexico. Passed by the Legislative Assembly, Session of 1858–1859* (Santa Fe: A. De Marle, 1859), 64–80. For a recent

article covering all aspects of the attempt to make New Mexico a state during the Secession Winter session, see Mark J. Stegmaier, " 'An Imaginary Negro in an Impossible Place'? The Issue of New Mexico Statehood in the Secession Crisis, 1860–1861," *New Mexico Historical Review* 84 (Spring 2009): 263–290.

8. Henry Winter Davis (A-MD) was devoted to maintaining the Union and desperate to play a leading role in devising compromise proposals which would attract Republican votes and satisfy southerners that they need not resort to secession. Davis was one of several American Party members who had chosen at the beginning of the 36th Congress to sit on the Republican rather than the Democratic side of the House. Despite his leadership abilities and a reputation as one of the best orators in the House, many people distrusted him. While Republicans in Congress liked him, the small clique of actual Republicans in Baltimore considered him anything but one of their number because of the actions taken to suppress Republicans there by Davis's nativists. On the other hand most Marylanders, especially the proslavery ones, considered Davis the least representative member of the Maryland delegation, in reference to the state's interests, whom Speaker Pennington could have selected for the Committee of Thirty-three. And, belying Davis's polished manners and statesman-like appearance was his association with and support from the most bullying and violent rowdies in Baltimore politics, the Catholic-hating nativist American Party machine known as the "Plug-uglies"; they characteristically would show up at the polls on election days with awls to jab any opponents who came to vote. Henry Winter Davis had even addressed one rally with a symbolic awl on the platform. He was a sincere southern opponent of secession though, and his Unionism even seems to have trumped his bigotry against Catholics during the secession crisis, for his plan to admit New Mexico to statehood would have added to the Union a new state which would possess an almost entirely Roman Catholic Mexican-Indian population. While Henry Adams admired Davis greatly and did not write in his letters about the brutal tactics of Davis's Americans in Baltimore, he would describe these tactics in some detail in his "Great Secession Winter" essay.

Another thing which Henry Adams chose not to inform readers about in his December 22 *Advertiser* letter was the leading role his father had taken in the committee at that time. Two days before this, on the

20th, the committee had been discussing the Nelson-Rust proposal for slavery recognition in present or future territories south of 36°30′ N. Lat. In the midst of this discussion Davis of Maryland had terribly upset the southern territorial strategy by suggesting the immediate admission of New Mexico as a state, with the choice on slavery left up to the New Mexicans themselves in drafting their state constitution. After the southerners, thoroughly startled by this break in their ranks, consulted among themselves, discussion of Nelson-Rust resumed, with Nelson delivering a speech passionately pleading for the Republicans of the committee to vote for the southern plan as an alternative to the destruction of the Union. Charles Francis Adams responded with vigor, in an address which must have shocked his fellow committee members, coming as it did from the usually mild-mannered Adams. In the wake of news that South Carolina had seceded that day, Adams attacked secession as nothing less than treason. He denounced the Nelson-Rust formula as totally incompatible with Republican principles and therefore ridiculous to offer as a compromise because Republicans would never support it. Adams had no faith that the southerners would abide by the resurrected Missouri Compromise line any more than they had in 1854, when they had voted to repeal it in the Kansas-Nebraska Act. Worst of all, Adams said, Nelson-Rust (and for that matter Crittenden's and all similar proposals) would convert the Constitution of the United States into "a mere guaranty" for the protection of southern slavery. Rather than alter the Constitution so fundamentally, Adams said in conclusion, he would prefer to see the Union destroyed.

Despite the supposed secrecy of the committee's proceedings, word did leak out as to what had transpired that day and Adams found himself surrounded by admirers when he walked back into the House chamber following his emphatic rejection of Nelson-Rust. When the Republicans on the Senate special Committee of Thirteen all voted the next day, December 22, against the Crittenden Compromise and helped defeat it in committee, a heart-sick, despondent Crittenden laid the blame for the defeat of his measures squarely on the Adams speech. At a dinner party that evening at Speaker Pennington's, Adams overheard Crittenden tell someone "The decision is in his hands." Adams looked around to see to whom Crittenden referred, only to find Crittenden putting his hand on Adams's shoulder and saying "This is the man." Adams tried to laugh it off but he knew Crittenden was not joking in singling him out. Actually, Crittenden was being unfair too. Even if Adams had not made the speech he had, the Republicans of the Senate committee would have voted down the Crittenden Compromise.

Although Henry Adams would make a vague reference to his father's speech in his next *Advertiser* letter (letter 6, dated December 28), he left out any reference in the December 22 letter and instead concentrated on criticizing the Crittenden Compromise itself and on illuminating the role of Henry Winter Davis. Adams was certainly not trying to denigrate his father's stand, of which he was very proud, by not giving an account of his father's committee address. Henry's biographer Edward Chalfant has written that Henry stressed the role of Davis in order to simplify publicizing Davis's New Mexico solution to the territories issue for the *Advertiser*'s readers. But another factor undoubtedly influenced Henry's decision on what to include and not include in the letter–his continuing concern with maintaining his anonymity as the Washington correspondent of the *Advertiser*. Even in his analysis of Davis's plan and its impact, Henry Adams wrote nothing that would indicate a correspondent who had inside information on the committee's secret proceedings. Providing an account of his father's speech in the letter might have put his jealously guarded anonymity at risk, and young Adams chose not to take that risk. C. F. Adams Diary, December 20, 22, 1860, roll 76, part 1, *MAP;* Levenson et al., eds., *Henry Adams Letters,* 1: 211; Henry Adams, "Great Secession Winter," 15–19; Stegmaier, "An Imaginary Negro," 267, 269, 286, n. 8; Samuels, *Young Henry Adams,* 85; Chalfant, *Both Sides of the Ocean,* 206; McClintock, *Lincoln and the Decision for War,* 98–99, 102; and Martin Duberman, *Charles Francis Adams, 1807–1886* (Stanford, CA: Stanford University Press, 1960), 231–234.

Newsmen in Washington generally respected the secrecy of the Committee of Thirty-three proceedings, as young Henry Adams did. But there was one glaring exception. James Gordon Bennett of the *New York Herald* maintained a contingent of five or six reporters in Washington, the largest single group for any newspaper, and these correspondents each filed daily telegraphic dispatches, unsigned, to the *Herald*. And these notoriously nosy newshounds had no scruples about printing material concerning speeches in the committee meetings, leaked to them probably by one of the disunionist Southern Democratic members. These reports led to considerable discussion and debate within the committee about the leaks in violation of their secrecy rule, but the *Herald* continued to publish summaries of committee speeches anyway. These included a synopsis of Charles Francis Adams's remarks on December 20. *New York Herald,* December 13, 14, 15, 18, 19, 21, 22, 30, 31, 1860, and January 6, 8, 9, 1861.

9. While some Republicans maintained a stiff-necked opposition to any measures which could be interpreted as compromise, concession, or back-down from party principles on their part, other Republicans realized that a palpable danger existed that the northernmost or border slave states of Maryland, Virginia, Kentucky, Tennessee, and Missouri might join the Deep South in secession before Lincoln took office on March 4, if Republicans chose to do absolutely nothing to influence the border states to remain in the Union. Border state Union men constantly made this plea to their Republican colleagues in Congress, sometimes almost tearfully, to give them some help as they fought against the disunionists in their states, something the border state Unionists could employ with their constituents as evidence of Republicans' good intentions toward them. Rep. Schuyler Colfax (R-IN) to Robert Carter, January 27, 1861, Robert Carter Correspondence, Houghton Library, Harvard University. Henry Winter Davis was able to convince Charles Francis Adams during a carriage ride to the Capitol on the morning of December 21 that his New Mexico statehood proposal would drive a wedge between the Border South and the Deep South. The Deep South would reject it because they really cared about guarantees for slavery in future territories, something of little practical interest to the border slave states. The border states, on the other hand, Davis believed, would be attracted to his New Mexico plan as a way of getting rid of the troublesome territorial slavery issue. Davis also argued that, if Republicans could support New Mexico statehood, even if New Mexico should then choose to be a slave state, the border slave states would interpret the move as an indication of the honesty and earnestness of the oft-made Republican pledge not to meddle with slavery in southern states. Adams was convinced and believed that Republicans should advocate Davis's plan. Adams saw this as a positive gesture Republicans could make to the Unionists of the Border

South to help retain those states in the Union, a gesture which he felt the party could make with no surrender of their cardinal principle of opposing slavery in national territories. Thus was born a position around which Republican moderates could rally, in between Republican radicals opposed to any compromise at all and most southerners and northern Democrats, who preferred the Crittenden Compromise. C. F. Adams Diary, December 21, 1860, roll 76, part 1, and Adams to W. D. Robinson, January 5, to B. Wood, January 8, and to E. C. Banfield, January 13, 1861, C. F. Adams Letterbook, roll 164, part 2, *MAP;* Henry Adams, "Great Secession Winter," 13–14; Stegmaier, "An Imaginary Negro," 266–267, 269; and David M. Potter, *Lincoln and His Party in the Secession Crisis* (New Haven, CT: Yale University Press, 1942), 295–296.

10. On December 17 the House of Representatives had passed two resolutions in relation to the personal liberty laws of northern states. The first, by Democrat Garnett Adrain of New Jersey, originally recommended repeal by northern states of all laws in conflict with the Constitution or with U.S. laws. Adrain accepted an amendment to the resolution by Democrat John Cochrane of New York to specifically include mention of personal liberty laws as objects of the resolution. The resolution passed 153-14; only a few Republicans voted against it because they wanted the words "nullification laws" also added as targets of the resolution. These Republicans had in mind unspecified, objectionable laws in the southern states. Democrat Thomas Florence of Pennsylvania quickly introduced a resolution to include the words desired by Republicans in a resolution nearly identical to Adrain's original version, and it passed 130-0. *Cong. Globe,* 36: 2: 107–109. On the next day, the 18th, the Committee of Thirty-three agreed to Henry Winter Davis's resolution to recommend that states get rid of any laws which obstructed enforcement of the Fugitive Slave Law of 1850; the committee approved the resolution without a division. "Committee of Thirty-three Journal," 11–12.

LETTER 6

Boston Daily Advertiser, January 1, 1861

Letter from Washington

[FROM OUR OWN CORRESPONDENT]

Washington, Dec. 28, 1860

Nothing has taken place here lately in either House of Congress, to create any remark; but almost every day some new rumor, true or false, makes this city actually shake and quiver all over. It is a paradise for sensation reporters.

Among the sensation reports which I have seen lately, has been one relating to some compromise in the Committee of Thirty-three which was to be offered by Mr. Adams on the part of the republican members. As it was mentioned as a back-down and as backing-down is a new style of movement for Mr. Adams to lead in, I have tried to discover what the whole affair really is, and unless I am wrongly informed, it amounts to this.[1]

I spoke in my last letter of a proposition offered by Mr. Winter Davis as his plan of a settlement of the territorial question. The main feature was the admission of New Mexico, including Arizona, as a State, taking her chance of being slave or free, and in this manner finally exhausting the source of dispute, as no more territory would remain south of 36°30′. In offering this proposition Mr. Winter Davis inflicted a blow on the southern democrats, for which they hate him if possible worse than they did before.

This measure was offered by Mr. Davis as an amendment to the ultimatum which was then pressed by the southern democrats; the Missouri compromise line with protection to slavery south of it, as an amendment to the Constitution.[2] After long debate, the republicans were evidently united in the rejection of this ultimatum, and the more advanced among them are reported to have declared very clearly that they could not agree to such a measure, whatever might be the consequences. Mr. Adams is reported to have declared his mind made up on that point, and not to be altered by any event whatever.[3] It was after this declaration and Mr. Davis's speech against the ultimatum, that all parties agreed to adjourn over a week.[4]

The republicans now found themselves in the position of refusing on the one hand to accept the demands of the South, and on the other, to make any offer of their own. This was a false position, and it was intended as such by the men who offered the ultimatum. They meant to place the republican party before the country as enemies of the South; enemies to every and any settlement of this question, except by the abolition of slavery, and as intending to respect the Constitution only until they should have the power to alter it. The southern men, not secessionists, hoped by this means to work on the doubtful men in the North, and so to force on a reaction which their friends, such as Gen. Cushing, declared to be already sweeping even Massachusetts.[5] There is a regular plan here of building up again the democratic party. It was for that that Gen. Cushing went to Charleston;[6] for that that Douglas and Pugh have renounced their squatter sovereignty heresies;[7] that is to be discovered under nearly all the manoeuvres now going on, and it has been said that the support of the Bell and Everett party is expected besides. Certain it is, that prominent Bell and Everett leaders have been here in consultation upon it.[8]

It became necessary, therefore, that the republicans should do something to set themselves right before the country, and to show that they did not wish to force a quarrel upon the South. Accordingly the republican members of the committee set to work in the recess. They held meetings nearly every day, and many hours each day. They called before them a gentleman from New Mexico, long a resident there and well acquainted with the country and the people; they questioned him and cross-questioned him until he had nothing more to say.[9] They did not take their steps in the dark. Of course, most that passed in their consultations is unknown, but before the committee reassembled, it was understood that they had agreed upon some course of action, and that Mr. Adams, the firmest, or among the firmest, in opposition to the ultimatum, was to be the one to offer their propositions to the committee.[10]

Meanwhile the same necessity had been felt in the Senate committee. There Mr. Seward had offered some measures which had decidedly cornered the southern men. There was no concerted action between the two committees, but the propositions were generally alike.[11]

But it was not merely the southern democrats that these measures were intended to affect. There is a strong party of southern whigs in the border States who appeal to the republicans for a helping hand. They ask some reasonable guarantee; something, if it be only an indication of good will and constitutional intentions, with which they may go before their constituents and resist secession. Otherwise they say that they are delivered up, bound hand and foot, to the democrats, without a hope of resisting the flood that is coming over them. Maryland and this city are especially open to this influence.[12]

As yet the propositions have not been offered, so that the details are not known. But undoubtedly the admittance of New Mexico as a State is one. Objections have been made to this as a concession; but if a concession, it cannot involve much principle. My own belief is, from what I can learn, that it will be found to be no concession at all, but simply a settlement. With very few exceptions, the republicans on both committees have assented to it, and it is understood that the southern democrats reject it. As for New Mexico being a slave State for perpetuity, people had better wait before believing it, until it is shown to be probable.

I may be mistaken in some points of this representation of the case, but in general I believe it to be correct. At all events, it is understood that Mr. Adams will consent to make no move which is not sustained by the republicans in a mass. Under these circumstances the North seems to have a tolerable guarantee against any serious backing down.

NOTES

1. Most likely Adams had gotten a look at the previous day's edition of the *New York Times*, copies of which probably reached Washington on the 28th before Adams wrote his letter for the *Advertiser*. On December 27 the *Times* had published a telegraphic dispatch from their correspondent "O. P. Q." in Washington, in which he reported in some detail

the New Mexico enabling bill and discussion of it by Republicans on the Committee of Thirty-three. He mentioned in his dispatch that Charles Francis Adams had offered the New Mexico proposition and added this comment: "Coming from the most radical man from the North this is regarded as a back-down." The use of that word "back-down" in Adams's *Advertiser* letter strongly suggests that this is the report he had seen. Henry Adams biographer Ernest Samuels indicated that the December 28 letter was in response to criticism of Charles Francis Adams in the Boston *Atlas and Bee*. However, that paper would not publish a lengthy criticism of his "back-down" until January 9. Boston *Daily Atlas and Bee,* January 9, 1861; and Samuels, *Young Henry Adams,* 85.

2. See letter 5, note 8.

3. Ibid.

4. ". . . Winter Davis has fairly cut himself loose and declared his intention to vote against the Mis. Comp. line as an amendment to the Constitution. He did this yesterday in a speech which followed one from C. F. A. . . ." Henry Adams to C. F. Adams, Jr., December 22, 1860, Levenson et al., eds., *Henry Adams Letters,* 1: 211. The committee adjourned on December 21 and did not assemble again until December 27. "Committee of Thirty-three Journal," 15; C. F. Adams Diary, December 21, 1860, roll 76, part 1, *MAP;* and Duberman, *C. F. Adams,* 233.

5. Caleb Cushing had achieved a general's rank during the Mexican War and was commonly referred to thereafter by that rank. Cushing must be considered one of the most unusual and difficult-to-categorize characters of the sectional crisis. A Massachusetts native and son of a wealthy ship-owner, Cushing had become a prominent lawyer. In the 1830s he had become a member of the nascent Whig Party, and combined a strong antagonism toward slavery with a conservative, legalistic Whig attitude which prohibited any interference with slavery in the southern states. In the early 1840s Cushing supported President John Tyler's side in his struggle against Sen. Henry Clay of Kentucky over the national bank issue and their personal contest for control of the Whig Party. When the Whig majority faction under Clay officially expelled Tyler from the party, Cushing completed his own transition from Whig to Democrat. He became a vigorous advocate of "Manifest Destiny" expansionism, Democratic President James K. Polk, and the Mexican War.

During the 1850s Cushing served as U.S. attorney general in President Franklin Pierce's administration and supported the Kansas-Nebraska Act's negation of the 1820 Missouri Compromise restriction against slavery in territories north of 36°30′N.Lat. Throughout that decade he played an active role in Democratic politics in Massachusetts and also nationally. He chaired the Democratic national convention at Charleston in April 1860 until enough southerners, dissatisfied that the northern Democrats supporting the presidential candidacy of Stephen Douglas of Illinois refused to endorse their demand for federal protection for slavery in national territories, walked out and forced the dissolution of the convention. When the convention reassembled in Baltimore in June and the Douglas Democrats refused to seat the southern delegations that had absconded at Charleston, chairman Cushing sided with the ones expelled and left the convention with them. Cushing then chaired a meeting of the radical southern Democrats in a separate Baltimore hall, where Vice President John C. Breckinridge of Kentucky was nominated for president.

Caleb Cushing believed that Breckinridge, with his slavery-protection-in-the-territories platform, represented the best hope for holding the Union of free and slave states together, and he loyally campaigned for the Kentuckian. When instead Abraham Lincoln of the Republicans emerged victorious in the election, Cushing desponded of hope for retaining the old Union. As several southern states began organizing secession conventions almost immediately after the election, Cushing delivered three public addresses in his hometown of Newburyport about the crisis facing the nation. In those speeches, he laid the blame for the crisis squarely at the feet of the Republicans and their constant agitation of the slavery issue over the years. Cushing stated his belief that the only hope for continued union of North and South would require the Republicans to totally repudiate the antislavery position that lay at the heart of the party and its platform. Realizing that the newly victorious Republicans would never do this, Cushing urged that if the South seceded, those states should be allowed to go in peace. He did not favor secession but also could not support any military coercion of seceded states back into the Union. Cushing himself remained staunchly loyal to the Union and, when the Civil War began in April 1861, he vehemently declared his loyalty to the northern cause. The war, and President Lincoln's consultation of him on legal matters, brought another political transition in the life of Caleb Cushing; by 1864 he identified with the Republican Party and remained a Republican for the rest of his life.

Henry Adams, in his December 28 letter, actually misjudged Cushing, associating him with those who, in their wishful thinking, believed that Massachusetts and other New England states were, when faced with southern secession, ready to soften their attitudes and make concessions to the South on the slavery issue. Cushing did not believe that Massachusetts would undergo such a transformation, and he had certainly not made any such statement in his public addresses. Adams may have read an editorial in the *Boston Courier* on December 15 in which that Democratic paper had listed evidence of such reaction against the Republicans and in favor of compromise developing in Massachusetts. Although the editorial did not mention Cushing by name, it would have been easy for Adams to have associated Cushing, a leading Massachusetts Democrat, with the views expressed in the *Courier*'s editorial. *Boston Daily Courier,* December 15, 1860; Levenson et al., eds., *Henry Adams Letters,* 1: 214; John M. Belohlavek, *Broken Glass: Caleb Cushing and the Shattering of the Union* (Kent, OH: Kent State University Press, 2005), especially 314–315; and Claude M. Fuess, *The Life of Caleb Cushing* (New York: Harcourt, Brace and Co., 1923), especially 2: 269–272. Sen. Henry Wilson (R-MA) wrote a long public letter in answer to Cushing's indictment of the Republican Party in his Newburyport addresses. Boston *Daily Atlas and Bee,* December 18, 1860.

6. As a last desperate gambit to persuade the South Carolinians to delay their move toward secession, President Buchanan chose to send Caleb Cushing—a northern Democrat trusted by the southerners—to Charleston with a letter for Gov. Francis W. Pickens advising that the governor delay the secession convention. Cushing undertook the mission as requested by the president, but he did not arrive in Charleston until the morning of December 20, only a few hours before the special convention passed its ordinance declaring South Carolina out of the Union. The celebrating disunionists invited Cushing to the formal ceremony of ordinance-signing and the subsequent festivities, but whatever sympathy Caleb Cushing may have shown for the South ended there. He

refused to lend any implied endorsement of secession by his presence at these activities and he quickly departed from Charleston for Washington. It was only natural for Republicans to interpret this last-minute effort by the Buchanan administration to stave off secession as part of an overall partisan strategy of the Democrats to ultimately regain national political power by keeping the slave states—nearly all of them dominated by the Democrats—in the Union. Henry Adams reflected this Republican thinking about Cushing's Charleston trip not only in his December 28 *Advertiser* letter but in a letter to his brother on the 26th. Levenson et al., eds., *Henry Adams Letters,* 1: 214; Belohlavek, *Broken Glass,* 316–317; Fuess, *Cushing,* 2: 273–274; and Nichols, *Disruption of American Democracy,* 411–413.

7. Sen. Stephen A. Douglas (D-IL) and Sen. George E. Pugh (D-OH) had consistently supported the doctrine of popular sovereignty in national territories during the 1850s, particularly in Kansas Territory after its organization in 1854, i.e., the northern Democratic rather than the southern Democratic version of the doctrine. When at the Democratic national convention in Charleston in 1860 the southern Democrats demanded a platform plank pledging the Democratic Party to pass a law in Congress establishing a federal slave code for the territories where the local population refused to protect slavery during the territorial stage, Sen. Pugh had bluntly informed the southerners that the northern Democrats would not agree to it. Successful substitution of a more moderate territorial plank in the platform by the Douglas Democrats rather than the federal slave code concocted by the southerners was what had triggered the walkout of southern delegations from the convention and the nomination of separate tickets by the northern and southern wings of the party. But after the election was over and the Union was imperiled by secession moves in the southern states, both Douglas and Pugh proved willing to advocate Crittenden's Compromise amendments as the best way to conciliate the South, prevent any states but fanatical South Carolina from seceding, and thus save the Union. Support for Crittenden's territorial amendment to positively protect slavery during the territorial period in all territory then held or thereafter acquired south of 36° 30′ N.Lat. did indeed force Douglas and Pugh to repudiate their earlier stand in favor of the northern Democratic version of popu-

lar sovereignty. On December 20 Pugh delivered a long Senate speech in favor of the Crittenden Compromise as an alternative to secession and civil war and challenged the Republicans to desert their Chicago Platform of 1860 and prove to the South their good intentions by voting for Crittenden's propositions. The *Louisville Journal*'s reporter said the speech sounded like an apology for and defense of secession, and pointed out that at its conclusion jubilant disunionists like Rep. William Barksdale (D-MS) crowded around Pugh to offer their hearty congratulations on his address. Two days later in the Senate's special Committee of Thirteen, Douglas voted in favor of Crittenden's territorial proposal, though it was defeated by a committee vote of 6-7. Henry Adams and other Republicans detected nefarious, partisan motives behind all this. Democrats certainly did promote the idea that if the southern states remained in the Union, the non-Republicans (Democrats and Americans) would have a majority in both houses of Congress and would thus have the power to block any antislavery moves attempted by the Republicans and the Lincoln administration. But partisan power considerations do not appear as the prime motivation for Douglas and Pugh in their support of the Crittenden Compromise; both made it clear that saving the Union lay at the heart of their effort. Pugh continued his Union-saving theme in a speech to a Union rally in Cincinnati on December 31. [Speech printed in *Cincinnati Daily Commercial,* January 1, 1861]. Throughout the session Douglas worked in tandem with Crittenden to achieve congressional passage of the latter's plan or any other plan they believed had a chance of passage. "Committee of Thirteen Journal," 36th Cong., 2nd sess., *Senate Reports* 288 (Ser. 1090): 5; *Cong. Globe,* 36: 2: Appendix, 31–32, 35; *Louisville Daily Journal,* December 25, 1860; *Morning Courier and New York Enquirer,* December 22, 1860; Levenson et al., eds., *Henry Adams Letters,* 1: 214; Robert W. Johannsen, *Stephen A. Douglas* (New York: Oxford University Press, 1973), 812–815; and McClintock, *Lincoln and the Decision for War,* 69–70, 98.

8. The Bell-Everett party, or Constitutional Union Party, were committed during and after the election to one basic goal—saving the Union—and everyone realized that their sympathies would lie with those other groups in Congress favoring compromise or concessions to the South. Since there had been much talk during the 1860 campaign of

possible fusion between the Douglas and Bell forces, Republicans naturally believed that consultation and cooperation by the two blocs would continue. Henry Adams in his December 28 letter portrays this in conspiratorial terms.

9. The person subjected to this five-hour grilling in chairman Corwin's rooms at Willard's Hotel on Christmas Day itself was John S. Watts, a former federal judge and New Mexico's delegate-elect. He had lived in New Mexico Territory for nine years. Amid questioning from the Republican committee members in relation to New Mexico's soil, climate, produce, resources, and population, Watts related his conviction that southern slave labor would never take hold as a labor system in the region's "barren" landscape. Stegmaier, "An Imaginary Negro," 271.

10. On December 26, the day after they had interviewed Judge Watts, the committee Republicans met again and Corwin proposed that they should offer two measures when the full Committee of Thirty-three held its next meeting. One of these would be a constitutional amendment prohibiting any congressional interference with slavery in southern states, and the second would be a bill for the immediate admission of New Mexico as a state, with or without slavery according to the state constitution its people should adopt. The purpose of the constitutional amendment would be to allay southern fears that the Republicans intended to abolish slavery in the South itself, and the purpose of the bill was to get rid of the slavery question in regard to national territories by forming a state in the only territory then held by the United States where slavery possessed even a theoretical chance of taking hold. The latter proposition would relieve Republicans from having to assume their traditional, steadfast opposition to slavery in national territories. The 1850 Compromise, of which the establishment of New Mexico Territory had been a part, had conveniently provided for the later admission of New Mexico to statehood under the popular sovereignty formula which Republicans on the committee were now ready to invoke. Corwin asked Charles Francis Adams, whom he referred to as "the Archbishop of antislavery," to draft the two proposals. A very reluctant Adams finally agreed to do it, under persuasion from Corwin and other committee Republicans, as an attempt to resolve the national crisis. Stiff-necked Republicans opposed to any compromise tried to dissuade Adams, while

most southerners treated the New Mexico statehood measure as a "dodge" to allow Republicans to avoid the territorial slavery issue. Adams of course believed that the Republicans needed to make some effort toward compromise in order to assist the Unionist element in the border slave states in their efforts to combat the secessionists in their states. He felt that Republicans, in offering these two measures, could impress the border state populations as to their good will toward them on the slavery issue, without having to sacrifice party principles or platform. Adams wished to drive a wedge between the secessionist Cotton South and the border slave states anxious to remain in the Union if they could. It was a courageous mission for Adams to undertake, for he realized that many Republicans would severely criticize his actions, as indeed they did. Ibid., 266–267, 271–276; and C. F. Adams to W. D. Robinson, January 5, and to E. C. Banfield, January 13, 1861, C. F. Adams Letterbook, roll 164, part 2, *MAP.* Henry Adams in his letters writes of his father and the committee in vague, rather detached terms; he knew a lot more than he was communicating but always wrote his newspaper correspondence with a consciousness of the need to preserve his anonymity.

11. Henry Adams here refers primarily to the similarity between propositions for a constitutional amendment against congressional interference with slavery in the southern states. In their Chicago Platform of 1860 the Republicans had pledged such non-interference from outside with "domestic institutions" of states. President-elect Lincoln had an interview at Springfield on December 20 with Thurlow Weed, editor of the *Albany Evening Journal* and mentor of and close advisor to Sen. William Seward of New York. Lincoln gave Weed several suggestions for resolutions for the Senate Committee of Thirteen; Weed first discussed these briefly with Sen. Seward on a train trip from Syracuse to Albany, but Seward did not receive Lincoln's written memorandum of suggested resolutions until December 26. In the meantime Seward, having arrived back in Washington on the 24th, had offered a set of three resolutions in the Committee of Thirteen and later claimed he assumed that they embodied the substance of Lincoln's proposals. Two of Seward's resolutions did involve the issue of fugitive slaves and the personal liberty laws used by some northern states to avoid enforcing the constitutional obligation to return fugitive slaves to their owners in the South. Lincoln's memo-

randum had mentioned both of these topics. But Seward also offered a resolution not included in Lincoln's written memorandum; this was for an amendment to the U.S. Constitution and it stated: "No amendment shall be made to the Constitution which will authorize or give to Congress the power to abolish or interfere within any State, with the domestic institutions thereof, including that of persons held to labor or service by the laws of said State." Seward here referred to slaves by the wording already employed in Article 4, section 2, clause 3 of the Constitution —the fugitive slave clause. It is not clear from existing records whether or not Lincoln had discussed such a constitutional amendment with Weed at Springfield. The proposal was certainly not in Lincoln's written memorandum. Roy P. Basler, ed., *The Collected Works of Abraham Lincoln* (New Brunswick, NJ: Rutgers University Press, 1953), 4: 156–157; and Burlingame, *Lincoln,* 712. Glyndon G. Van Deusen in *William Henry Seward* (New York: Oxford University Press, 1967), 240–241, mistakenly lists the constitutional amendment among Lincoln's proposals. See also letter of December 20 from Springfield correspondent of *Cincinnati Daily Commercial,* December 26, 1860; and letters of December 20 and 21 from Springfield correspondent [Henry Villard] of *New York Herald,* December 25, 27, 1860. The wily Seward may have cooked the amendment up on his own and then claimed to have derived the idea as one of Lincoln's during Seward's oral discussion with Weed. Seward's letter of December 26 explaining all this to Lincoln is reproduced in Frederick W. Seward, *Seward at Washington as Senator and Secretary of State. . . 1846–1861* (New York: Derby and Miller, 1891), 484–485. Lincoln himself never disputed the notion that he may have supported it to Weed, and indeed the president-elect supported the proposition once it was made. Still, the question remains why Lincoln did not include it in his written statement, even if he had suggested it to Weed. Given Seward's history of acting based on his own calculations and without consulting others and in his desire to exercise the leadership role among congressional Republicans that everyone seemed to expect from the New Yorker, it would not be surprising for Seward to have undertaken this amendment proposal on his own. Lincoln would have then been faced with the choice of either repudiating the man whom many Republicans still considered the party leader and whose support Lincoln would definitely need when he took office, or of letting Republicans think Lincoln had a hand in the amendment and endorsing it. Since Seward's amendment contained nothing obnoxious to Lincoln's sensibilities, the president-elect could easily choose the latter option. Ideas for constitutional amendments to prevent congressional interference with slavery in various ways had been talked of earlier in the session (e.g., several House proposals introduced on December 12 and referred to the Committee of Thirty-three included such constitutional amendments. *Cong. Globe*, 36: 2: 76–79). Seward could simply have put together his suggested amendment based on these earlier congressional ideas and in a form which he felt Republicans could vote for.

However, Seward probably looked no further than the Senate Committee of Thirteen for the source of his amendment, giving even more indication that the amendment originated in Washington and not in Springfield. Three major newspapers, the *Philadelphia Inquirer*, the *New York Times*, and the *New York Tribune*, traced the origin of Seward's amendment to a compromise plan devised by Sen. James W. Grimes of Iowa, with some input by Sen. Jacob Collamer of Vermont. Both were Republican colleagues of Seward's on the Committee of Thirteen. The aforementioned papers referred to the Grimes initiative as the "ultimatum" of the Republican members of both the House and Senate special committees. The *Times* listed his first proposal as if it were merely a resolution, which stated: "that the Constitution shall never be so amended as to permit the interference of the Federal Government with Slavery in the States, and that this shall be secured by legislative enactment." When Seward, probably working closely with Grimes, framed this proposal as a constitutional amendment, he substituted the circumlocution of the fugitive slave clause to avoid placing any direct mention of "slavery" in the Constitution. He also limited the scope of the amendment to actions by Congress to avoid any congressional interference with the other two federal branches. Grimes's next two proposals, on fugitive slaves and personal liberty laws, also became part of the package offered by Seward in the committee on December 24. A fourth Grimes proposal—to enable New Mexico to enter the Union as a slave state—was not offered by Seward. For one thing he probably concluded that the Adams bill of the House Committee of Thirty-three sounded more equitable to the North and less proslavery. For another, Seward would have had a very hard time explaining to Lincoln how he could have misinterpreted Weed's oral version of Lincoln's suggestions to specifically include one on New Mexico statehood. *New York Times*, December 28, 1860; *New York Daily Tribune*, December 25, 1860; and *Philadelphia Inquirer*, December 25, 27, 1860.

Rep. Charles Francis Adams devised a constitutional amendment very similar to that of Seward and submitted it to the Committee of Thirty-three on December 28, four days after Seward had introduced his. Adams's measure stated: "Resolved, That it is expedient to propose an amendment to the Constitution of the United States providing that no amendment having for its object any interference within the States with the relation between their citizens and those described in the second section in the first article of the Constitution (the three-fifths clause) as 'all other persons' shall originate with any state that does not recognize that relation within its own limits, or shall be valid without the assent of every one of the States composing the Union." Adams's wording was more cumbersome than Seward's and not so specifically limited to prohibition of congressional interference as was Seward's. Seward and Adams were very close friends and consulted with each other, but no record indicates that they discussed their respective constitutional amendments.

The Committee of Thirteen approved Seward's suggested amendment on December 24, the day it was offered, by a vote of 11-2, while the Committee of Thirty-three voted 21-3 in favor of Adams's resolution just after it was proposed on the 28th, and voted formally for the amendment itself 20-5 on January 11. Seward's proposal was the only one strongly endorsed by the Senate committee, but the committee dissolved on December 28 in frustration over their inability to arrive at any agreement on an overall settlement of the issues. The committee made no report except that it could not agree and saw no use in continuing its deliberations. Adams's amendment did become part of the Committee of Thirty-three's majority report on January 14, 1861; after that time it became known as the Corwin amendment, after the committee chairman who delivered the majority report.

There was less similarity between the Senate and House committees in relation to the territories. Following sometimes heated discussions with other congressional Republicans, Adams brought forward a resolution on December 29 declaring it was "expedient" to admit New Mexico Territory, including the Arizona region, as a state. The Committee of Thirty-three adopted the resolution that day by a less-than-overwhelming 13-11, and on January 11 voted 14-9 for the New Mexico statehood bill itself. During its one week of meetings the Senate Committee of Thirteen considered several proposals on territorial slavery, including Crittenden's. Finding no general consensus on any of these, the committee was near to collapse when Sen. Henry M. Rice (D-MN) offered a plan which garnered considerable support. On December 12 Rep. John Sherman (R-OH) had proposed in the House that the existing territories should be admitted to the Union as states of convenient size. Southerners feared such an arrangement because it would definitely create more free states than slave states and only add to the already-predominant political clout of the free states in both houses of Congress. On December 27 Sen. Rice refined this idea into a resolution for the establishment of only two states, one on each side of the 36°30' N. Lat. line, including within the bounds of the two states all organized or unorganized territories. The northern one would be named "Washington," and it would absorb the Territory of Kansas which was applying for admission as a free state at this session of Congress. The southern one would be admitted as the state of "Jefferson." Rice introduced this in the Senate on the 27th for reference to the Committee of Thirteen, and the next day brought it up as a member of that committee. The committee's Republicans found the idea repulsive since they saw the admission of a separate state of Kansas as the culmination of their struggle to win that territory for freedom since 1854. They did not want it to now disappear and become just another part of a gigantic state called "Washington." Sen. Seward moved to amend Rice's resolution to exempt Kansas from it. The vote on Seward's amendment was 6-6, with the committee's five Republicans and Douglas voting for it. When this motion thus failed, the resolution itself was voted down 3-10. Rice introduced a modified version of his two-state plan in the Senate on January 16, and some congressional interest in Rice's formula for a compromise on the territories issue continued for the rest of the session. "Committee of Thirteen Journal," 11, 17–18; "Committee of Thirty-three Journal," 19–21, 35–37; "Disturbed Condition of the Country," 36th Cong., 2nd sess., *House Reports* 31 (Ser.

1104): 11–12; *Cong. Globe* 36: 2: 76–79, 195, 401; Stegmaier, "An Imaginary Negro, " 271–272, 277; and R. Alton Lee, "The Corwin Amendment in the Secession Crisis," *Ohio Historical Quarterly* 70 (January 1961): 12–19.

12. Southern Unionists in the border slave states consisted primarily of former Whig Party members who, after the demise of that party in the mid-1850s, had mostly joined the Know-Nothing or nativist, anti-Catholic, anti-foreign immigrant movement as an alternative to the Democrats in their states. They operated under various labels, as the American Party in some places, simply as the Opposition in others. Strongly pro-Union as they were in the secession crisis, these border staters wanted more definitive guarantees from the Republicans on slavery than the Republicans believed they could give, if they did not reject compromise altogether. Southern Unionists chiefly desired that Republicans agree to the Crittenden Compromise, with its very explicit recognition of slavery where it already existed and in present or future territories below the old Missouri Compromise line. While southerners on the Committee of Thirty-three might appreciate Adams's amendment and his New Mexico bill as a gesture of good will by moderate Republicans, these measures were not the concessions they wanted. Among the southern Unionists, only Henry Winter Davis fully supported the Adams measures. Francis Bristow of Kentucky, the only other border slave state Unionist to vote for the New Mexico bill, later told Adams he had voted for it only to acknowledge it as a Republican effort toward conciliation but that Kentuckians would consider it an insult to them. Adams became so discouraged by the southern Unionists' lack of enthusiasm for his amendment and bill that he voted against both of his own proposals when the committee majority approved them on January 11. Later in the session, under the urging of Cassius M. Clay of Kentucky, a rare moderate Republican in the Upper South, Adams would reverse himself and resume his support of the Committee of Thirty-three proposals. Stegmaier, "An Imaginary Negro," 272, 276–278, 283.

LETTER 7

Boston Daily Advertiser, January 5, 1861

Letter from Washington
[FROM OUR OWN CORRESPONDENT]

Washington, Jan. 1, 1861[1]

New Year's Day is over, with all its calls, it eggnog and apple toddy, its commiserations over national affairs, and its threats of murder and arson. From noon to dark every gentleman in Washington almost, has been rushing about from house to house, toiling to be amusing and, if a republican, striving to keep his temper and avoid politics. One might as well try to avoid death. The ghost of this murdered republic rises everywhere, and meets everyone. I am told that this has been comparatively a dull New Year's day, that many houses are closed and that the callers have been comparatively few. I can say from my own experience that in spite of the troubles nearly every one has seemed tolerably gay and willing to amuse himself so long as possible. And this, too, although almost everyone has talked of certain civil war; of streets drowned in blood, and of the city a prey to the flames. Many of the residents here are preparing to remove their families; many more talk of it; but the majority are contented with lamenting their lot, and hoping some improvement.

From all that I hear, I am convinced that there is certainly somewhere some concerted plan by which it is hoped to prevent Mr. Lincoln's inauguration, and if possible secure this city to the seceders. Men who know more about it than I, say that such a plan was concerted early in the campaign, under the idea that the whole South would vote for Breckenridge [Breckinridge], and on Lincoln's election would seize the Capital and declare their candidate President. They declare that three at least of the President's Cabinet were concerned actively in this plot, and there are persons enough who believe firmly that Mr. Buchanan himself was privy to it. The election defeated this plan by dividing the South;

the hasty action of South Carolina disconcerted the parties to it still more;[2] the resignation of Cobb and now of Floyd and the substitution of honester men[3] in their places, have completely defeated it, but every blow has only made the seceders more bitter and now the whole city is in a paroxism of fear at the boldness of their threats and the openness of their parade.[4]

The ramifications of the plan are enormous; indeed this whole idea seems to have formed only a part of a grand design, according to which the southern States, after seceding and seizing this city, were to have invited the northern States to a reconstruction of the Union on terms which should suit the South. New England was to have been left out, but it seems to have been hoped that New York city would acquiesce in it, if bribed sufficiently high. It was thought that California would come in also, thus securing the whole southern half of the continent.[5]

Most sensible northern men would laugh at such a story as this, and say that none but mad-men could really expect success from such a crazy plan. Still, I am convinced that it is so. I have heard it from quarters that give it great weight, and all the acts of the southern men, including Mr. Sickles,[6] tally with it. It is to the evident defeat of the idea, that I believe the growing bitterness of the seceders is due, and when almost every soul in Washington, except the seceders, became actually light-hearted last Saturday over the rumored appointment of Gen. Scott as the acting Secretary of War, they only felt it as a death-blow to these plans, and a guarantee to the safety of this city.[7]

Today I have had a chance to see what the real course of opinion is here, and in all the oceans of punch, and floods of company-talk, and acres of paste-board,[8] there has been nothing so very prominent as this dread of violence. If once, I have been told fifty times, and that by young and old, men and women, that within a month these streets would be drenched in blood. They *knew* it. Yes! I might laugh and pooh-pooh as much as I chose. I should see it soon enough. One band was organized in Baltimore. Another in this city. More in Virginia. A conflict was certain, whatever the result might be.[9]

This is pleasant talk over cake and egg-nog, and an agreeable change from the usual vapidity of New Year calls. To one who believes as I do, that the tide has turned and that the worst to be expected here is a possible attempt at riot, it is hard not to laugh and joke over such talk; but to those who really believe that the whole city is in the greatest danger of utter destruction from day to day, it must be rather difficult to keep up a sufficient stock of good spirits. Altogether this has been as extraordinary a New Year's day as any one could wish to see.

NOTES

1. Adams's scholars—biographers and the editors of his letters such as Samuels, Levenson, and Chalfant—somehow never spotted this or the subsequent letter, no. 8, as they researched in the *Advertiser.* Edward Chalfant even wrote in his biography of Henry Adams that the young man may have taken a New Year's break from his newspaper correspondence due to a bad cold. How, one may ask, did these scholars miss the two letters in the *Advertiser* issue of January 5? Chalfant provided a clue to the answer when he wrote that the Adams letters "uniformly" appeared on page 2 of the paper. But editors of newspapers were not uniform in their layout, and sometimes would shift material which they ordinarily published on one page to a different page for various reasons. Unfortunately, the earlier searchers for Adams's *Advertiser* letters assumed that since the letters were regularly on page 2, they always were. They failed to look on page 1 of the January 5 issue. It was the only issue in which two separate Adams letters appeared, and maybe the editor, Charles Hale, felt that they would best fit on page one of that particular issue. Chalfant, *Both Sides of the Ocean,* 201, 212.

2. Adams's letter of January 1 conveys a strong sense of the paranoia that gripped Washington during the Secession Winter and dampened much of the usual New Year's festivities and gaiety. It is not difficult to understand why the residents of the District, surrounded as it was by the slave states of Maryland and Virginia, were consumed incessantly during these months with rumors of disunion plots to seize control of Washington, disrupt the official counting of the electoral vote in February, and prevent Lincoln's inauguration on March 1. The version of the southern plot which Henry Adams related in his letter was based on

what Sen. Douglas told Charles Francis Adams in a conversation on New Year's Day. Douglas apparently felt that his efforts in the Upper South during the campaign had helped to break up the slave state unity which the plotters had depended upon in order to fulfill their plan. C. F. Adams Diary, January 1, 1861, roll 76, part 1, MAP; C. F. Adams to Richard H. Dana, Jr., February 9, 1861, box 16, Dana Family Papers, Massachusetts Historical Society, Boston; *New York Herald*, February 4, 1861; and Henry Adams, "Great Secession Winter," 8–9. For another version of the same plot, as related by Attorney General Edwin Stanton to Sen. Charles Sumner (R-MA), see Sumner to Gov. John A. Andrew of MA, January 26, 28, 1861, Andrew Papers, roll 2, Massachusetts Historical Society, Boston, also in Sumner Papers, roll 74, Houghton Library, Harvard University, Cambridge. See also F. W. Seward, *Seward at Washington*, 497, 502.

3. The "honester men" Adams mentions replacing Cobb and Floyd were Philip F. Thomas of Maryland as secretary of the treasury and Joseph Holt of Kentucky as secretary of war. When the secession-sympathizing Floyd resigned at the end of December, President Buchanan transferred the fervently Unionist Holt from his position as postmaster-general to the more vital cabinet position in charge of the war department. In early January 1861 Thomas would resign the treasury post and be replaced by John A. Dix of New York. See also Henry Adams, "Great Secession Winter," 9–10, 21.

4. Adams, in writing of disunionists openly parading their secessionism in Washington, probably had in mind the particular display by some government employees. As he would later write:

> The most flagrant treason was openly proclaimed, accompanied by threats that reminded one of the days of Catiline. Clerks in the Government Departments mounted the disunion badge and talked openly of oaths they had taken never to permit the inauguration of Abraham Lincoln. Before that should happen Washington would be a heap of ashes. Some of them appeared in costumes of homespun, and announced that it was the uniform of a corps of five hundred who were bound by solemn oaths never to allow the election to be declared or the inauguration to be consummated. Persons whose busi-

ness led them to keep late hours were alarmed by meeting bodies of men drilling at midnight in the environs of the city. Henry Adams, "Great Secession Winter," 7.

Not all the sentiment displayed in Washington, of course, was pro-secession. The commissioners sent from South Carolina to see President Buchanan became quite indignant when they discovered on Sunday morning, December 30, that a Unionist wag had managed to emplace a U.S. flag in the hand of the equestrian statue of Andrew Jackson, near the White House, with a blue secession cockade attached to the horse's rear end. *Cincinnati Daily Commercial,* January 1, 1861. The most egregious flaunting of secessionism took place at the New Year's Day reception given to the public for two hours that day by President Buchanan and the bachelor president's niece Harriet Lane. Though the reception was not as well attended as it traditionally had been, many of the attendees at this function were government employees and their families sympathetic to the South. Now disdainful of President Buchanan for refusing to relinquish the Charleston forts to South Carolina when their commissioners had demanded it, for refusing to order Maj. Robert Anderson to evacuate Ft. Sumter, and for shuffling the membership of his cabinet to eliminate disunionists from it, some government clerks and others came to the reception in order to show their contempt for the chief executive. As he greeted people in the reception line, some swept by the president and refused to shake his hand. Others avoided paying their respects to him altogether and simply went directly over to the East Room for food and drink. Many of the men and women sported their secession cockades. The South Carolina badges or cockades consisted of three layers of dark blue cloth, notched at the edges and fastened together by a shiny brass button. The button depicted a palmetto tree, emblem of that state, with two arrows crossed and fastened with a bow of ribbon where the two intersected. Around the button were the words of the state motto: "Animis opibusque parate," i.e., "ready with our minds and means." As if to underscore the industrial weakness of the South, the cockade, as one Boston reporter related, on its reverse side read "Manufactured by the Connecticut Manufacturing Co." Apparently anticipating or having heard that secession cockades would be worn in abundance at the event, about a dozen Union-sympathizing reporters attended the reception decked out in Union blue rosettes and badges. These Union cockades consisted of a red silk center surrounded by a white silk rosette with blue pendants below, all fastened together with a gilt button showing an American eagle encircled by stars. Despite the opposing displays, no fights reportedly broke out at the reception. President Buchanan looked worn and haggard to reporters, but he was all politeness and smiles to his guests who acted graciously. For detailed descriptions of the cockades, see Baltimore *Sun,* December 5, 1860; *New York Herald,* December 15, 1860; Richmond *Daily Dispatch,* December 17, 1860; and *Springfield* (MA) *Daily Republican,* December 17, 1860. The reverse side of the South Carolina badge is mentioned in *Boston Herald,* December 14, 1860. For accounts of the reception, see: *Boston Morning Journal,* January 65, 1861; Boston *Daily Evening Traveller,* January 5, 1861; *Cincinnati Daily* Commercial, January 5, 1861, which deemphasized the secessionist presence; Louisville *Daily Journal,* January 7, 1861; New York *Evening Post* (semiweekly), January 5, 1861; New York *World,* January 4, 1861; St. Louis *Sunday Morning Republican,* January 6, 1861; and Nichols, *Disruption of American Democracy,* 433.

5. In this paragraph of his letter, Henry Adams refers to one of the most protean concepts in the secession crisis, that of "reconstruction." The idea had emerged as soon as the possibility of southern secession as a result of Lincoln's election became likely. If the southern states, or some of these, seceded, could the Union be then put back together again? And on what terms? Was it an idea seriously considered by moderates or just a ploy or "dodge" tossed out by secessionists to cover their moves to achieve permanent disunion? Reconstruction was a concept fraught with the potential for numerous interpretations, shapes, and rumors. Adams in his letter of January 1 refers to one of the rumors about "reconstruction" as part of a sinister southern plot to ultimately have the rest of the country, except New England, reshape the Constitution to satisfy the South. In the various reconstruction scenarios, rumored or seriously suggested, New England, upstate New York, and the Upper Midwest—the most antislavery areas—were to be excised to form their own confederacy or to join with Canada. Adams's reference to New York City arose from New York Democratic newspaper editorials and a De-

cember 10 speech by Rep. Daniel Sickles (D-NY) in Congress suggesting that if the Union dissolved, New York City should secede from the rest of New York state. New York's Democratic mayor, Fernando Wood, would actually propose this to the city's Common Council in early January.

Sometimes closely related to the reconstruction idea was the notion that several possible confederacies might result from a general dissolution of the Union. General Winfield Scott had outlined several possible subdivisions of the old Union in October 1860 for President Buchanan. On January 7, 1861, Gov. John Letcher of Virginia described a four-confederacy scene in his message to the Virginia state legislature. Basically these schemes envisioned a lower South, the Pacific and southwest areas, a Central or Middle Confederacy of northern and southern border states, and an upper North. Whether these confederacies would combine further or make war on each other or simply coexist was beyond prediction. The most definite proposal in this regard was that of a Central Confederacy or "Federal Republic of Washington," an idea advocated primarily by southern border state moderates in December and January. The plan initially included Missouri, Kentucky, Tennessee, Virginia, Maryland, Delaware, New Jersey, Pennsylvania, Ohio, Indiana, and Illinois. Since the Old Northwest states were adamant about having access to the length of the Mississippi River for transportation of their produce, proponents of the Central Confederacy also advocated inviting Louisiana, Texas, Arkansas, and Mississippi to join them.

Some of those desperate for compromise to avoid civil war latched onto the reconstruction panacea as hopes for any practicable adjustment diminished during the session. Proposals for the calling of a national convention to formulate a settlement were often touted as a prelude to reconstruction. Sen. Stephen Douglas (D-IL), identified by Charles Francis Adams as the source for the southern conspiracy plot story portrayed in Henry's January 1 letter, was later in January reported as becoming a prime mover in promoting reconstruction if compromise efforts failed. Whatever interest Douglas may have expressed in secession-and-then-reconstruction, by early February he was urging the border slave states to remain in the Union as an important step in enticing the seceded states of the Deep South back into the Union. All of those in Congress who urged the reconstruction formula were southerners or northern

Democrats such as Sen. William Gwin of California and Sen. Joe Lane of Oregon who were close allies of the southerners. Southern Unionists were genuinely sympathetic to reconstruction as a possible solution to the crisis. The same might be said for reluctant secessionists such as Sen. Jefferson Davis of Mississippi and Sen. Robert M. T. Hunter of Virginia. The motivations of fire-eating disunionists such as Sen. Louis T. Wigfall (D-TX) and Rep. Muscoe Garnett (D-VA), when they mentioned reconstruction possibilities, were highly suspect.

Hopes for reconstruction as a solution to the secession crisis foundered for the same reasons that compromise plans did. There simply was no basis for a meeting of the minds of northerners and southerners on the underlying issues. Republicans steadfastly condemned reconstruction as a fraud and delusion employed by southern disunionists to seduce the border slave states into secession. Republicans instinctively realized that, if they made any favorable comments about reconstruction possibilities, it would imply Republican recognition of a right to secede in the first place. In addition they argued that if disunion became complete, North and South would never agree to reconstruction. Radical southern disunionists also disdained reconstruction; they wanted a government of their own and interpreted reconstruction as simply another gimmick resorted to by "submissionist" border state southerners. Staunch disunionists argued that the natural division should be between free and slave states, and they ridiculed southern Unionist ideas for a Central Confederacy as an impossible alliance of slavery with the enemies of slavery. When secessionists in Congress broached the idea of reconstruction after secession, they always made eventual reconstruction dependent on there being no federal coercion used against the seceded states. Such coercion, they said, would bring civil war and destroy all possibility of reconstruction. Even southern Unionist advocates of reconstruction demanded as a condition for it that the Constitution be amended to protect slavery along the lines of the Crittenden Compromise. Republicans, of course, saw this as only another move in the old southern game of forcing the North to recognize and protect the right of property in slaves as a national institution.

As events progressed in and out of Congress during the Secession Winter, talk of reconstruction gradually diminished. The actual secession of seven southern states, South Carolina's firing on the unarmed steamer *Star of the West* in early January as President Buchanan attempted to use that ship to reinforce the beleaguered U.S. garrison at Ft. Sumter, the formation of a Confederate government at Montgomery, Alabama, in early February, and a general stiffening of resolve by both northerners and southerners pretty much ended discussion of reconstruction by early February. At the beginning of that month, however, the idea began a curious resurrection in an unlikely source–the *Cincinnati Commercial,* one of the leading Republican newspapers in the Midwest and considered a voice for the interests of radical Republican leader Salmon P. Chase. In a series of editorials this newspaper began arguing that secession was a fact which the North should accept and allow the South to separate peaceably. The *Commercial*'s editors believed this was an alternative preferable to civil war. But they did not expect that situation to last very long before southern mismanagement and government ineptitude had ruined the southern Confederacy economically and politically. Then a reconciliation and reconstruction of the old Union would begin. It all proved to be just a last, very strange twist in the reconstruction notion.

On the plot described in Adams's January 1 letter, see also: C. F. Adams Diary, January 1, 1861, roll 76, part 1, C. F. Adams to John G. Palfrey, January 5, and to Richard H. Dana, Jr., February 9, Adams Letterbook, roll 164, part 2, *MAP;* Henry Adams, "Great Secession Winter," 8–9; and Rep. John M. Ashley (R-OH) to S. P. Chase, December 18, 1860, John Niven, ed., *The Salmon P. Chase Papers: Microfilm Edition* (Frederick, MD: University Publications of America, 1987), roll 14. On the scheme to have New York City secede from New York state, see *Cong. Globe,* 36: 2: 41; *New York Daily News,* December 20, 22, 1860, January 8, 9, 12, 1861; and Jerome Mushkat, *Fernando Wood: A Political Biography* (Kent, OH: Kent State University Press, 1990), 111–113. On various ideas related to the establishment of several confederacies, especially a Central Confederacy, see: *Cong. Globe,* 36: 2: App., 98–99; *Charleston Mercury,* December 29, 31, 1860, January 24, 26, March 2, 1861; *Cincinnati Daily Enquirer,* December 22, 1860, January 8, 1861; *Louisville Daily Courier,* December 19, 1860, January 19, 21, 1861; *Louisville Daily Journal,* December 4, 1860, January 8, 1861; *Memphis Daily Appeal,* December 30, 1860, January 8,

February 3, 1861; *New Orleans Daily Crescent*, January 17, 1861; *New York Times*, December 12, 19, 31, 1860; Richmond *Daily Dispatch*, December 28, 31, 1860, January 8, 1861; St. Louis *Daily Missouri Republican*, December 1, 20, 22, 1860, January 8, February 4, 1861; John P. Kennedy, *The Border States: Their Power and Duty in the Present Disordered Condition of the Country* (Philadelphia: J. B. Lippincott & Co., 1861), 22–23, 35; Smith, *Presidency of Buchanan*, 167; and F. N. Boney, *John Letcher of Virginia: The Story of Virginia's Civil War Governor* (University: University of Alabama Press, 1966), 101–103. For Republican criticism of the reconstruction idea, see: V. W. Kingsley to M. Fillmore, January 23, 1861, Lester W. Smith, ed., *Microfilm Edition of the Millard Fillmore Papers* (Buffalo: Buffalo and Erie County Historical Society and State University College at Oswego, 1975), roll 49; Rep. Eldridge G. Spaulding (R-NY) to Thurlow Weed, December 30, 1860, Thurlow Weed Papers, Rush Rhees Library, University of Rochester; Henry Adams, "Great Secession Winter," 24; *Cong. Globe*, 36: 2: 341, 379, 624, 797, 801, 1392, and App., 47, 159–160; *Chicago Daily Tribune*, December 29, 1860, January 9, 29, and February 8, 11, 1861; *Morning Courier and New York Enquirer*, December 21, 1860, February 12, 1861; *New York Daily Tribune*, December 28, 1860, January 14, 1861; and Philadelphia *North American and U.S. Gazette*, January 8, 11, 28, February 6, 1861. A note from Sen. Douglas critical of reconstruction is in *Macon* (GA) *Daily Telegraph*, February 8, 1861. Southern disunionists' opposition to reconstruction is in : Rep. W. W. Boyce (D-SC) to Sen. R. M. T. Hunter (D-VA), February 5, 1861, Papers of R. M. T. Hunter, 1817–1877, University of Virginia Library, Charlottesville, roll 7 (Lamont Library, Harvard University copy); *Cong. Globe*, 36: 2: App., 226; *Charleston Mercury*, January 24, 26, 31, February 11, 18, 25, March 6, 1861; *New Orleans Daily Crescent*, December 12, 1860, February 5, 14, 22, 1861; Richmond *Daily Dispatch*, December 31, 1860; and Washington (DC) *Evening Star*, January 29, 1861. Northern and southern statements favorable to reconstruction are in: John P. Kennedy to Robert C. Winthrop, December 3, 1860, roll 29, and Winthrop to Kennedy, December 22, 27, 1860, roll 39, Marjorie F. Gutheim, ed., *Microfilm Edition of the Winthrop Papers* (Boston: Massachusetts Historical Society, 1976); *Cong. Globe*, 36: 2: 144–145, 189, 310, 328, 330, 331, 360, 459, 495, 589, 590, 667, 720, 728, 1071, 1366, 1370, and App., 96, 138, 153, 167, 198–199, 260; *Cin-*

cinnati Daily Enquirer, December 8, 1860, January 20, 22, 1861; *Louisville Daily Courier,* December 21, 1860, January 19, 22, 1861; *Macon* (GA) *Daily Telegraph,* November 30, December 1, 1860, January 16, 1861; *New York Evening Express,* December 10, 13, 1860, January 14, 16, 1861; *New York Herald,* November 26, December 9, 10, 11, 16, 1860, and January 3, 4, 5, 7, 22, 1861; St. Louis *Daily Missouri Republican,* December 11, 16, 1860, January 8, February 26, 1861;Washington (DC) *Evening Star,* December 8, 24, 1860, January 7, 10, 1861; and Crofts, *Reluctant Confederates,* 135–136. On the peculiar position assumed by the *Cincinnati Daily Commercial,* see its editorials of February 1, 2, 4, 5, 9, 11, 15, 18, 1861; and Columbus (OH) *Crisis,* February 7, 1861.

6. Rep. Daniel E. Sickles (D-NY) was probably the most notorious northern Democrat in the House. He owed this notoriety mainly to the infamous 1859 incident when he had shot his wife's lover to death in Lafayette Park near the White House. Sickles had then secured acquittal on grounds of temporary insanity, and even managed to keep his wife after forgiving her for her adultery. He also had been one of the most pro-southern of free state Democrats in Congress. Sickles continued in that vein at the opening of the Secession Winter session; on December 10 he addressed the House briefly to defend the right of southern states to secede as a last refuge from the antislavery aggression of Republicans, whom he blamed for driving the South into secession. A week later on December 17 he even proposed a resolution, referred to the Committee of Thirty-three, for a constitutional amendment which would provide a process by which states might withdraw from the Union. However, his defense of the South had its limits, and he considered South Carolina's individual state secession to be an outrage. Sickles by late December and early January transformed into a stiff-necked defender of the Union and a strong supporter of forceful measures undertaken by the Buchanan administration. He opposed any removal of Maj. Robert Anderson's U.S. troops from Ft. Sumter and denounced South Carolina's firing on the *Star of the West.* Sickles did favor the Crittenden Compromise as a settlement but absolutely opposed the South's separate state secession tactic. During the Civil War he would serve in the Union Army as a major general of U.S. Volunteers with the Army of the Potomac. *Cong. Globe,* 36: 2: 40–41, 107, 508–509; and W. A. Swanberg, *Sickles the Incredible* (New York: Charles Scribner's Sons, 1956), 106–113.

7. Gen. Winfield Scott, general-in-chief of the U.S. Army whose military brilliance had played a major role in winning the Mexican War of 1846–1848, stood 6 ft., 5 in. tall and weighed over 300 pounds. At 74 years old he was in frail health when President Buchanan requested him in December 1860 to come to Washington from his headquarters in New York. The president needed Scott's considerable military expertise as he attempted to wrestle with real threats by southern secessionists to seize federal forts and other installations in their states and rumored conspiracies by disunionists in Maryland and Virginia to attack and seize control of Washington itself. General Scott, originally a Virginian and suspected of sympathizing with southern secession, nonetheless felt duty-bound to defend the U.S. government and the Buchanan administration from whatever threats it faced. Despite his advanced age and infirmities and lack of any sizable U.S. forces at his immediate disposal, Scott had arrived in Washington determined to do what he could to prop up the faltering government. Given his military record, many in the District of Columbia instinctively took heart from his presence, as Henry Adams's January 1 letter indicated. Buchanan chose Joseph Holt of Kentucky to be secretary of war, rather than Scott, but Scott continually provided the administration with what advice he could and set about to militarily secure the District against any disunionist notions of capturing it. Scott placed a trusted officer, Col. Charles P. Stone, in charge of building up local defenses and of making a display of military might, small as it was, to discourage disunionist plots within or from outside the District. Some locals and southern politicians naturally complained about Washington gradually taking on the appearance of a military camp, but Scott and Stone were able to bring companies of U.S. troops and batteries of artillery into the District and also to organize a local militia there. The show of force worked, and the rumors and threats about Washington falling into southern hands before Lincoln took office evaporated. Smith, *Presidency of Buchanan*, 167–168, 175, 182, 186; Furgurson, *Freedom Rising*, 28–30, 35–36, 39; and Margaret Leech, *Reveille in Washington, 1860–1865* (New York: Harper & Sons, 1941), 1–5, 27–32.

8. "Acres of paste-board" represents an interesting combination of both hyperbole, or exaggeration, and synecdoche, or in this case referring to an object by the material from which it is made. Henry Adams, in using the phrase he does, is describing tables covered with calling cards

at the places he visited on New Year's. Calling cards were made from pasteboard consisting of several layers or plies of paper pressed together. Henry discussed some of the people he visited with on New Year's Day in a letter to his brother Charles on January 2. Levenson et al., eds., *Henry Adams Letters,* 1:217.

9. See note 7 above. Stoking the rumors and fears in Washington about armed groups in Maryland and Virginia preparing to attack the District were articles proposing such action in the *Richmond Enquirer* and the *Richmond Examiner.* Former Virginia Gov. Henry A. Wise, though he vacillated between Unionism and secession, made some public statements of a similar nature. His son, O. Jennings Wise, edited the *Enquirer.* Baltimore, where the *Sun*'s editorials leaned toward secession, was a hotbed of disunion plotting. Two groups of well-armed militia in Washington itself, the National Rifles and the National Volunteers, were known to be drilling at night and both included many secessionist-minded members. Baltimore *Sun,* December 10, 17, 1860 and January 2, 1861; *Cincinnati Daily Commercial,* December 28, 1860; *Philadelphia Inquirer,* December 20, 1860; *Daily Richmond Enquirer,* December 17, 1860; *Richmond Semi-Weekly Examiner,* December 21, 1860; Washington (DC) *Evening Star,* December 27, 1860 and January 2, 1861; Leech, *Reveille in Washington,* 28–29; and Craig M. Simpson, *A Good Southerner: The Life of Henry A. Wise of Virginia* (Chapel Hill: University of North Carolina Press, 1985), 220, 228–231, 234–241, especially 240–241.

LETTER 8

Boston Daily Advertiser, January 5, 1861

Washington, Jan. 2, 1861

The capitol was thronged again today. Ladies are now in the habit of going up there as early as nine o'clock, with books, or their work-baskets, and their luncheon; and they sit with a patience that is much more than feminine though all the performances.[1] The Senate is a mere debating society, and the honorable Senators talk for the galleries. Today the new Senator from Oregon[2] declared his opinions, but what was of more consequence than that, or than anything else that has yet happened in that body, was the desperate resistance of the southern men to going into executive session on the nomination to the Charleston Collectorship.[3] Of a piece with this was the conduct of the southern side of the other House in fighting the committee of inquiry into the proceedings of Mr. Floyd and other shady matters till now untouched. They fought this as if their lives depended on it, calling the ayes and noes on everything, and raising points of order, interspersed with motions to adjourn, with perfect desperation.[4] This behavior leads every one to suppose, of course, that they are afraid of a development which would do them great harm. It's of no use, however, for the investigation must come in one form or another, and it will probably be voted upon soon. No speeches need be expected in the House for some time to come, for all parties seem agreed to shut them off.

The Senate crisis committee has expired, though it perhaps may be resuscitated some day.[5] The House committee is reduced to a conveniently small number, as some ten members have seceded. The last batch that went did not do it gracefully. Mr. Adams and Mr. Corwin got them into an exceedingly tight place, for when they offered their list of grievances they exploded, every one of them. Mr. Miles Taylor[6] and his friends performed a regular dance from one slippery place to another.

First they pirouetted on the Personal Liberty Laws, when up came the North in a mass with a proposition to repeal or modify anything unconstitutional in those measures. Next they hopped over to the intentions of the North to abolish slavery in the southern States, and here again they were gently tipped over by a proposition to amend the Constitution in such a way that no compulsory abolition should be possible. Then they jumped to the Fugitive Slave Law; it was referred to a sub-committee from the border States. Finally they all united in a howling Irish jig on the territorial question, but here Mr. Adams utterly swamped them by his proposition as to New Mexico, and Mr. Corwin let them down still lower by his motion to strike out the words "hereafter acquired" from their ultimatum. As there was nothing left to dance on, Mr. Miles Taylor and his associates could only make their bow and say that though they had intended a much more extended exhibition of their celebrated feats in ground-and-lofty tumbling, unforeseen circumstances, &c., &c., &c., and retire, which they did.[7]

Joking apart, I do not see but what they have succeeded in completely destroying themselves. The effect that the leading republicans seem to have aimed at has been wholly gained. The seceders have literally been driven from one position to another, till at last they assert their real grievance to be that the republicans will not guarantee slavery in Territory they haven't got; will not mortgage some one else's property; will not pledge themselves to force an institution hateful to God and men on a country that no more belongs to them now than Liliput or Brobdignag.[8] If the seceders are willing to dissolve the Union on this issue, they will immortalize themselves to all time as a very brilliant set of statesmen perhaps, but their own day and generation will hardly sustain them.

The committee will probably report within a fortnight, but as yet there are only two propositions I think which have been almost unanimously agreed upon.[9] We have not as yet heard here what Mr. Corwin proposes to say in the report.

Everyone is talking of a riot which is to take place on the day of declaring the election, and thus to vitiate the whole thing.[10] But the rioters have given such generously early and definite notice that the republicans will be altogether too polite not to make use of their well-meant-attentions, and act accordingly. There is treason enough in this city to hang several Cabinet officers, a number of Senators, a large fraction of the House, and a quarter of the citizens, on a rough calculation. It is by no means certain that some such process may not take place, if people act as they talk; it is still less certain, however, that they will ever venture to act in that way.

NOTES

1. For another description of ladies whiling away the morning hours in the Senate gallery as they waited for debate on slavery and secession to begin (at one p.m.), see *Boston Post,* January 12, 1861. On the relative attractiveness of various senators to the ladies of the Senate gallery, see a correspondent's column in *New York Daily Tribune,* January 11, 1861.

2. Adams here refers to the first part of a two-day speech by Sen. Edward D. Baker (R-OR). Originally from England, Baker had lived in poverty in Philadelphia as a boy weaver, moved to Illinois and became a lawyer and a Whig congressman, served gallantly as a colonel in the Mexican War, and finally migrated to California and then to Oregon. A close friend of Lincoln's since his Illinois days in the 1830s, Sen. Baker had just returned from a visit to the president-elect in Springfield. Having just taken his seat at the start of this session, Baker in this speech of January 2–3 made his first display of Senate oratory. The New York *Evening Post* correspondent described him as: "A tall, military-looking man, of large frame, with his head, which is partially bald, whitened with the snows of perhaps fifty years. He has a high-keyed, distinct and pleasing voice, . . ." This correspondent also noted his good enunciation and animated gestures and speaking style. While ostensibly Baker's address was on some resolutions for constitutional amendments offered earlier on December 13 by Unionist Democrat Andrew Johnson of Tennessee, Baker more specifically delivered his speech in response to a secessionist address by Sen. Judah Benjamin (D-LA) on December 31. Given Benjamin's reputation for legislative argument, the *Post*'s reporter was most impressed with Baker's ability to deftly spar with Benjamin during the Louisiana disunionist's frequent interruptions over the two

days. Baker vehemently denied Benjamin's assertions that the Union was a mere compact of sovereign states and that the 10th Amendment of the Constitution gave states a reserved right to secede. In reply to Benjamin's claims, Baker quoted James Madison, Daniel Webster, John Quincy Adams, and Andrew Jackson. The Oregon Republican denied at length that southern states had any justification for secession on the basis of a right of revolution, stating the North had committed no intolerable oppression against the South, despite acts by individuals like John Brown. Baker provided an orthodox Republican expression of the "freedom national, slavery sectional" doctrine against any southern assertion of a constitutional right to expand slavery. He said southerners feared a cordon blocking them from expanding slavery, but he declared that such a cordon was already in place and that the South would have to accept that there was no place into which they might expand the "peculiar institution." When Benjamin complained of northern antislavery attitudes, Baker defended the North's right of free speech on the issue. He did reiterate the Republican mantra that the Republicans and the Lincoln administration would not interfere with slavery in the southern states. Baker also demonstrated moderation in favoring repeal of any unconstitutional personal liberty laws in the North and the admission of remaining territories as states. On the coercion issue, Baker defended the authority of the federal government to enforce obedience to its laws by all individual citizens of the country. Baker's speech constituted a rather comprehensive review of Republican doctrines on all the major issues, and it undoubtedly pleased his friend Lincoln. Baker's speech is in *Cong. Globe,* 36: 2: 224–229, 238–243. For newspaper commentaries on the speech, see: *Boston Morning Journal,* January 5, 1861; *Chicago Daily Tribune,* January 7, 1861; *Cincinnati Daily Commercial,* January 4, 1861; Columbus *Daily Ohio State Journal,* January 5, 1861; *Louisville Daily Journal,* January 10, 1861; *New York Commercial Advertiser,* January 3, 1861; New York *Independent,* January 10, 1861; New York *Evening Post* (semiweekly), January 5, 1861; New York *World,* January 3, 5, 1861; *Philadelphia Inquirer,* January 3, 4, 1861; and Springfield *Daily Illinois State Journal,* January 8, 1861. The *Philadelphia Inquirer* published a particularly adulatory biographical sketch of Baker on January 11, 1861. A Springfield correspondent provided an excellent description of Baker during his visit with Lincoln. *Cincinnati Daily Commercial*, December 31, 1860. See also Harry C. Blair and Rebecca Tarshish, *The Life of Colonel Edward B. Baker, Lincoln's Constant Ally* (Portland: Oregon Historical Society, 1960). Once the Civil War began, Baker joined the Union Army with the rank of colonel, and died leading his troops at the battle of Ball's Bluff, Virginia, on October 21, 1861.

3. President Buchanan, newly bolstered in his resolve against South Carolina secession by General Scott and cabinet members Jeremiah Black, Joseph Holt, and Edwin Stanton, had decided that he was going to enforce the collection of federal tariff duties at Charleston on board U.S. Navy vessels as the only available means to perform this task. Buchanan had earlier made an informal agreement with South Carolina emissaries not to reinforce the Charleston forts as long as South Carolina took no military action against those positions. After Major Anderson suddenly and secretly transferred his forces from the vulnerable Ft. Moultrie to the much more defensible Ft. Sumter, the federal customs officials at Charleston had resigned their positions, and the angry South Carolinians had seized Ft. Moultrie and Castle Pinckney. These actions by South Carolina had cancelled in President Buchanan's mind any earlier understanding he may have had with the South Carolinians. But in order to collect the customs at Charleston, the president needed to appoint a new collector at Charleston. He chose an old friend from York, Pennsylvania, named Peter McIntire, described in a *Cincinnati Commercial* article as an older, well-respected, conscientious, firm-minded, and dutiful man of Scottish descent who had held positions mainly in York and had campaigned for Breckinridge in the recent election.

When the president sent this nomination in to the Senate on January 2, it fell as a "thunderbolt" on that chamber, as reported by the New York *World*'s correspondent. Sen. Baker had just completed the first part of his speech and pleaded exhaustion as he asked the indulgence of his fellow senators to allow him to complete his address the next day, prior to Sen. Stephen Douglas's scheduled speech. When the McIntire nomination arrived Sen. Preston King (R-NY) moved that the Senate proceed to an executive session to consider the nomination. The report of debates in the *Congressional Globe* provides only a tame rendition of what happened next, but Henry Adams and other Washington correspondents accurately portrayed the sense of turmoil, confusion, and excitement which ensued. Southerners absolutely wanted to block this nomination of a U.S. collector for a port in a state which had declared itself seceded from the U.S. as a "complete declaration of war against the secessionists by the President." Thomas Clingman of North Carolina, Jefferson Davis of Mississippi, and several other southern senators first took up Senate time with a useless discussion of whether Baker should be permitted to complete his speech the next day. Following that the southerners marshaled their forces, with the help of a few northern Democratic friends, to turn back three Republican moves for an executive session. A southern motion to adjourn then barely passed 27-23, with William Gwin of California, Joe Lane of Oregon, Henry Rice of Minnesota, and John Thomson of New Jersey helping the southerners defeat the Republicans, some northern Democrats, and the only slave state senator to vote against the adjournment, Lazarus Powell of Kentucky.

A few days later on January 7 Sen. William Bigler (D-PA), President Buchanan's closest ally in the Senate, moved for an executive session in the late afternoon. This time the motion passed quickly by a vote of 30-23, with John Crittenden (A-KY), Andrew Johnson (D-TN), and Willard Saulsbury (D-DE) joining the northern majority against the southern bloc and Democrats Pugh of Ohio, Lane of Oregon, and Rice of Minnesota. Once in the closed-door executive session, the Senate voted to refer the McIntire nomination to the Committee on Commerce for further consideration. Several reporters interpreted this reference to be a deathblow to the nomination, and therefore a southern victory, since that committee was dominated by southerners. In anticipation that the Commerce Committee would get the nomination, the committee chairman and longtime secessionist Clement C. Clay (D-AL) arrived in Washington on the 8th and took his seat in the Senate for the first time that session. He had been very ill at home until then and appeared "very feeble in health" to one observer. One reporter said Clay looked the very part of Catiline: "That dark, sinister face–those sunken glittering eyes–that long black beard and hair–they would become a bandit of the Appennines [*sic*]. . . ." Initially it seemed that Clay and his southern colleagues on the committee would enjoy the upper hand against the McIntire supporters. Besides Clay, Robert Toombs (D-GA) and Thomas Clingman (D-NC) were certain to oppose the nomination. Willard Saulsbury was questionable. Hannibal Hamlin (R-ME), vice-president-elect, had resigned his Senate seat. That left as the only sure votes for McIntire on the committee William Bigler (D-PA) and Zachariah Chandler (R-MI). But circumstances soon changed the prognostications. Alabama declared itself seceded on January 11 and Sen. Clay withdrew from the Senate on the 21st. Toombs meanwhile left Washington to attend the Georgia secession convention. It appeared then that Bigler would become committee chair and be able to push the McIntire nomination through the committee at least. But the nomination struggle ended there. Neither President Buchanan nor his friend Sen. Bigler pressed the matter further, probably in hopes of avoiding a military confrontation with South Carolina, a confrontation which might provoke some of the border slave states to secede. *Cong. Globe*, 36: 2: 23–231, 271–272; *Boston Morning Journal*, January 5, 7, 9, 10, 14, 1861; Boston *Daily Evening Traveller*, January 11, 1861; *Charleston Daily Courier*, January 8, 11, 1861, the latter issue reprinting an article on McIntire from the *Cincinnati Commercial; Cincinnati Daily Enquirer*, January 9, 1861; *Louisville Daily Journal*, January 12, 1861, describing Clay's physical appearance; *New York Herald*, January 3, 7, 8, 10, 17, 1861; New York *World*, January 2, 1861; and Nichols, *Disruption of American Democracy*, 433–434.

4. Although Henry Adams here singles out newly resigned Secretary of War John Floyd for mention as the target of the proposed inquiry by the House, the resolutions of inquiry offered in that chamber on January 2 concerned the situation at Charleston and questions of what contact administration officials might have had with South Carolina officials in regard to the forts and other federal property. The possibility of sending reinforcements to and collecting federal revenues at Charleston were included in a resolution by William Howard (R-MI). None of the House inquiry resolutions of January 2 specifically targeted Floyd, although Republicans were convinced that he had aided southern secession by transferring arms and artillery to the South while secretary of war. An inquiry by the House Committee on Military Affairs on December 31 would exonerate Floyd of any treasonous behavior. Floyd was, however, incompetent and had mismanaged his department. As to the resolutions of January 2, Adams's letter correctly reports the efforts of southern-

ers in the House, by raising points of order on procedure and taking up time with numerous roll call votes, to block the northern-sponsored resolutions in reference to Charleston. A week later, on January 9, another resolution by Rep. Howard to have an inquiry into the Charleston situation conducted by a select committee of five passed the House 133-62, following a message from President Buchanan about his attempt to reinforce Maj. Anderson at Ft. Sumter. That was also the day on which South Carolina artillery fire forced the unarmed reinforcement ship *Star of the West* to retreat without ever landing its troops. *Cong. Globe,* 36: 2: 221, 231–237, 295–296; Smith, *Presidency of Buchanan,* 187; and George T. Curtis, *Life of James Buchanan: Fifteenth President of the United States* (New York: Harper & Bros., 1883), 2: 413–417.

5. The Committee of Thirteen, after a long meeting on December 28 which resolved none of the crisis issues, decided to adjourn "sine die" unless the committee chairman decided that there might be some use in a future meeting. On December 31 the committee assembled to hear the journal of its proceedings read, but that was the last time they would meet. "Committee of Thirteen Journal," 14–19.

6. Rep. Miles Taylor, Louisiana Democrat. Not considered a secessionist per se, Taylor was described by the *Baltimore American*'s correspondent as an able, rather conservative southern member of the House. But Taylor also believed strongly that the Crittenden Compromise formula of unamendable constitutional amendments offered the only real security for what southerners deemed their rights regarding slave property against the expected antislavery measures of the incoming Republican administration. After the Republicans on the Committee of Thirty-three managed on December 28 to strike out from the southern-sponsored committee version of the Crittenden Compromise any reference to protecting slavery in future territorial acquisitions south of 36° 30′ N. Lat., Taylor recorded a protest in the committee journal indicating his despair that the committee would make any effective changes to the Constitution and declared his intention to no longer participate in committee sessions. He did not, however, resign his seat on the committee, since, as he stated, he wished to participate with some other committee southerners in a minority report against whatever majority report the committee produced. See Letter 12, note 2. Following Louisiana's secession

on January 26, Rep. Taylor delivered a withdrawal speech in the House on February 5; in this address he repeated his views on the need for iron-clad constitutional amendments to protect slave property, blamed the North for having caused the crisis, warned that the South would fight if the North attempted any coercion, and proclaimed that European powers would intervene on the side of the South in any civil war because of their economic dependence on southern cotton. "Committee of Thirty-three Journal," 19, 21–22; 36th Cong, 2nd sess., *House Reports* 31 (ser. 1104), majority and minority reports of Committee of Thirty-three, part 4–report of Taylor et al., 1–20; *Cong. Globe,* 36: 2: 751–754; and *Baltimore American and Commercial Advertiser,* December 7, 1860.

7. Henry Adams's paragraph here does not refer to any particular events in the Committee of Thirty-three on January 2. Rather it is his humorous summation of what had transpired in the committee up to that time. Given Adams's obvious Republican bias in the summary, his account does conform to the basic facts of what had occurred. In his portrayal of the southerners as dancers, one can sense Adams's fun in writing this literate, masterful analysis. Every time the southerners had demanded concessions, the Republicans and Henry Winter Davis of Maryland had devised counter-proposals which the committee majority had voted to adopt: Davis's resolution on December 18 for states to repeal their personal liberty laws, Adams's resolution on December 28 for a constitutional amendment to prevent federal interference with slavery in the states, and Adams's resolution on December 29 on the expediency of admitting New Mexico as a state. Southerners, of course, desired the more explicit guarantees for slave property in the Crittenden Compromise, for which Republicans could never vote. Corwin's successful maneuver on December 29 to eliminate the words "hereafter acquired" from the Crittenden Compromise territorial amendment emasculated the proposition in southerners' eyes, for Taylor and his friends saw this as the essential concession of "principle" by Republicans on the territorial question. Republicans instead proposed New Mexico statehood to avoid the issue of slavery in national territories, especially future ones, altogether. Henry Adams probably singled out Taylor for personal mention in his "dancing" analogy because Taylor on the 29th had offered resolutions in the committee demanding explicit constitutional recog-

nition of the right of property in slaves, and had then filed his written protest for the Crittenden Compromise. The Committee of Thirty-three on January 11 would approve the specific constitutional amendment and the New Mexico statehood bill, both framed by Charles Francis Adams. C. F. Adams Diary, December 29, 31, 1860, roll 76, part 1, *MAP;* "Committee of Thirty-three Journal," 11–12, 19–22, 24, 35–37; and Henry Adams, "Great Secession Winter," 2–21.

8. "Liliput or Brobdignag" should be spelled more accurately "Lilliput or Brobdingnag." In Jonathan Swift's satirical and imaginative novel, *Gulliver's Travels* (1726), Lilliput is a land of pygmies and Brobdingnag a land of giants.

9. Davis's resolution on the personal liberty laws had met no recorded opposition on December 18, while Adams's resolution for a constitutional amendment had passed the committee by a 21-3 vote on the 28th. Adams's resolution for New Mexico statehood had encountered stiffer opposition the next day, winning approval by only a 13-11 vote. "Committee of Thirty-three Journal," 11, 19, 21.

10. One of the many rumors circulating in Washington during the Secession Winter was that disunionists planned to stage a riot in Washington on February 13 to disrupt the official counting of the electoral votes in Congress. If anyone seriously considered planning a riot that day, General Scott's military preparations to provide security in the District gave any expectant rowdies a sober second though. No disturbance occurred on February 13, and Abraham Lincoln was declared officially elected as president.

LETTER 9

Boston Daily Advertiser, January 11, 1861

Letter from Washington
[FROM OUR OWN CORRESPONDENT]

Washington, Jan. 7, 1861

The plot is thickening. So many striking events have been crowded into the last few days that it is hard to keep the account. Tomorrow reinforcements will have reached Major Anderson, or else there will be war begun by South Carolina; which of the two, you will know long before this reaches you.[1] There is the sound of war in Washington. Troops are concentrating here; the militia is organizing; officers are ordered off, and we hear no more of that weak hesitation which lasted up to the retreat of Floyd. Mr. Buchanan is redeeming himself. He is absolutely showing vigor and courage, and is said to be very defiant towards the secessionists. Wonder of wonders, he is supported by the republicans and is now to most intents and purposes as good as a republican. Some future Shakespeare will have a grand field in his weakness and timidity, and "Leave me sir; leave me! I must go pray."[2]

Mr. Lincoln's Cabinet is understood to be nearly settled. I suppose there is no doubt that Mr. Seward will be its head.[3] Of course the friends of Mr. Seward are delighted, and even those who would have preferred some other man as a matter of policy, have nothing to say against it. New England will be represented by Mr. Welles of Connecticut,[4] it is understood; and though Massachusetts thought her services worth a Cabinet place, still I do not believe she finds any fault with this appointment.

Mr. Seward will soon speak in the Senate and his speech will be, I suppose, a plan of policy for the administration. After the stuff that Toombs and Benjamin, Mason and Wigfall talk, it will be refreshing.[5]

Things look darker again about a compromise. Out-generalled in committee, the southerners under the lead of Mr. Crittenden, are trying to turn the flank of the republican party on its weakest side. Mr. Crittenden is an extraordinary man; he does not seem to suppose that the North has any honor. He comes forward in his plausible way and asks the North to yield all they have fought for and gained; to give up any amount more of territory to slavery and what is worse still, to recognize this grant in the Constitution. I really do not see that Mr. Jefferson Davis asks much more than this, practically. Mr. Crittenden, too, has no party and speaks for no one. He is not a man of great weight and such a proposition from him is of value only as he can bring it to suit men, not as he can bring men to support it. Finally, for any southern man to propose a return to the Missouri compromise line is so cool that some fanatical creatures who still preserve a little self-respect, might call it an insult.[6]

Still it might pass Congress possibly, and worse than that, it might make ill-feeling among the republicans. There was a story some days ago that Mr. Seward favored it. This of course is mere nonsense. I believe there could not be invented a story crazy enough not to be snapped up by the New York reporters[7]. All the real republicans are against it, and John Hickman[8] is said to have made a very effective speech in caucus on the matter. Mr. Weed,[9] by the way, who came on here with various compromise measures of his own, has gone back today, without having found the first republican to give them countenance. The truth is, that no compromise can be invented that will do any good. Congress can do nothing to keep the South, except by overthrowing the North, and if any one still thinks they can do that, he must be curiously blind.

There was violent kicking in the House today over the resolution as to Major Anderson, and of support to the administration in sustaining him, but it was passed by a large majority.[10] Various changes of tactics on the part of the secessionists are spoken of; among others that the seceding members are to go home to their States, but the Senators will remain here, in order, I suppose, to stop all legislation that displeases them. It will be a curious sight, that of a State which claims to be independent, still allowing herself to be represented in Congress.[11]

NOTES

1. A reference to the *Star of the West*'s mission. At General Scott's behest, President Buchanan at the beginning of January decided to send reinforcements to Maj. Robert Anderson at Ft. Sumter. An unarmed side-wheel steamer–a merchant vessel–was chosen for the mission; troops and supplies were not-so-secretly loaded aboard the vessel, and the ship steamed from New York harbor on January 5. From the beginning the mission went badly. Southerners up North learned of the reinforcement attempt and forewarned South Carolina by telegraph. On the other hand, Maj. Anderson did not know the ship was coming. As the *Star of the West* approached Charleston harbor early on January 9, South Carolina's shore artillery opened fire. The ship had no choice but to retreat back to New York, undamaged and with no casualties. It was a humiliating debacle for the Buchanan administration. Many people in the North and their state legislatures quickly reacted with commitments to maintain the Union and to take military action against South Carolina. Some state legislatures pledged armed forces to carry out any military operations undertaken by the government. But no military action proved forthcoming. Maj. Anderson and Gov. Francis Pickens of South Carolina established an informal truce at Charleston, and the cautious President Buchanan planned but did not carry out any further missions to reinforce Ft. Sumter during the remainder of his administration. The threat of war, which Henry Adams deemed so imminent in his January 7 letter if South Carolina attacked the *Star of the West,* did subside during the weeks after the event.

2. Given the intense strain under which President Buchanan operated during the Secession Winter, with his own cabinet initially divided between southerners sympathetic to secession and northerners urging a forceful stand against disunion and with his own natural sympathies in favor of resolving southern grievances by compromise and for maintaining peace, it is understandable why the president appeared mired in vacillation. Ever since his annual message of early December when, on the one hand, he denied any state's right to secede from the Union but then, on the other hand, denied that the federal government had a right

to employ military coercion against seceding states, politicians in Washington had engaged in ridiculing the "Old Public Functionary," as he was known. Republicans especially had made him the brunt of jokes. When President Buchanan on December 15 published a proclamation urging the nation to observe January 4 as a day of fasting and prayer to invoke the aid of Providence in the crisis, his proposal only increased the sarcasm. Henry Adams declared in a December 18 letter to his brother that Buchanan alternated between crying and praying, and he included a similar statement in his later "Great Secession Winter" essay. On January 4 the special prayer services held in Washington at the House of Representatives drew a reported audience of some six thousand people, crammed into every nook and cranny of the chamber, to hear an eloquent Union sermon by Rev. Thomas H. Stockton, chaplain of the House. Various churches in the District and elsewhere also conducted services that day. The *Boston Courier*'s Washington correspondent reported that the members of Congress mainly congregated in the clubs, bars, and hotels on that day. President Buchanan did seem quite prayerful himself, understandably under the circumstances. On December 28, when a South Carolina delegation consisting of Robert W. Barnwell, James H. Adams, and James L. Orr came to the White House to demand that the president recognize the legitimacy of South Carolina's secession by withdrawing the federal troops from Ft. Sumter and turning over all federal installations in South Carolina to that state, President Buchanan grew weary after two hours of the delegation's badgering.. In order to finally get rid of the three emissaries, the president invoked his need to pray over the matter. As J. L. Orr remembered Buchanan's statement over a decade later, he said: "Mr. Barnwell, you are pressing me too importunely. You don't give me time to consider. You don't give me time to say my prayers. I always say my prayers when required to act upon any great state affair." By that time Buchanan, under the influence of General Scott and secretaries Black and Holt, had no intention of caving in to South Carolina's demands, and, when he did reply in writing, he refused to agree to what they wanted. Barnwell, Adams, and Orr headed back to South Carolina empty-handed. Undoubtedly President Buchanan had verbally responded on the 28th in words very similar to what Orr later remembered, even if Orr's version may not have been, with the passage of time, an exact rendition of the president's actual words. As Buchanan's statement to the South Carolinians traveled through the gossip-and-rumor mill of Washington, it wound up in Henry Adams's January 7 letter as a plaintively desperate statement. President Buchanan had his faults but he was not at this stage quite so pathetically inept or weak as Republicans like Adams portrayed him. Adams's reference to Shakespeare in the sentence indicates that Henry may have had in mind, as he wrote this, one of Hamlet's short statements to Horatio: "I hold it fit that we shake hands and part:. . . Such as it is, for mine own poor part, Look you, I'll go pray." *Hamlet,* act 1, scene 5. The president's "Recommendation" for the fast day is in Washington (DC) *Constitution,* December 15, 1860. On the fast day observances, see *Boston Daily Courier,* January 9, 1861; *Cincinnati Daily Commercial,* January 5, 1861; *New York Commercial Advertiser,* January 5, 1861; *New York Times,* January 5, 1861; *Address: by Thomas H. Stockton, Chaplain U.S.H.R. Delivered in the Hall of the House of Representatives, on the Day of National Humiliation, Fasting, and Prayer, Friday, January 4, 1861* (Washington: Lemuel Towers, 1861); Nichols, *Disruption of American Democracy,* 409, 555, n. 28; and Philip S. Klein, *President James Buchanan: A Biography* (University Park: Pennsylvania State University Press, 1962), 372. On the "crying and praying," see Mrs. Roger A. Pryor (Sara A. R. Pryor), *Reminiscences of Peace and War* (New York: Macmillan Co., 1905), 110; Levenson et al., eds., *Henry Adams Letters,* 1:208; and Henry Adams, "Great Secession Winter," 6. Philip Klein, due to a misreading of Pryor's work, mistakenly attributed the statement to Buchanan's former secretary of state, Lewis Cass, but Pryor did not name her source for the "crying and praying" phrase. Klein, *Buchanan,* 374–375. On Orr's version of Buchanan's statement to the South Carolinians, see ibid., 387; and especially Nevins, *Emergence of Lincoln,* 2: 371.

3. Lincoln had offered Seward the state department on December 8, and after due consideration Seward had accepted the position on December 28. Seward would reconsider his decision in early March 1861 but would finally agree to stay in the cabinet as secretary of state. Van Deusen, *Seward,* 239–241, 253; and Henry Adams to C. F. Adams, Jr., January 2, 1861, Levenson et al., eds., *Henry Adams Letters,* 1: 217; and F. W. Seward, *Seward at Washington,* 481, 487. For a recent, detailed account of Lincoln's selection of his cabinet, see Burlingame, *Lincoln,* 1: 719–745, 2: 52–58.

4. As with other presidents-elect, Lincoln's choices for cabinet positions reflected attempts to satisfy various factional and sectional blocs within the Republican Party. In early January when Henry Adams penned this letter to the *Advertiser,* there was still a great deal of public speculation about the cabinet posts, except for the state department which Seward had already accepted. Gideon Welles of Connecticut was high on the list of other likely choices for Lincoln's cabinet as one who would satisfy the need to award a seat to the former Democrat wing of the Republicans and also to a New Englander. Welles was a Democratic newspaperman in the Jacksonian era, who had then become a Free Soil Democrat and finally a Republican. Some thought that Charles Francis Adams might get a cabinet post under Lincoln, and young Henry certainly hoped his father might, but Welles appeased more groups and Adams's closeness to Seward tainted his chances. Lincoln kept Welles and everyone else in suspense until the beginning of March when he appointed Gideon Welles his secretary of the navy. He would perform efficiently and energetically in that vital role during the Civil War. John Niven, *Gideon Welles: Lincoln's Secretary of the Navy* (New York: Oxford University Press, 1973), 303–323; and Henry Adams to C. F. Adams, Jr., January 2, 1861, Levenson et al., eds., *Henry Adams Letters,* 1: 217.

5. Robert Toombs of Georgia, Judah P. Benjamin of Louisiana, James M. Mason of Virginia, and Louis T. Wigfall of Texas were all extremist southern Democrats in the Senate, if not outright disunionists. Wigfall had given formal speeches on December 5, 12, and 13, Benjamin on December 31, and Toombs on January 7. *Cong. Globe,* 36: 2: 12–14, 71–76, 85–87, 212–217, 267–271, respectively. Mason had given no formal speech yet but had actively expressed his views in shorter remarks. Ibid., 35, 55–57, 156, 158.

6. Another incisive Henry Adams critique of the Crittenden Compromise, as in Letter 5, written on December 22. See also Henry Adams, "Great Secession Winter," 10–11.

7. Sen. William Seward of New York, given how much the public at large looked to him for leadership in forging a congressional resolution of the secession crisis, walked a more precarious tightrope during these months than anyone else in Washington outside President Buchanan himself. Seward's position had been complicated from the beginning of

the session after his mentor and close advisor Thurlow Weed in late November had editorialized in his *Albany Evening Journal* in favor of a compromise involving restoration of the Missouri Compromise line in the territories as a way to avoid civil war. Although this seems to have been Weed's own idea, many detected the hand of Seward in it too. When Crittenden proposed his famous compromise a few weeks later, one also including the 36°30′ N. Lat. line, it was natural for some to conclude that Seward might support it or similar proposals. More radically anticompromise Republicans were among those who suspected Seward would divide the party by favoring some proposition to which the great majority of Republicans could never assent. Border slave state Unionist leaders hoped that Seward might finally vote for the Crittenden Compromise or something like it, which would assist them in fighting the secessionists in their home states. Despite Republican fears that Seward would betray them, Seward steadfastly refused to adopt any stand which would violate the party's principles and platform. Seward instead adopted a delaying action, hoping to keep as many border slave states in the Union as possible until March 4, when the Lincoln administration could take over and handle the secession crisis. Therefore Seward in these months always appeared calm, exuded his usual charm and gregariousness, smiled a lot, constantly assured people that the crisis would be amicably settled, and spoke softly and moderately without ever committing himself to any particular set of compromise proposals which would have satisfied the southerners. The New Yorker said many things to many people, and he sometimes fueled speculation that he would vote for the Crittenden Compromise or another plan by implying that he might support such compromise plans under certain conditions or with certain amendments to them. The *New York Herald*, that city's leading Democratic paper, was a source of speculation on Seward's pro-compromise intentions in late December, as was the Washington *Evening Star*. Seward frustrated all such speculation, however. *New York Herald*, December 26, 1860; and Washington (DC) *Evening Star*, December 27, 1860. For comments on Seward in early January by Washington correspondents, who were sometimes mystified at his calm demeanor in the midst of the crisis, see: *Baltimore American and Commercial Advertiser*, January 8, 1861; *Boston Daily Courier*, January 11, 1861; *Boston Morning Journal*, January 5, 1861; *Morning*

Courier and New York Enquirer, January 17, 1861; *New York Evening Express,* January 9, 10, 1861; and St. Louis *Daily Missouri Democrat,* January 9, 1861, reprinting a column by Washington correspondent of *Cincinnati Commercial.* See also: F.W. Seward, *Seward at Washington,* 477–515; Chalfant, *Both Sides of the Ocean,* 213; Van Deusen, *Seward,* 238–249; Crofts, *Reluctant Confederates,* 219; and Van Deusen, *Thurlow Weed: Wizard of the Lobby* (Boston: Little, Brown and Co., 1947), 266–268.

8. Rep. John Hickman of Pennsylvania had originally been elected as a Democrat to the 34th and 35th Congresses and as an Anti-Lecompton (i.e., anti-Buchanan administration) Democrat to the 36th Congress. During that Congress he completed his transition into a Republican and participated in their caucuses. The particular caucus to which Henry Adams referred in his January 7 letter was probably the House Republican caucus held on January 5. The focus of their concern at the caucus, however, was not the Crittenden Compromise but a similar one that had been put together by a self-appointed "Committee of Fourteen" from northern and southern border states in the last days of December and the first days of January. This comprehensive settlement, like Crittenden's, would protect slavery in territories south of the old Missouri Compromise line but, unlike Crittenden's, would not apply to future acquisitions of territory and would require a two-thirds vote of both House and Senate to approve the addition of any new territory or two-thirds of the Senate if the acquisition was done by treaty. *Louisville Daily Journal,* January 11, 1861; *New York Herald,* December 26, 30, 1860; and January 5, 6, 7, 8, 1861; *New York Times,* December 29, 1860, January 5, 7, 1861; *New York Daily Tribune,* January 7, 1861; New York *World,* December 29, 1860, January 7, 1861; *Philadelphia Inquirer,* December 31, 1860, January 3, 7, 1861; Philadelphia *North American and United States Gazette,* January 7, 1861; Philadelphia *Press,* December 31, 1860; Springfield *Daily Illinois State Journal,* December 31, 1860, January 7, 9, 1861; and Washington (DC) *Evening Star,* December 28, 29, 1860, January 3, 5, 1861. Nearly all of the Republicans considered the border state compromise as providing for constitutional recognition of slavery, particularly in national territories, just like Crittenden's, and so they opposed it. Though the Republican caucus of January 5 was supposed to be secret, Washington correspondent James Harvey ("Independent") of the Philadelphia *North*

American became privy to the details of the meeting, as did a correspondent of the *New York Tribune.* Harvey reported that Hickman joined noted Republican radicals Owen Lovejoy of Illinois, Thaddeus Stevens of Pennsylvania, and John Bingham of Ohio in denouncing the border state, Crittenden's, or any other compromises as an abandonment of the 1860 Chicago Platform of the party. On January 7 when Rep. Emerson Etheridge (A-TN) attempted to get House rules suspended so that he could introduce the border state plan into that chamber, the motion received a majority of 83-78 but not the two-thirds required to suspend the rules. Hickman was one of the Republicans who voted against reception of the plan. *Cong. Globe,* 36: 2: 279–280; Philadelphia *North American and United States Gazette,* January 7, 1861; *New York Daily Tribune,* January 7, 1861; and New York *World,* January 10, 1861. Republican rejection of the border state plan greatly discouraged southerners, especially Unionists, and led several southern congressmen to write angry letters which were published in their home states. *Louisville Daily Courier,* January 19, 1861; *Macon* (GA) *Daily Telegraph,* January 14, 1861; *Philadelphia Inquirer,* January 9, 1861; and Springfield *Daily Illinois State Journal,* January 10, 11, 1861. See also Crofts, *Reluctant Confederates,* 201, 204, 232–233.

9. Weed had come to Washington from New York, arriving on January 5, with a delegation of New York business and political leaders–Erastus Corning, W. H. Aspinwall, Hamilton Fish, James W. Beekman, Moses Grinnell, and others–to urge members of Congress, especially Republicans, to compromise in order to save the Union (and retain New York's good business relations with the South in regard to the cotton trade with Europe). Weed and his associates wanted any compromise, even Crittenden's or the border state plan. In particular, they pushed for a compromise introduced into the New York legislature by Assemblyman Lucius Robinson; it was very similar to the compromise proposed by Sen. Henry Rice (D-MN), and included the admission of all remaining territory, in addition to Kansas, as two states divided at the 36° 30′ line (Letter 6, note 11). Weed et al. found the Republicans impervious to their pleas. Even Democratic leader Stephen Douglas of Illinois told the New York delegation that their plan would only make free states throughout the West in a matter of months and do nothing to appease the South. After a few days of such chilly reception, Weed departed for Albany on January

7, anxious at least to press the New York legislature to adopt Robinson's plan. More radical Republicans in the legislature were able to block the proposal offered by moderate Republican Robinson. Charles Sumner to John A. Andrew, January 8, 1861, roll 2, Andrew Papers; *Cincinnati Daily Enquirer,* January 8, 11, 1861; *Cincinnati Weekly Gazette,* January 9, 1861; *New York Evening Express,* January 8, 1861; New York *Independent,* January 10, 1861; New York *Evening Post* (semi-weekly), January 9, 1861; *New York Times,* January 7, 8, 1861; *New York Daily Tribune,* January 5, 7, 1861; *Philadelphia Inquirer,* January 9, 10, 1861; Philadelphia *Press,* January 8, 1861; St. Louis *Daily Missouri Democrat,* January 9, 1861, reprinting column from *Cincinnati Commercial;* St. Louis *Daily Missouri Republican,* January 12, 1861; Washington (DC) *Evening Star,* January 7, 1861; Van Deusen, *Weed,* 268–269; McClintock, *Lincoln and Decision for War,* 129–131, 137, 157, 178; and Potter, *Lincoln and His Party,* 178.

10. The resolution, by Anti-Lecompton Democrat Garnett B. Adrain of New Jersey, not only supported Maj. Robert Anderson's decision to move his troops from Ft. Moultrie to the safer Ft. Sumter, but also endorsed President Buchanan's new determination to support Maj. Anderson. The resolution passed the House 124-56 despite southern condemnation of it. *Cong. Globe,* 36: 2: 280–282; and C. F. Adams Diary, January 7, 1861, roll 76, part 1, *MAP.*

11. Henry Adams here pointed out a dilemma for the southerners. They had discussed in their caucuses the idea of remaining in Congress after their states seceded, in order to block legislation hostile to the South. Practical as that tactic might have initially appeared, southerners from seceding states did not attempt to employ it. To do so would have called into serious question the southern assertion that their states had a right to secede and were no longer part of the old Union. As their states declared themselves seceded and sent official notification of that to Washington, the southern congressmen and senators gave farewell addresses in their respective chambers and departed for home. For an account of the southern senators' caucuses at which they first supported and then rejected the idea of remaining in the Senate, see: (Sen.) Thomas Bragg (D-NC), Diary, January 11, 12, 1861 , Southern Historical Collection, University of North Carolina Library, Chapel Hill; Clement Eaton, *Jefferson Davis* (New York: Free Press, 1977), 124; and Cooper, Jr., *Davis,* 321–322.

LETTER 10

Boston Daily Advertiser, January 15, 1861

Letter from Washington
[FROM OUR OWN CORRESPONDENT]

Washington, Jan. 11, 1861

The political barometer fluctuates violently from day to day. The news from Charleston, the last plan of compromise, the action of the seceding States, the opinions of the Cabinet and Gen. Scott, are the points of discussion and curiosity with the crowd. But if I understand the state of affairs here rightly, the real and deep anxiety of all the Union leaders centres on one point, or perhaps two. Whether Fort Sumter is reinforced or not is in point of fact of little actual importance. Whether the Cotton States will secede or not, is now not the most vital question. But the question which really goes deepest is, what will be the action of Virginia and Maryland? Their secession would bring about an immediate collision with all its consequences. If they do not secede, the troubles can be comparatively easily managed. The struggle is very great in both these States, but I am told this evening that Maryland is tolerably secure. There was a Union meeting in Baltimore last night,[1] which has encouraged the Union men here very much. I understand that it is now thought certain that Northern troops can pass through Baltimore without trouble,[2] and that Gov. Hicks[3] will be sustained by the State. Any man here would understand what an immense point this is to be gained.

As for this city, you can rely upon it that there will be no great trouble. In a few days there will be a force here large enough to maintain it. I am told that the wish is, not to have too strong a force here; only enough to hold their ground twenty-four hours or so in case of attack, until aid should come from the North. All this is arranged, I believe, and it is not wished to do too much. It will need only a telegraphic word to set a host of bayonets in motion towards this city.

Mr. Jefferson Davis's speech is regarded here as subdued, illogical and weak. He seemed very much troubled by the evident intention of the Union men to fight, if need be, and hinted at a reconciliation. Some of his remarks called up Andrew Johnson of Tennessee, against whom Mr. Davis tried to be sarcastic, but without success.[4] If that is the best Mr. Davis can do, Andrew Johnson is worth six of him. There is probably no man who is now hated so violently by the extremists as this Mr. Johnson. Originally a tailor, his wife first taught him to read, and helped him to what book-education he has. Of all the southern men in Congress, he is the only one who has not played at hide-and-seek with treason. His speech in the Senate[5] is to my mind the best that has been delivered there on the subject, except perhaps Mr. Wade's,[6] which was of the same sort; that is, plain common sense without much show or polish. The Southerners say that Johnson will be tarred and feathered when he goes home, but others declare that his State will support him. If all the Southern Union men had had his courage, there would be no question about it, but they have almost without exception played directly into the hands of the secessionists.

The Committee of Thirty-three are winding up their labors. Today all the seceders were called back again to vote finally on the propositions which have been carried. It is rather hard for an outsider to unravel the confused threads of their proceedings,[7] but so far as I can make it out the Southerners are now unwilling to take the responsibility of rejecting the report, but before committing themselves to it, want to see if they cannot make something out of Mr. Crittenden's propositions. The Northerners on the other hand want to force them to take one side or the other. This seems to be the object of some resolutions which Mr. Adams introduced, the first of which asserted the duty of acquiescing in Mr. Lincoln's election. Seven of the Southern men refused to vote on this, and filed a paper declaring their reasons,[8] whereupon Mr. Adams introduced another resolution, setting forth that since seven States had refused to acknowledge the duty of acquiescence in a Presidential election, there could be no use in further discussion and that the chairman be authorized to report a disagreement and ask that the committee be excused from further duty.[9] This hit them again and they fought it off, and so the matter now stands. Tomorrow there is to be a republican caucus to decide whether they will go on, or at once stop all further talk on the matter.

There is an immense amount of intrigue and confusion about the Cabinet; at least, it looks so to an outsider. I do not believe that Mr. Cameron will take the Treasury.[10] No doubt he will be in the Cabinet, but not, I think, in that department. Who will have it is another question, and as there are a variety of cross-influences, I rather think the matter will remain open a little while yet.

Mr. Seward speaks tomorrow. His effort will be, I take it, to unite the North and divide the South. This must be the policy of every great statesman. We have seen how it has been done in the Committee of Thirty-three. Tomorrow we shall see how the future Secretary of State manages it.

NOTES

1. Much depended in the secession crisis on what the border slave states would do. To the people of the District of Columbia, surrounded as it was by Maryland and Virginia, the concern all boiled down to what actions those two states would take. The rumors flying around the District in December had made it appear as if Washington was virtually under siege from secessionists in the neighboring states, and disunionists in Baltimore loudly vocalized their desires for Maryland to secede and then to capture the District. But gradually Unionists began to organize and to unfurl their U.S. flags in Baltimore. As Henry Adams's letter indicated, the holding of a Unionist mass meeting in that city on the evening of January 10 relieved the minds and warmed the hearts of Unionists in Washington. The meeting was held at the Maryland Institute Hall, and, soon after the doors to that large room were opened at 7 p.m., it "was thoroughly packed in every part" of the lower floor and galleries, according to the Baltimore *Sun*'s report. A band struck up "Hail Columbia," the "Star-Spangled Banner," and "Yankee Doodle" as the huge crowd filed in. The gathering then heard and cheered Unionist speeches opposed to the calling of any secession convention in the state, speeches delivered by William H. Collins, Augustus W. Bradford, Reverdy Johnson, and others. The assembled multitude approved resolutions proclaiming loyalty to the Union and, just before adjournment, listened to a supportive letter from Sen. John J. Crittenden, read to the assemblage. Even though

disunionists in Baltimore were holding meetings on January 10 and 11 to urge the governor to call a state convention, the Union rally demonstrated that Baltimore was a divided city in its attitude toward disunion. Henry Adams to C. F. Adams, Jr., January 8, 1861, Levenson et al., eds., *Henry Adams Letters,* 1: 219; *Baltimore American and Commercial Advertiser,* January 11, 12, 1861; Baltimore *Sun,* January 11, 12, 1861; and J. Thomas Scharf, *The Chronicles of Baltimore;. . .* (Baltimore: Turnbull Bros., 1874), 584–585.

2. Baltimore was most essential to the military security of the District some forty miles to the southwest, for any northern troops coming into Washington by rail had to come through Baltimore. The Philadelphia-Wilmington-Baltimore Railroad and the Northern Central Railroad were the lines northern forces would have to travel to Baltimore, and from there the Baltimore & Ohio Railroad would transport them into the District. Gary L. Browne, *Baltimore in the Nation, 1789–1861* (Chapel Hill: University of North Carolina Press, 1980), 164–165. Advertisements and some schedules for the respective railroads can be found in any issue of the Baltimore newspapers.

3. Gov. Thomas H. Hicks of Maryland had been elected in 1857 as an American. During the secession crisis Hicks played a pivotal role in keeping that border state in the Union. Despite intense pressure from disunionist members in the legislature, agents sent to him from seceding states, and resolutions from public meetings in Baltimore, Hicks firmly resisted demands that he call a special session of the legislature which would then call a state convention which might then pass a secession ordinance. Many Marylanders, of course, fervently supported their governor's Unionist stand. Hicks strongly supported Sen. Crittenden's compromise as a solution to the sectional issues, and he believed its passage would surely keep Maryland and the other border slave states in the Union. As divided as sentiment on secession was in Maryland, the state might have drifted into the southern orbit had it not been for Gov. Hicks. For Hicks's communications during the crisis, see *Executive Letter Book, 1854–1861,* 145–192, Maryland State Archives, Annapolis; and Thomas H. Hicks to John J. Crittenden, December 13, 1860, January 9, 19, 1861 (roll 12), January 25, 1861 (roll 13), Crittenden Papers, Manuscripts Division, Library of Congress. See also Ella Lonn, "Thomas Hol-

liday Hicks," in Dumas Malone and Allen Johnson, eds., *Dictionary of American Biography* (New York: Charles Scribner's Sons, 1933), 5: 8–9.

4. In a message sent to Congress on January 9 but dated the day before, President Buchanan discussed his exchange of communications with the South Carolina commissioners and placed the responsibility squarely on Congress to declare war on seceded states or to authorize a military force to enforce federal law in those states. Sen. Jefferson Davis of Mississippi, whose home state was seceding that day, succeeded in getting printed into the public record the final, bitter, and insulting letter sent by the commissioners to the president and which Buchanan had left out of the documents accompanying his message. Continuing the next day with a long formal speech in relation to the president's message, Jefferson Davis on the 10th seemed angry at President Buchanan's new-found resolve to maintain federal occupancy of Ft. Sumter and his apparent contemplation of employing military force to subdue South Carolina. Davis argued that Maj. Anderson had been wrong in moving his troops to Ft. Sumter, that the South would resist any federal coercion, and that only peaceful secession, including the withdrawal of federal soldiers from southern forts, would make an eventual reconciliation or reconstruction possible. The Mississippi senator defended secession both as a reserved right under the Constitution and on the basis of the right of revolution against oppression. This brought staunch southern Unionist Democrat Andrew Johnson of Tennessee to interrupt Davis's speech with a brief assertion that it would be much better for the South to battle for her rights within the Union, that Democratic majorities in the Senate could block any Republican moves hostile to southern rights or block any Republican patronage appointments inimical to the South, and that the South in the Union could effectively control not only Lincoln's job appointments but also the military appropriations. Davis's "sarcastic" response, to which Henry Adams referred, consisted of a declaration that Johnson and unconditional Unionists like him seemed determined only to subvert the government to which they supposedly clung, an act of revolution. Johnson and his friends would do this rather than fight; for himself, Davis said, he would choose the type of revolution which the founding fathers had fought. Senator Davis devoted the last part of his speech to an indictment of the Republicans for having

caused the crisis through their policies of hostility to slavery. He accused them of inciting the slaves to revolt–they were too ignorant, he said, to do that on their own–and he believed that the Republicans, using federal troops, would instigate a slave revolt in the South reminiscent of that on St. Domingue at the turn of the century. Davis's speech was basically a synthesis of favorite southern themes; it contained no new ideas and its delivery did not positively impress most reporters who heard it. *Cong. Globe,* 36: 2: 284–289, 306–312; Crist, ed., *Jefferson Davis Papers,* 7: 8–9; Richardson, comp., *Messages and Papers,* 5: 655–659; Boston *Daily Evening Traveller,* January 11, 1861; Louisville *Daily Journal,* January 16, 1861; New Orleans *Sunday Delta,* January 20, 1861; *New York Evening Express,* January 11, 1861; *National Anti-Slavery Standard* (New York), January 19, 1861; New York *Evening Post* (semi-weekly), January 12, 1861; Springfield *Daily Illinois State Journal,* January 14, 1861, reprinting correspondent's column from *Cincinnati Commercial;* Nichols, *Disruption of American Democracy,* 443–444; W. C. Davis, *Jefferson Davis,* 292–293, 725, n. 28; and Cooper, Jr., *Davis,* 323–324.

5. Andrew Johnson, Democratic senator from Tennessee, was an anti-secessionist and one of the firmest southern Unionists in the Senate. Charles Francis Adams, Jr., described him as "a rather tall, strongly built man, with black hair and a swarthy complexion," possessed of pleasant but "slightly formal" manners, a clean-shaven face, and the look of someone both physically and intellectually strong. Johnson believed that the southern states had just grievances which needed redress, but he believed that nothing the South had suffered so far justified the revolutionary act of secession. Johnson, whose elocution fellow Democratic congressman Samuel S. Cox of Ohio found "more forcible than fine–more discursive than elegant," argued at length in his speech of December 18–19 that the South's rights could best be protected and their problems solved by remaining in the Union. He denied the existence of any right of secession under the Constitution, and defended the right of the federal government to recapture any federal property which seceding states might seize. Disunionists reacted with outrage to Johnson's speech and views while northerners of all parties lavishly praised it. *Cong. Globe,* 36: 2: 117–119, 134–143; Leroy P. Graf and Ralph W. Haskins, eds., *The Papers of Andrew Johnson* (Knoxville: University of Tennessee

Press, 1976), 4: 3–51; C. F. Adams, Jr., *C. F. Adams, 1835–1915*, 79; Henry Adams, "Great Secession Winter," 11; Samuel S. Cox, *Union–Disunion–Reunion: Three Decades of Federal Legislation, 1855–1885* (Washington, DC: J. M. Stoddart & Co., 1885), 71; and Hans L. Trefousse, *Andrew Johnson: A Biography* (New York: W. W. Norton & Co., 1989), 130–132.

6. See Letter 4, note 1.

7. Another Henry Adams statement to protect his identity and to cover up the fact that, through his father, he did have inside information about the committee's proceedings.

8. The southerners and Charles Francis Adams on the Committee of Thirty-three were frustrated and facing dilemmas. The southerners had wanted the Crittenden Compromise, with its explicit recognition of slavery and its protection for slavery in present or future territories south of 36°30′ N. Lat. The more moderate Republicans on the committee instead offered Adams's propositions for a constitutional amendment opposing any interference with slavery in the southern states, and the bill to establish New Mexico statehood, encompassing the then-held territory of the United States below the 36°30′ line. Southerners considered neither of these to be the concession of "principle" on the recognition of slavery which they wanted. At the same time, the southern members did not want to appear as opponents of any compromise by voting against the committee's propositions. Adams was very frustrated too. He had stuck his neck out for compromise, drafting the constitutional amendment and the New Mexico statehood bill. These measures had gained him a torrent of criticism back in Massachusetts from those who believed Adams was backing down in the face of southern threats. To extricate himself from his quandary, Adams had announced in committee on January 8 that, unless the southerners assented to or at least expressed their views on his measures, he intended to oppose both the bill and amendment when they came up for vote. That, he hoped, might mollify his angry constituents. When the committee next met on the same day as Henry Adams penned his *Advertiser* letter, January 11, Charles Francis Adams called up a resolution he had introduced on the 8th, which declared that acquiescence in the election of a president was "the paramount duty" of every good U.S. citizen. The exasperated Adams wanted to force the southerners to take a firm stand one way or the other on

Lincoln's election. Members from the slave states did not want to so unequivocally endorse the election. John S. Millson of Virginia therefore moved to substitute "a high and imperative" for "the paramount"; his amendment to Adams's resolution passed 11-10. Adams confided to his diary that Millson had pulled out his "sharpest tooth" in the resolution by the change. He also noted that the substitute only passed because Freeman H. Morse (R-ME) removed himself to the next room to avoid voting. Adams's resolution, amended by Millson, then passed 22-0. Before the final vote was taken, Millson embarrassed the southern extremists by declaring his intention to vote for the amended resolution. Seven of them retired to consult in the next room–Democrats Miles Taylor of Louisiana, John S. Phelps of Missouri, George H. Houston of Alabama, Peter E. Love of Georgia, Albert Rust of Arkansas, Andrew J. Hamilton of Texas, and William G. Whiteley of Delaware. The seven wrote out and signed a statement of their reasons for not voting on the resolution at all, and they had it recorded in the committee journal. After having signed the document, Hamilton changed his mind, and expressed his approval of the resolution as amended by Millson. The brief written statement asserted that the Adams resolution, no matter how amended, could not contribute in any way toward a settlement of the crisis nor lead to passage of laws by Congress or amendments to the Constitution. Thus the signers considered voting on the measure a useless gesture. Millson and two Americans–Francis M. Bristow of Kentucky and Thomas A. R. Nelson of Tennessee–also provided a written testament in the journal explaining their reasons for voting in favor of the resolution, among which were their conviction that a vote against or withheld from the resolution would imply that they believed that there would be no acceptance of the election result by the South no matter what settlement might be reached, and also their belief that refusal to vote on the resolution would erroneously signify to people that the grievances claimed by southerners were only a pretext to cover their resistance to the election of a president they did not like . C. F. Adams Diary, January 8, 11, 1861, roll 76, part 1, *MAP;* "Committee of Thirty-three Journal," 32–35; Duberman, *C. F. Adams,* 246; and Stegmaier, "An Imaginary Negro," 276–277.

9. Henry Adams is mistaken here in stating that his father offered this as a resolution in the committee on the 11th, for there is no such

resolution recorded in the committee journal for that day. Charles Francis Adams, however, recorded in his diary for that day that he did verbally state to the committee substantially what Henry claimed he offered as a resolution. C. F. Adams wrote in his diary entry that southern resistance to the election of Lincoln, as indicated by the refusal of southern members to vote on his previous resolution, indicated "a deeper disease" than Congress would be able to reach. Adams admitted in the diary that his language at this point had become quite heated in the committee when he suggested that it should break up. After several members complained that Adams, usually a person of very calm demeanor, was being unfair, Adams asked for some time to consider his objections further. As Adams had promised to do on January 8, he voted against both of his own measures–the constitutional amendment and his New Mexico statehood bill–on the 11th. The committee, nonetheless, voted 20-5 and 14-9, respectively, to approve both of them. C. F. Adams Diary, January 11, 1861, roll 76, part 1, *MAP;* "Committee of Thirty-three Journal," 35–37; Duberman, *C. F. Adams,* 246; and Stegmaier, "An Imaginary Negro," 277.

10. One constituency which Lincoln knew he would have to satisfy with a cabinet position was Pennsylvania, and Sen. Simon Cameron, a strong protectionist on the tariff issue and one of the more conciliatory Republicans toward the South in Congress during the Secession Winter, seemed certain to be Lincoln's choice for Pennsylvania's seat in the cabinet. Cameron's opponents in Pennsylvania raised objections that Cameron was tainted with participation in corruption and bribery, but the charges were not well substantiated and Cameron had a great deal of support. Some thought Lincoln might appoint him as secretary of the treasury, but, as Lincoln juggled all of the positions, personalities, and factions, he decided to offer the treasury to Salmon P. Chase of Ohio and to offer Cameron the war department. Lincoln did not finally make the offer to Cameron until the beginning of March, just prior to his inauguration. Cameron did not prove satisfactory as secretary of war and Lincoln replaced him in 1862 with Edwin M. Stanton. The best of many accounts of Cameron's selection for Lincoln's cabinet is Erwin S. Bradley, *Simon Cameron, Lincoln's Secretary of War: A Political Biography* (Philadelphia: University of Pennsylvania Press, 1966), 159–174. See also Burlingame, *Lincoln,* 1: 726–737, 2: 52–54. Henry Adams discussed the

controversy surrounding Cameron's appointment and the attempts to keep him out of the cabinet in a letter to his brother on January 11. In this letter Henry rightly predicted that Cameron would end up with the war department. Levenson et al., eds., *Henry Adams Letters,* 1: 220.

LETTER 11

Boston Daily Advertiser, January 16, 1861

Letter from Washington
[FROM OUR OWN CORRESPONDENT]

Washington, Jan. 13, 1861

As early as eight o'clock yesterday morning the throng began to assemble at the Capitol. Soon after ten the galleries of the Senate Chamber were full, and swarms of people were hurrying about the corridors trying to find an opening. The cloak-rooms and lobbies themselves were filled with a crowd of ladies, and the Senators driven out. Long before the Senate came to order, the great mass of men in the gallery to the right of the President's chair, were swaying about, and seemed on the point of forcing the foremost ones over the railing. Many came up from Baltimore, and it seemed as though all Washington were there. Men say that so great a demonstration never was seen before in the Capitol.[1]

Before anything was done, the Vice President had the lobbies cleared, and as they were filled with women, many of them very important personages, there was a storm of complaint, and I doubt if Mr. Toombs or Mr. Hale or the Vice President will ever be forgiven or recover any social standing. Out they had to go, however, and out they did go before the Senate would proceed to business. The surplus crowd almost filled the great galleries of the House of Representatives, where many of them retreated on finding the Senate galleries closed.[2]

Mr. Seward spoke about two hours, being interrupted a little while to allow the right gallery to be cleared on account of the noise there. The crowd was so dense that a boy was nearly suffocated and was passed out over the heads of the people. This made so much confusion and laughter that the Vice President ordered that part of the galleries to be cleared. At the end of the speech there was an attempt at applause, but it was stopped short by the Chair.[3]

It is hard to say what sort of an impression the speech has made here.[4] The southern men call his concessions insulting, as they have a way of calling everything that does not go the whole length they ask.[5] Many of the republicans think it yields too much. They believe conscientiously that the North ought to rest satisfied with being in the right, and that any advance is necessarily an abandonment of principle.[6] Mr. Seward believes conscientiously that it is not enough to be in the right, but that the South must be convinced that they are in the wrong. Lord North[7] had a right to tax the American colonies, he said, and his obstinacy lost them to the English crown. Time will show whether Mr. Seward's doctrine or Lord North's is true statesmanship.

Still the concessions which Mr. Seward does make are very guarded, and it is rather hard to see what he does mean about the Territories.[8] As I heard a senator say: he is willing to vote for the Rice proposition, except for two objections. One is that it is bad; the other that it is unconstitutional and impossible.[9]

Meanwhile the House has finished the appropriation bills, except one,–and the seceding senators are going off so as to leave the republicans in a majority in the Senate, which is very lucky. The Union men have been much comforted by the news from Virginia[10] which shows a chance of saving that State at least till the 4th of March or later, and if it goes then it will be only after a tremendous contest. The course of Mr. Seward will no doubt aid the Union party in Virginia very much, possibly turn the scale.[11]

There was a republican House caucus Saturday evening, but it seems to have left things much as it found them.[12] The Committee of Thirty-three will report tomorrow and the debate in the House will begin as soon as the Army Appropriation bill has passed. I do not believe it is likely to effect any good whatever.

NOTES

1. Having said so many things to so many people earlier in the session about the crisis shortly being settled peacefully and with his immense political stature as the anticipated "premier" of the incoming Lincoln

administration, Seward was looked to by those in the public hopeful of compromise to deliver a speech which would propose a formula to magically resolve the crisis. On the day before the speech the Washington *Evening Star* had perfectly reflected the public's expectation by declaring that the speech "will be the most momentous one in its results ever delivered" before the Senate. How Seward could have remained calm in this intense atmosphere with so much responsibility for saving the Union hoisted onto his shoulders by the public is itself incredible–somewhat akin to the unflappability of President Millard Fillmore, whom Seward had loathed, during the earlier sectional crisis of 1850. The Baltimore *Sun* said that the speech was heralded as a "great pacificator," an undoubted reference to the former Whig "Great Pacificator" Henry Clay of Kentucky and his compromise proposals of 1850. John Forney, clerk of the U.S. House and publisher of the Philadelphia *Press*, sent a note to Seward on the 11th urging him to rise above party platforms and to use his every effort to save the country from disunion and civil war. Meanwhile, radical Republican Salmon P. Chase wrote from Ohio advising Seward to offer no compromise then but to tell the southerners that the Republicans would make a fair adjustment once they had assumed power. Forney to Seward, January 11, 1861, roll 61, Seward Papers; Chase to Seward, January 10, 1861, Niven, ed., *Chase Papers–Microfilm Ed.*, roll 14; *Baltimore American and Commercial Advertiser*, January 10, 12, 1861; Baltimore *Sun*, January 14, 1861; *Boston Herald*, January 15, 1861; *National Anti-Slavery Standard* (New York), January 19, 1861; and Washington (DC) *Evening Star*, January 11, 1861.

From just what vantage point in the Senate chamber Henry Adams witnessed the proceedings is not clear from his description, but it would not have been the reporters' gallery since he was not an accredited correspondent for a newspaper. Some of the other observers of the scene added interesting details in their accounts, but Adams's description of the huge crowd and the congestion agreed with other reports. The throng did begin arriving very early and the Senate galleries were full by 10 a.m. Only Adams mentioned the men in their gallery swaying to and fro and nearly forcing some to fall over the railing. The Washington diplomatic corps, their wives, some of the Supreme Court justices, and many House members attended, and the contest for seats in the chamber and galleries became fierce. Coats were torn and hats crunched in the melee. Ladies took over the passages to the Senate and the cloak rooms when their gallery became so packed that one of its doors broke from its hinges. Many of the estimated two thousand or so could not even find standing room by 11 a.m. and had to wait outside the chamber. One incident in the lobby raised momentary alarm when a young man from Virginia dropped his coat on the marble floor and a loaded revolver in a coat pocket accidently fired a shot. Luckily, no one was injured. How the crowd maintained any semblance of order for as long as they did is a testament to their restraint and stamina, for the Senate did not even begin its session until noon. C. F. Adams Diary, January 12, 1861, roll 76, part 1, *MAP; Baltimore American and Commercial Advertiser,* January 14, 1861; *Boston Herald,* January 15, 1861; Boston *Daily Evening Traveller,* January 18, 1861; *New York Commercial Advertiser,* January 14, 1861; *National Anti-Slavery Standard* (New York), January 19, 1861; St. Louis *Daily Missouri Democrat,* January 17, 1861; St. Louis *Daily Missouri Republican,* January 17, 1861; *Springfield* (MA) *Daily Republican,* January 18, 1861; F. W. Seward, *Seward at Washington,* 493–494; and Van Deusen, *Seward,* 244.

2. Following the opening prayer in the Senate at noon, Vice-President John C. Breckinridge of Kentucky, ex-officio president of the U.S. Senate, decided to enforce the Senate's rule no. 48 against the presence on the Senate floor of anyone except senators, representatives, foreign diplomats, Supreme Court judges, and a few other officials listed under the rule. Sen. Simon Cameron (R-PA) urged that the rule be dispensed with for the occasion of this speech, as it had been on earlier such occasions. The exotic Georgia secessionist with long black hair and bombastic rhetorical style, Robert Toombs (D-GA), immediately objected to any suspension of this rule, knowing that it could only be suspended by unanimous consent of the Senate. "Bully Bob"–he relished the appellation–did not like Seward and would do anything to diminish the audience for his speech. Whether the ladies present–and they were the intended targets of the chamber-clearing move–resented this as meanspirited did not matter to Toombs; he was preparing to leave Washington the next day to attend the Georgia secession convention. On the Republican side of the chamber, Sen. John P. Hale of New Hampshire decided to extend the rule enforcement further and advised the vice-president that the rule

included anterooms, lobbies, and passageways leading to the chamber. The fat, round-faced Hale, noted for his humor and sarcasm, represented the radical wing of the Republicans who feared and distrusted Seward. Breckinridge, a Kentuckian who supported the Crittenden Compromise as a sine qua non for his remaining a Unionist, also wanted to hinder Seward's address and agreed with Hale. Despite Cameron's continued pleas to the contrary, Breckinridge ordered the floor vacated by all unauthorized persons. Some of the ladies stood their ground, but the vice-president refused to continue the proceedings until the women, and some men, left the areas within the rule. Many of them matriculated over to the House galleries. Senate business resumed at 12:22 p.m. Sen. Seward had not yet even arrived. *Cong. Globe,* 36: 2: 340; *Louisville Daily Journal,* January 12, 1861 (on Toombs); and *Springfield* (MA) *Daily Republican,* January 18, 1861. For biographies of the three individuals who lessened the numbers present to hear Seward's speech, see: William Davis, *Breckinridge: Statesman, Soldier, Symbol* (Baton Rouge: Louisiana State University Press, 1974); Richard H. Sewell, *John P. Hale and the Politics of Abolition* (Cambridge: Harvard University Press, 1965); and William Y. Thompson, *Robert Toombs of Georgia* (Baton Rouge: Louisiana State University, 1966).

3. At about 12:40 p.m. or so, a slightly built, unimposing man with a pale, wrinkled face and dressed in a gray suit quietly entered the Senate chamber. Exuding a calm demeanor and with a face so placid and expressionless that one reporter wrote that it reminded him of "a piece of chalk," Sen. Seward first went to his own seat and then took up a position in front of it next to that of Vermont's Sen. Collamer and nearer to the center of the hall. Delay ensued when the men's gallery became so noisy that Vice-President Breckinridge ordered it partially cleared. The New York senator began his address just before 1 p.m. and continued until just before 3 p.m.

If the crowd expected to hear a dynamic Websterian oration, they stood to be disappointed. Seward spoke in a husky voice so low that even those seated near him on the Senate floor had difficulty hearing him. Knowing the quality of his voice beforehand may explain why Kentucky's Sen. Crittenden took a seat only three feet from him. Despite his weak voice and gestures which seemed forced and even "grotesque" as one commentator described them, Seward still impressed listeners as intelligent, scholarly, and able. One detects in Henry Adams's *Advertiser* letter a bit of initial disillusionment with his champion's performance; the letter provided little indication of the speech's content. That may have reflected Adams's own problems with hearing Seward's words clearly. Those in the galleries must have strained to hear anything Seward said.

To some observers it appeared that Seward declaimed without preparation, but that was not the case. The manuscript of his speech lay on the desk in front of him and he had already sent printed copies to some newspapers. In a sort of dress rehearsal four days earlier he had attempted to gauge the response of radical Republicans to the speech by sharing the address personally with Sen. Charles Sumner of Massachusetts. Now he could present it before a Senate packed with fellow politicians and plenty of other citizenry, all anxious to hear and witness this highly anticipated event. Later in January, Seward would address a letter to conservative Robert Winthrop of Massachusetts, in which he proclaimed: "It is a glorious theme–Union and Peace." Those words certainly encompassed the overall theme of his January 12 speech.

Starting with an introduction which extolled the public's adherence to the Union and recognition of the dangerous challenge to it presented by the threat of secession, Sen. Seward then declared his belief that the Union could not be saved in this crisis by merely singing its praises; nor by further debates and recriminations over slavery in the territories, the right of secession, or the right of coercion; nor by the chimerical notion of peaceful dissolution and eventual reconstruction; nor by congressional compromise achieved under armed threat and involving sacrifice of cherished principles. The New Yorker then argued that disunionists deluded themselves if they believed some right of secession had been acknowledged by the Founders under the Constitution, and he specifically cited the declaration in Article 6 of that document on the supremacy of the Constitution and federal laws made under it in contradiction of disunionist claims. Congress, he said, should act to redress any real grievances of the states and also to provide the president with whatever means were necessary to maintain the Union.

This first section of the speech led next to the longest part of it, the main body of the address. At length Seward contrasted the historic strength, safety, and security which the Union under the Constitution had provided for the people of the republic against the certain dangers to result if the Union degenerated into two or more confederacies. Among these latter were the greater threats of foreign wars, wars between the indigenous confederacies, and resultant loss of republican freedoms and representative government in favor of standing armies and military despotism. Amidst his litany of looming disasters consequent upon disunion, Seward certainly had southern white fears in mind when he stated that a "ferocious" slave population of millions desirous of freedom would inevitably rise up in revolution in the event of a civil war between confederacies. Southern senators listening in "breathless silence" to the speech reportedly looked rather "grave" in countenance as Seward described the horrors which war would bring them.

In ascribing causation for the secession crisis, Seward mentioned the longtime grievances of southerners about interference of northern states with the recovery of fugitive slaves and resistance by Republicans to demands by southerners to carry slaves into and hold them as property in national territories. But the immediate cause of the secession of slave states at that time, the senator declared, was their refusal to submit to the election of Abraham Lincoln as president by the traditional constitutional process. Lincoln and the Republicans had done nothing and would do nothing to interfere with or abolish slavery in the southern states, he said, despite southern apprehensions of that based on misrepresentation of Republican policy. Seward deemed it "unwise" for the Deep South states to think that secession and the establishment of a separate confederacy would be advantageous to their interests.

Seward then proclaimed, in what some listeners considered the most movingly eloquent passage of the speech, that consideration of party must be subordinate to the Union. "Republican, Democracy, every other political name and thing; all are subordinate–and they ought to disappear in the presence of the great question of Union." Twice in subsequent lines he said "it shall be so." Old Crittenden, seated nearby, had wept openly at times in the earlier course of the address, but Seward's remark about subordinating party to Union brought a "joyful expression" to the old compromiser's face. The New Yorker's words "it shall be so" were apparently voiced in such an emotionally appealing way that many men, women, and children shed tears.

Yet, having just raised the hopes of many in his audience that he was about to offer some dramatic new plan of compromise, Seward offered nothing new when he listed specific proposals to which he could commit himself. Nothing he mentioned departed from Republican principles or the party's 1860 Chicago platform. In regard to slavery in the southern states, he reiterated the basic Republican dogma that state law which recognized property in slaves was supreme in those states. Seward supported the enforcement by northern states of the constitutional obligation to return fugitive slaves to their owners in the South, but he desired that the current fugitive slave law be amended to drop the requirement that private individuals assist in the recapture of fugitive slaves and to protect northern free blacks from being claimed as fugitives and fraudulently reduced to slavery. At the same time Sen. Seward also urged the repeal of all unconstitutional laws in free or slave states; that would have included personal liberty laws by which northern states had sometimes interfered with southern attempts to recapture fugitive slaves, and Negro seamen laws of southern states which denied black sailors who were citizens of northern states their "privileges and immunities" under Article 4, section 2, of the Constitution by requiring that they be incarcerated in local jails while their ships visited southern ports. Though Seward believed any amendment of the Constitution unnecessary, he restated his willingness to support an amendment to prevent the Constitution from being amended in future to give Congress any power to abolish or interfere with slavery in southern states. Just as this proposal duplicated what he had offered earlier in the Committee of Thirteen, so it was with the senator's method of finally resolving the territorial slavery issue. As he had in the committee, Seward proposed, in addition to the pending admission of Kansas as a free state, the admission of two states to contain within their respective limits all the remaining territory then possessed by the United States. Adams's New Mexico statehood bill from the House Committee of Thirty-three would have provided the southernmost of these two states. Seward also suggested that in one-to-three years, after the secession excitement had calmed down, the nation could assemble a convention to consider additional amendments to the Constitution; he had suggested this in a letter to Weed at the end of December as a measure to mollify the border slave states. Seward completed his recommendations by expressing his support for a law to guard against invasion by citizens from one state into another, i.e., John Brown-type raids, and his support for further binding the Union together by the construction of two transcontinental railroads to the Pacific Coast, one northern, one southern. This two-route Pacific Railroad bill was then under consideration in Congress.

These proposals, he said, were not exactly what he himself desired but they reflected his desire to do his utmost in "moderation, forbearance, and conciliation" during the crisis. Seward believed his position represented the furthest extent to which he and other Republicans could go to alleviate southern fears about Republican intentions and the policies which the incoming Lincoln administration would adopt toward the South and slavery. He was telling the South that this program constituted the best they could hope for within the Union, that this program was fair and honorable to their interests, and that the Union as it existed was the only venue in which those interests could find any real protection.

Sen. Seward concluded his address with a final expression of his boundless faith in the Constitution and the Union, and he declared his belief that the American people were too wise and calm to allow the U.S. government to fall. "Woe! Woe! To the man that madly lifts his hand against it," Seward warned. "It shall continue and endure; . . ." As he finished, the pent-up emotions of the gallery audience burst forth in loud applause, mixed with some hisses, until the sergeant-at-arms began ushering people out of the overcrowded galleries as directed by Vice-President Breckinridge on a motion from the floor. The Senate then adjourned for the day. The only senators who immediately came to Seward to shake his hand and congratulate him were his fellow moderates among the Republicans (those not opposed to some compromise), James Dixon of Connecticut, Henry Anthony of Rhode Island, James Grimes of Iowa, and Edward Baker of Oregon. Crittenden, who only a short while before had cherished hopes that Seward would endorse something like his own compromise, now sat dejected, feeling that Seward had offered the South no substantial concessions. None of the other slave state senators moved toward Seward to congratulate him, even if they appreciated his conciliatory spirit, for fear that their being seen in close company with the New Yorker might be misinterpreted as an anti-southern gesture in their home states. Republicans, other than the four moderates named above, also avoided contact with Seward. William P. Fessenden of Maine and Jacob Collamer of Vermont, seated near Seward, walked off without saying a word to him. Most Republican senators gathered in little knots of two to four members to discuss the speech. Wade, Hale, and Sumner looked displeased, and Wade was overheard to proclaim about Seward: "Great was the fall thereof." The foreign diplomats who had listened to the speech were profoundly interested in the international ramifications of the union-disunion issue. The Russian minister in Washington, Baron Edouard de Stoeckl, was particularly active in circulating among the senators on the floor to gauge their reactions to Seward's address.

As for Seward himself, he seemed pleased and seemed to feel that he had come through this ordeal at least without having done any irreparable damage to the Union cause or to his own reputation. A few nights later when he dined with Congressman Adams, Adams described his friend as in a very positive, high-spirited frame of mind. Above all he could enjoy the satisfaction of knowing that he had remained consistent with his principles and his political strategy in the crisis. He had wanted to appear conciliatory without appearing to capitulate to southern demands; as Charles Francis Adams, Jr., phrased it in a letter to his father describing Seward's tactics: ". . . concession is asked & is gently to be refused or, if granted, is to be granted in such a manner as to make a penny look as much as possible like a dollar." Seward had not set out to enrage anyone by inventing polarizing and memorable phrases, and he had never intended to present a compromise plan which would rally both North and South behind him in a great Union-saving crusade. Seward had no such illusions; he realized that the sentiments he uttered could have no positive effect on the secession-bent Gulf states of the South and also that his January 12 speech could not melt the icy resolve of the radical Republicans opposed to compromise per se. He had not read his speech earlier to Sen. Sumner thinking to convert the Massachusetts radical to his idea on compromise. Sen. Seward's focus in the speech was consistent with the rest of his conduct in the secession crisis–to offer enough concessions to retain the loyalty to the Union of as many of the upper tier of slave states as possible until Lincoln took office on March 4. His speech's emphasis on the values of the Union, the multiple dangers which southern slave states would encounter if they did choose to secede, and a program of mild concessions to demonstrate a lack of Republican hostility toward slavery in the southern states was primarily targeted toward the border slave states. As Seward's speeches went, this one did not become either famous or infamous in history. That is understandable, given that Seward does not appear to have desired to say anything very consequential; if the border slave states did not leave the Union because of anything he said on January 12, then Seward could consider his effort a success. On the setting for the speech and descriptions of Seward, see: C. F. Adams, Jr., *Autobiography*, 81; *Baltimore American and Commercial Advertiser*, January 14, 1861; *Boston Herald*, January 15, 1861; Boston *Daily Evening Traveller*, January 18, 1861; *New York Herald*, January 13, 14, 15, 16, 17, 1861; *Charleston Mercury*, January 16, 1861; *Louisville Daily Journal*, January 17, 1861; *National Anti-Slavery Standard* (New York), January 19, 1861; New York *World*, January 15, 1861; Philadelphia *North American and United States Gazette*, January 14, 1861; Philadelphia *Press*, January 14, 1861; St. Louis *Daily Missouri Democrat*, January 17, 1861; St. Louis *Daily Missouri Republican*, January 17, 1861; and Ben: Perley Poore, *Perley's Reminiscences of Sixty Years in the National Metropolis* (Philadelphia: Hubbard Brothers, 1886), 2: 54–55. Seward's January 24 letter to Winthrop is in roll 29, Gutheim, ed., *Microfilm Ed.—Winthrop Papers*. For the speech itself and reactions during it, see: *Cong. Globe*, 36: 2: 341–344; Baker, ed., *Seward's Works*, 4: 651–669; Boston *Daily Evening Traveller*, January 18, 1861; F. W. Seward, *Seward at Washington*, 494–495; Van Deusen, *Seward*, 244–247; and Crofts, *Reluctant Confederates*, 236–238. Seward's convention suggestion is in his letter to Weed, December 29, 1860, Weed Papers. On the scene following the speech, see: *Boston Daily Courier*, January 16, 1861; Boston *Daily Evening Traveller*, January 18, 1861; *Charleston Mercury*, January 16, 1861; and St. Louis *Daily Missouri Democrat*, January 17, 1861. On Seward's upbeat mood after the speech, see Adams Diary, January 15, 1861, roll 76, part 1, *MAP*. C. F. Adams, Jr.'s letter to his father, January 14, 1861 is in Letters Received, etc., roll 551, part 4, *MAP*. See also Letter 9, note 7 above on Seward.

4. One difficulty for Henry Adams in judging what impression the speech had made was that many who heard or read the speech remained

uncertain about Seward's attitude on compromise. It was difficult for old conservatives to reconcile the anti-southern provocateur Seward of the previous decade with the conciliatory Seward of the secession crisis. Edward Everett of Massachusetts wrote two letters on January 21, in one declaring that "Seward's whole political system has been an attempt to set the upper part of a keg of gun powder on fire without blowing up the cask" and in the other that, having done so much to ignite the crisis, Seward could not now remedy the problems "by a few vague generalities of a conciliatory nature." In the same vein William C. Rives of Virginia confided to his diary that Seward had "more faces than Janus" [the two-faced Roman god] and that his remedies amounted to "a tea spoonful of spirits of nitre [an old preparation used often as a diuretic] given to heal a compound fracture of the leg." Everett to William Everett and to Sir Henry Holland, both dated January 21, 1861, in Frederick S. Allis, Jr., ed., *Microfilm Edition of the Edward Everett Papers* (Boston: Massachusetts Historical Society, 1971), roll 31; W. C Rives Diary, pp. 13–14 (January 13), 28 (January 24), and 44 (February 18, 1861), container 2, W. C. Rives Papers, Manuscripts Division, Library of Congress. Besides the letter of C. F. Adams, Jr., cited in note 3 above, other comments on the vagueness of Seward's speech and proposals were in: C. F. Adams Diary, January 15, 1861, roll 76, part 1, *MAP;* J. P. Kennedy Journal, January 14, 1861, roll 3, volume 12, John B. Boles, ed., *The John Pendleton Kennedy Papers Microform* (Wilmington, DE: Scholarly Resources, 1972); R. C. Winthrop to J. P. Kennedy, January 16 and to Hugh B. Grigsby, January 11, 1861, roll 39, Gutheim, ed., *Microfilm Ed.–Winthrop Papers;* Boston *Daily Courier,* January 17, 21, 1861; *Louisville Daily Journal,* January 19, 1861; *New York Evening Express,* January 14, 1861; Richmond *Daily Dispatch,* January 16, 1861; and St. Louis *Daily Missouri Democrat,* January 17, 1861.

5. Southern radical journalists understood how open to different interpretations Seward's speech had been. The *Charleston Mercury*'s Washington correspondent referred to it as "Delphic," after the ancient Greek oracle noted for sometimes uttering prophecies misinterpreted by those who heard them. Similarly a *Louisville Courier* editorial called the speech "Jesuitical," after the reputedly sinister equivocality of Jesuit priests. Southern radicals not only did not trust anything Seward said, but saw no value to the South in the propositions Seward had mentioned

in his address. The principal remarks of Seward which southern radicals emphasized were his statements about empowering the federal government to preserve the Union; to southern extremists such declarations meant only one thing: federal military coercion of the seceding states. They concluded after Seward's January 12 speech that no reasonable hope of any adjustment between North and South remained. Sen. Robert Toombs telegraphed to Georgia that the speech was a "cheat," while Sen. John Slidell telegraphed to Louisiana that it was "temporizing" and only designed to delay southern secession. For various radical southern commentaries, see: Baltimore *Sun,* January 14, 1861; *Charleston Mercury,* January 16, 1861; *Louisville Daily Courier,* January 15, 1861; *New Orleans Bee,* January 15, 1861; New Orleans *Daily Delta,* January 23, 1861; Richmond *Daily Dispatch,* January 17, 1861; Washington (DC) *Constitution,* January 12, 1861 (evening ed. only); and Wilmington (NC) *Daily Journal,* January 15, 1861. On the Toombs and Slidell telegrams, see: Boston *Daily Evening Traveller,* January 18, 1861; and Thompson, *Toombs,* 156.

6. Foremost among the Republicans angry with Seward over his speech was Sen. Charles Sumner, to whom Seward had shown his speech four days before its public delivery. This absolutely uncompromising radical Republican believed that Republicans should firmly stand their ground against secessionist traitors and offer the South no concessions, even at the expense of possibly having the border slave states secede. Sumner interpreted any deviation from rigid adherence to the Republican platform as weakness in the face of threats, which could split the Republican Party. Sumner, after having read Seward's speech, had pleaded vehemently with the New Yorker to change it and remove every hint of concession to "traitors" from it. He wanted Seward to return to his earlier, more radical position, but Seward ignored Sumner's comments and delivered the more moderate address he had prepared. Sumner openly attacked Seward in correspondence and personal conversation for the rest of the session, to the point where the Adamses thought Sumner a bit crazed in his obsession. Charles F. Adams, Jr., Diary, February 22, 1861, roll 1, C. F. Adams, Jr., Papers, Massachusetts Historical Society; C. F. Adams Diary, January 13, 1861, roll 76, part 1 *MAP;* C. F. Adams, Jr., to John A. Andrew, February 22, 1861, Andrew Papers; Charles Sumner to Samuel G. Howe, January 17, 1861, roll 64, and Sumner Let-

ters to John M. Forbes, Dorothea L. Dix, John A. Andrew, John Jay, and Salmon P. Chase, January 13–19, 1861, roll 74, Sumner Papers; and David Donald, *Charles Sumner and the Coming of the Civil War* (New York: Alfred A. Knopf, 1961), 372. For other comments by Republicans that Seward was surrendering his principles or conceding too much, see: Benjamin H. Brewster to Simon Cameron, January 13, 1861, roll 6, Simon Cameron Papers, Manuscripts Division, Library of Congress; Salmon P. Chase to John G. Whittier, February 1, and Thaddeus Stevens to Chase, February 3, 1861, Niven, ed., *Chase Papers–Microfilm Ed.,* roll 14; Rep. John A. Bingham (R-OH) to Joshua R. Giddings, January 14, 1861, roll 4, J. R. Giddings Papers, Ohio Historical Society, Columbus; Samuel G. Howe to Sumner, January 20, and Henry W. Longfellow to Sumner, January 29, 1861, roll 74, Sumner Papers; Ebenezer Tucker to Rep. Elihu B. Washburne (R-IL), January 28, 1861, container 13, E. B. Washburne Papers, Manuscripts Division, Library of Congress; and Earle Field, "Charles B. Sedgwick's Letters from Washington, 1859–1861," *Mid-America: An Historical Review* 49 (April 1967): 138.

7. Frederick, Lord North (1732–1792), served as prime minister under King George III in 1770–1782. His stubborn retention of the tax on tea as symbolic of Parliament's authority to tax the American colonies (1770), the Tea Act of 1773, and the Coercive Acts of 1774 following the Boston Tea Party became major events in the coming of the American Revolution. In his *Advertiser* letter, Henry Adams cast the radical, uncompromising Republicans in the role of Lord North.

8. Some newspapers, mostly Democratic, criticized Seward's proposals near the end of his speech as offering no real measures of adjustment. Boston *Daily Atlas and Bee,* January 16, 1861; *Boston Daily Courier,* January 17, 1861; *Cincinnati Daily Enquirer,* January 13, 1861; and Columbus *Daily Ohio Statesman,* January 16, 1861; *New York Herald,* January 14, 1861. Southern Unionist John J. Crittenden, so disappointed initially that Seward offered nothing which he believed the South could support, recovered his hopeful spirit enough a few days later to interpret Seward's propositions as a first step toward meaningful conciliation. *Charleston Daily Courier,* January 16, 1861; and *New Orleans Daily Crescent,* January 26, 1861. Moderate northern Republican papers and correspondents argued that Seward's suggestions in the address should form the ba-

sis for a settlement which all reasonable southerners could advocate. New York *World*, January 15, 1861; and Philadelphia *North American and United States Gazette*, January 14, 1861. Moderates particularly felt that the kindly tone of the incoming secretary of state presaged a disposition to arrange a fair adjustment with the South. The *North American* issue cited above; and Washington *Evening Star*, January 14, 1861. As the latter paper opined, Seward had not outlined a compromise plan of his own but had simply stated some terms upon which he was prepared to settle differences with the South. The *Star* estimated correctly that Sen. Seward had not framed his program as a plan which he would present as a comprehensive settlement. At a Republican caucus a few nights after his speech, Sen. John Ten Eyck of New Jersey declared his readiness to support Seward's measures. But Seward responded that he would not bring any plan forward in the Senate, having decided from the generally negative reception of his speech by his fellow Republicans that such a set of proposals on his part could split the party. Charles Sumner to John A. Andrew, January 18, 1861, Andrew Papers. Thus Seward's January 12 ideas for a settlement could remain "very guarded," as Henry Adams termed it, and southern Unionists would continue to wait in vain for Seward to offer a compromise plan.

9. On Sen. Rice's compromise, which Sen. Seward favored as a settlement of the territorial slavery issue, on condition that Kansas be admitted separately as a free state, see Letter 6, note 11, above. It is not clear why the unnamed senator whom Adams overheard declared that Rice's proposal was "unconstitutional." The senator may have thought it "impossible" because southerners wanted slavery protected in national territories and considered the quick admission of all remaining territory as states a subterfuge for avoiding the need for any northern concession on the territories issue. The senator may have deemed Rice's plan as "bad" simply because he opposed any compromise at all.

10. Union men of both North and South were encouraged by the actions of Virginia's governor and state legislature. Gov. John Letcher, in the same January 7 address to the legislature in which he discussed the possible division of the Union into several confederacies [Letter 7, note 5], had delivered a strong plea for preserving the Union, if possible. The legislature then took up consideration of two bills. One of these, the

contents of which were immediately transmitted to Washington by telegraph, provided for calling a state convention. But rather than appear to be a prelude to Virginia's quick secession from the Union, this bill virtually ensured that Virginia would remain in the Union at least until after Lincoln assumed the presidency on March 4. The more disunionist legislators from the plantation-slaveholding eastern Virginia counties knew they must accommodate the strongly Unionist, largely nonslaveholding "white" counties in the western half of Virginia (much of which became the Union state of West Virginia during the Civil War). To do this, the easterners agreed to allot convention seats on the basis of free population only and to submit any proposal by the convention to the final decision of the Virginia electorate. The elections for convention delegates would not be held until February and the convention would not assemble until February 13. The second bill before the legislature would issue a call for all the states to send delegates to Washington, D.C., for a Peace Convention to begin on February 4 and to devise a Union-saving compromise to be submitted to Congress. The legislature enacted the convention bill on January 14, the day after Henry Adams penned his *Advertiser* letter, and approved the Peace Convention bill on January 19. These actions by Virginia severely dampened the disunion movement, at least temporarily, in that state and in other border slave states such as Kentucky. Richmond *Daily Dispatch,* January 8, 17, 19, 1861; Washington (DC) *Evening Star,* January 14, 1861; Crofts, *Reluctant Confederates,* 135–136; Boney, *Letcher,* 103–105; Henry T. Shanks, *The Secessionist Movement in Virginia, 1847–1861* (Richmond: Garrett & Massie, 1934), 142–150; and William A. Link, *Roots of Secession: Slavery and Politics in Antebellum Virginia* (Chapel Hill: University of North Carolina Press, 2003), 224.

11. Henry Adams wrote an even more positive evaluation of the effect of Seward's speech on the border states to his brother on January 17: "Seward's speech has done great good. As you must see, it sustains and relieves our father on one side, and cut the ground right from under the feet of the agitators in the border-states. . . ." By the time he drafted his "Great Secession Winter" essay after the end of the session, Adams became rapturous as he assessed the impact of the speech: "The effect of the speech was instantaneous. From that day the rumors of war began to subside; the Union men in the South took new courage; public confi-

dence began to re-establish itself, the country breathed more freely and hope rapidly rose." Levenson et al., eds., *Henry Adams Letters*, 1: 222; and Henry Adams, "Great Secession Winter," 23–24. For some similar expressions of faith that Seward's speech would have a positive impact on the loyalty of the border slave states, see: Rep. E. B. Washburne (R-IL) to Lincoln, January 13, 1861, Lincoln Papers; Springfield *Daily Illinois State Journal*, January 16, 1861, quoting Washington correspondent of *Cincinnati Gazette;* and Washington *Evening Star*, January 14, 1861. Other strongly positive assessments of Seward's speech can be found in: C. F. Adams, Jr., to C. F. Adams, January 14, 1861, Letters Received, etc., roll 551, part 4, *MAP;* James E. Harvey to Thurlow Weed, January 15, and Weed to William H. Seward, January 19, 1861, roll 61, W. H. Seward Papers, Rush Rhees Library, University of Rochester; *Baltimore American and Commercial Advertiser*, January 14, 16, 1861; Boston *Daily Atlas and Bee*, January 14, 1861; *Boston Evening Transcript*, January 12, 1861; *Chicago Daily Tribune*, January 16, 17, 1861; New Haven *Daily Palladium*, January 15, 18, 1861; *New York Commercial Advertiser*, January 14, 1861; *Morning Courier and New York Enquirer*, January 16, 1861; *New York Times*, January 14, 16, 1861; *Philadelphia Inquirer*, January 14, 1861; Philadelphia *Press*, January 14, 1861; and St. Louis *Daily Missouri Democrat*, January 15, 1861.

12. Adams here downplays the significance of the House Republican caucus held on the evening of January 12, but the meeting was a good indicator of just how desperate southern Unionists were to persuade the Republicans to agree to a compromise that the border state Unionists could accept, and also of how concerned some House Republicans were becoming about their continued relations with the southern Unionists. Seward's friend Sen. James W. Grimes (R-IA) sent a note to Seward on that day warning him that some House members planned to attack his speech and its propositions at their caucus, and he urged Seward to provide printed copies of his speech for his friends at the meeting in case any radicals resorted to criticism of Seward. Actually, however, the purpose of that caucus was to discuss compromise measures, and none of the members apparently even alluded to Seward's Senate address earlier that day. In a very irregular proceeding, the House Republicans invited Rep. Emerson Etheridge (A- TN) to expound on the merits of the border state committee's compromise plan [Letter 9, note 8], about which the

Republicans had unceremoniously voted on January 7 against its introduction into that chamber. That Etheridge was even willing to visit the Republican caucus attested to his perseverance and magnanimity. The Republicans requested Etheridge's presence as a good will gesture toward a leading southern Unionist whom they had offended by their vote on January 7. Etheridge tried to convince the Republican caucus that the border state compromise was, in his opinion, the only measure which could retain the border slave states in the Union. The debate lasted three hours before the meeting adjourned. No votes were taken at the caucus. Whatever Etheridge hoped to achieve or thought he had achieved by his efforts that evening, the Republicans remained steadfastly opposed to the border state compromise. When the House met again on Monday, January 14, radical Republican Owen Lovejoy of Illinois objected to Etheridge's renewal of his attempt to introduce the border state committee's proposals into the House, a move that required unanimous consent. Lovejoy's objection stopped the plan a second time. Grimes to Seward, January 12, 1861, roll 61, Seward Papers; John Stryker to Weed, January 9, 1861, Weed Papers; *Cong. Globe,* 36: 2: 364; *Cincinnati Daily Enquirer,* January 13, 1861; *Louisville Daily Courier,* January 11, 1861; *New York Evening Express,* January 15, 1861; *New York Herald,* January 14, 15, 1861; *New York Daily News,* January 11, 1861; *New York Times,* January 14, 1861; *New York Daily Tribune,* January 14, 1861; New York *World,* January 10, 14, 1861; and *Philadelphia Inquirer,* January 14, 1861.

LETTER 12

Boston Daily Advertiser, January 17, 1861

Letter from Washington
[FROM OUR OWN CORRESPONDENT]

Washington, Jan. 14, 1861

Mr. Corwin has at last succeeded in getting his report in, but if the country is not more unanimous about it than the Committee, nothing will be gained but time. I understand that the vote on submitting the report to the House stood sixteen to thirteen, and of those sixteen there are about half who voted for it with the reservation that they should oppose it hereafter. At least, if not half, enough voted for it to carry it, on the ground that it would be a mistake in policy to kill it before it was fairly tried by a larger court.[1] There will be a small library of minority reports which will straggle in one by one, but as the matter is made a special order for next Monday, we shall then see how it stands. I believe that Mr. Adams voted against it, so that there will probably be a minority report from him as well as from eight or ten others.[2]

On the whole I think there is a general feeling of satisfaction that the Committee has succeeded in doing something, and though most of the stronger republicans will vote against and resist its recommendations, still, even their passage would be no practical disaster provided it made no serious split in the party. If this secession trouble can once be weathered with no greater sacrifice than that, the rest is plain sailing. The real danger is on the one side that Virginia and Maryland will go out, which will be a bad blow; or on the other, that the Crittenden compromise will pass. If the committee's plan will cut between these two and defeat both, it will be a most masterly stroke.[3] Under any circumstances, however, this committee has been a good thing, for it will have saved nearly two months, and now the cotton States are quietly off, the appropriation bills are passed, the seceders are feeling the end of their tether, and the House can talk without doing half the harm it might have done six weeks ago.

Mr. Cox of Ohio made a speech today. It was such a speech as a northern democrat might be supposed to make. In order to conciliate both parties, he threatened and abused both. He told the South that the republicans would not fight, but that the Mississippi must always remain in the Union and not a hair of Major Anderson's head must be touched. He told the republicans that they were only after the spoils, and that their talk of principles and threats of war were all moonshine. Mr. Cox is a demagogue, and thinks he can form an independent Union party which will tip the republicans over.[4]

So far as the President is concerned, I have not heard lately of any new trouble. Last week he was very shaky and indeed it always takes ten men to hold him up, and it is hard work for them. Tomorrow evening he is to have his first reception this winter and the company will be something new to the White House. I suspect there will be something of a republican demonstration, in the hope of encouraging and sustaining the old man, and provided such a change of surroundings does not frighten him back, it may do some good. All or nearly all the secessionists and traitors have at last been driven away from him, and with their pressure off, and the strong Union pressure on him, he may prove capable of standing up for a few more rounds, until we can get our champion into the ring.[5]

Society here is extinct, so far as entertaining goes. No one dares give a ball and even dinners are very scarce. Many families refuse to show themselves at all, except in their own houses, and those that do still dance and make calls, talk of nothing but destruction and ruin. It is not uncommon to see ladies weep in talking over the troubles; at least so I am told, though I have myself been lucky enough to have escaped that trial.[6]

NOTES

1. On Monday, January 14, the House Committee of Thirty-three gathered together for their final session. Officially the meeting began at 10 a.m. but it was nearly noon before enough members had arrived

to constitute a quorum for conducting business. Eventually twenty-nine presented themselves. The committee over the course of several weeks' deliberations had approved a number of resolutions, two bills, and a constitutional amendment by various majority votes, and these were incorporated into the report which Corwin had already written. The amendment was Adams's measure to prohibit any future constitutional amendment to abolish slavery (Adams used the wording of the three-fifths clause to refer to slaves) from originating in the free states. Letter 6, note 11]. One of the bills was Adams's New Mexico statehood bill. [Letter 5, notes 8–9; Letter 6, notes 10–11] and the other was Henry Winter Davis's bill to amend the Fugitive Slave Law of 1850 [Letter 4, note 4]. The amended bill had passed the committee on January 7 by a vote of 13-11. It changed the 1850 law by providing that an alleged fugitive slave captured in a free state would be entitled to a jury trial on the question of his or her status in federal district court in the area from which the accused had allegedly fled. The bill also eliminated a major northern complaint against the 1850 law by striking out the requirement that northern citizens assist in the capture and detention of alleged fugitive slaves, except in cases where a marshal or slave-owner encountered powerful opposition to the capture. "Committee of Thirty-three Journal," 28–32.

At the beginning of the final committee session, Chairman Thomas Corwin proposed a further bill for consideration, a measure to more effectively guarantee the extradition of fugitives from justice who had allegedly committed crimes in one state and then escaped into another. Traditionally the practice had been for the governor of the state where the crime had taken place to apply for the extradition of the fugitive to the governor of the state where the fugitive had taken refuge. Southern governors, however, had encountered difficulty in getting Republican Gov. William Dennison, Jr., of Ohio to cooperate in this process on matters relating to slavery. Gov. Dennison had rejected the extradition request by Virginia Gov. Henry Wise for Owen Brown and Francis Meriam, two of John Brown's confederates who escaped after the 1859 raid on Harpers Ferry. Dennison had also refused the request by Kentucky's governor for the extradition of a fugitive involved in helping Kentucky slaves escape to Ohio. He turned down both of these extradition requests on the basis of legal technicalities, but to southerners his actions fit a pattern of northern attempts to interfere with slavery. The timing of Corwin's bill may seem a bit odd, with Corwin waiting until the last committee meeting to introduce it, but Corwin may have suddenly produced his bill as a Republican gesture to please the border slave states in general and Emerson Etheridge of Tennessee in particular. While Republicans could not support major features of the border state compromise plan which Etheridge vigorously promoted, Corwin's bill embraced one of the lesser parts of that plan. This measure would have the governor of the state where the crime allegedly took place make his extradition request to the U.S. district judge in the area where the fugitive was located. The committee did not debate the bill much before passing it 12-11; only three Republicans—Corwin of Ohio, Dunn of Indiana, and Kellogg of Illinois—voted for the new bill. Adams, who thought the transfer of extradition authority from governors to federal judges open to "dangerous abuse," voted in the negative with eight other Republicans. Ibid., 37–38. For discussion in the House and Senate of the fugitives-from-justice issue in this session, see *Cong. Globe,* 36: 2: 55, 101–102, 197–198, 268, 271, 328–329, 411, 453, 479, 486, 506–508, 565–566, 578, 1007, and App., 29, 95, 119–120, 141, 146, 204, 209. See also Rep. Ferry's condemnation of the bill as the "most dangerous law" of the last fifty years in its impact on a state's ability to protect its citizens. New Haven *Daily Palladium,* January 23, 1861.

Charles Francis Adams described what followed the passage of Corwin's bill as "one of the most curious scenes" in the history of legislation. It quickly became clear that no single majority of the committee favored recommendation of the whole package—bills, amendments, and resolutions—passed individually in the committee as the majority report. Albert Rust of Arkansas, unhappy that the committee had not adopted the Crittenden Compromise or something similar, proposed a resolution to essentially break up the committee altogether by declaring that they could not agree and requesting to be discharged from further action. But a clear majority rejected Rust's move by a vote of 19-10. Corwin then stated that he would introduce the committee's approved measures into the House on his own responsibility. However, John S. Millson, a Virginia Democratic moderate, devised a resolution giving Corwin the committee's authority to report all the committee propositions to the

House and to include his own commentary on them. The committee approved Millson's resolution by a vote of 16-13, hardly an enthusiastic endorsement of their labors over the previous weeks. Corwin presented his report to the House as soon as the committee adjourned. C. F. Adams Diary, January 14, 1861, roll 76, part 1, and C. F. Adams to C. F. Adams, Jr., January 15, 1861, "Letters Received, etc.", roll 551, part 4, *MAP;* "Committee of Thirty-three Journal," 38–40; "Disturbed Condition of the Country," 36: 2: *House Reports* 31 (ser. 1104): 1–13; *Cong. Globe,* 36: 2: 378; and Duberman, *C. F. Adams,* 247–248.

2. Actually seven minority reports were produced, involving fourteen members of the committee. Individuals filed three of these—Republicans Charles Francis Adams of Massachusetts, Orris S. Ferry of Connecticut, and American Thomas A. R. Nelson of Tennessee. Two signers apiece filed three other reports—Republicans Cadwallader C. Washburn of Wisconsin and Mason W. Tappan of New Hampshire, northern Democrats John C. Burch of California and Lansing Stout of Oregon, and southern Democrats Peter E. Love of Georgia and Andrew J. Hamilton of Texas. Five southern Democrats—Miles Taylor of Louisiana, John S. Phelps of Missouri, Albert Rust of Arkansas, William G. Whiteley of Delaware, and Warren Winslow of North Carolina—joined together to endorse one drafted by Taylor.

The three minority reports filed by the southerners possessed a common thread in the compromise solution they believed to be the only one which would satisfy the South—the Crittenden Compromise. From the strongly Unionist Nelson to the more extremist southern Democrats, nearly all the southerners preferred the Kentucky senator's set of comprehensive amendments. While Love and Hamilton registered a short dissent from the majority report, the ones by Nelson and Taylor both addressed the grievances which southerners believed required remedies in order to save the Union. Taylor's lengthy essay in particular outlined a history of northern aggressions against slavery from 1820 onward, which he said had perverted the original purpose of the Constitution to provide security for the rights and property of all into an instrument to subjugate the South by warring upon the institution of slavery. The southerners charged that Republicans were simply disingenuous in pledging on one hand that they and Lincoln would not interfere with slavery in southern states while on the other hand these same Republicans virulently and constantly denounced slavery as an unmitigated evil. While Nelson and Taylor both saw value in the committee's constitutional amendment to protect slavery in the southern states, both of their reports portrayed the other parts of the plan as inadequate and flawed. Both reports opposed the New Mexico statehood bill as something unwarranted by the circumstances in New Mexico and designed only to relieve Republicans from having to make any concession on the issue of southern rights to slave property in national territories.

The three Republican reports were quite discrete in content. The lengthiest and most elaborate was that by Washburn and Tappan, both among the irreconcilables in the party who opposed any compromise as unnecessary and humiliating to the Republicans. They argued that southern claims of northern aggressions on southern rights lacked any solid foundation and served only to cover up a longtime South Carolina disunion plot which now had ensnared other slave states, following the election of a Republican as president. Washburn and Tappan, seeing no compromise as valid, attacked each and every part of the majority plan: the constitutional amendment offered the South a needless guarantee since Republicans consistently declared that they had no right to and would not interfere with slavery in the South; the amendments to the fugitive slave law would do nothing to help an alleged fugitive slave who was actually a free black; New Mexico was unworthy of statehood for numerous reasons and was only among the measures of the committee because of its slave code and potential for becoming a slave state; and the fugitives-from-justice bill wrongly transferred authority in the matter from state officials to federal judges. Adams in his briefer report confessed his support for the committee plan until he discovered that nearly all the southern members disdained it in favor of the Crittenden plan. He wrote that he finally turned against the committee plan on January 11, after Adams introduced a resolution proclaiming the duty of all citizens to acquiesce in the election of Lincoln; the fact that seven southern members refused to vote on the resolution, saying in a written statement that it would do more harm than good, indicated to Adams that these southerners intended to act against the substance of the resolution and not accept the outcome of the election. Under those conditions, Adams became convinced that the root of the crisis was too deep to be resolved by the committee plan. Representative Ferry of Connecticut limited himself to a statement that, while he liked some committee proposals, he opposed other parts and therefore believed that he could not advocate the measures as a package. Northern Democrats Burch and Stout, in a short statement, professed support of most of the committee's proposals but dissented because they believed the plan would not settle the crisis. Instead they championed, as they had in the committee, the calling of a national constitutional convention as the most efficacious road to an adjustment. The individually paginated minority reports can be found as the last seven parts of "Disturbed Condition of the Country" cited in note 1 above.

3. An insightful analysis by young Adams, from the viewpoint of moderate Republicans, of the two basic dangers which these Republicans sought to avoid until March 4, and also of the Committee of Thirty-three measures which moderate Republicans hoped would appease the border slave states and distract congressional and public attention away from the Crittenden Compromise. See also his comment on the Virginia-Maryland secession question in his January 8 letter to his brother. Levenson et al., eds., *Henry Adams Letters,* 1: 219.

4. Adams here gives a definite Republican spin to Cox's speech, emphasizing his attack on both the secessionists and the Republicans as part of a design on the Democrat's part to start up a new Union party. Radical Republicans accused moderates like Seward of attempting to do the same thing. However, those who talked of a Union party, whether Democrats or Republicans, always spoke of it as a coalition developing within the existing party framework, not a separate political party. What Henry Adams failed to stress in his account was the speech's reflection of ardent Unionism and hatred for secession among Democrats of the Old Northwest states. Adams apparently did not attend the House's session on January 14 in time to hear the address just prior to Cox's, one given by another northwestern Democrat, John A. McClernand of Illinois. McClernand had been a key lieutenant of Sen. Douglas for years, but during the disunion crisis session he, Cox, and some other northern Democrats had gradually drifted away from Douglas, believing that the senator was cozying up to southerners like Jefferson Davis too much

and not assuming as strong a condemnation of secession as these other northern Democrats would have liked. They too, like Douglas, favored compromises to save the Union, but they felt that Douglas's efforts to appease southern leaders prevented Douglas from attacking disunion to the extent his former close allies did. McClernand in particular had become disgusted at southern braggadocio and threats in House debate; at one point on December 31, the Illinois Democrat had shaken his finger at disunionists William Barksdale of Mississippi and Thomas Hindman of Arkansas and loudly exclaimed on the House floor: "Come on! come on! now we are ready to meet you and settle it quickly!" *New York Times,* January 1, 1861.

Although McClernand and Cox organized their back-to-back speeches differently and allotted the content of them differently, both congressmen covered the same topics. McClernand's was certainly the more ponderous of the two; for the first half he presented one of the more comprehensive attacks on the southern assumption that a right of secession existed. In citation after citation, quote after quote, McClernand sought to demonstrate that the Founding Fathers had framed the Constitution to be the foundation for a permanent government, not one that could be dissolved by the secession of states. The more flamboyant Cox, with better oratorical skills, also refuted any right of a state to secede from the Union but allotted less space to the argument.

Another issue covered by both speakers, a topic of special significance to the Old Northwest states, was the palpable threat that seceding southern states on the lower part of the Mississippi River would interfere with or block commerce from the northern states in transit to the Gulf of Mexico through New Orleans. Northwestern Democrats had typically not been hostile to southern interests, but the possibility that southerners in any way might use their stranglehold over the sole commercial outlet to the Gulf in order to control the politics of the Northwest alienated those free states upriver from the South like no other issue in the secession crisis. John McClernand devoted much of the second half of his speech to this subject, while "Sunset" Cox expressed the same determination, albeit in fewer words than his Illinois colleague, to keep navigation of the Mississippi open to all. Despite the constant pledges by southerners not to interfere with the free navigation of the Mississippi through an independent southern confederacy, northwesterners had received telegraphic news in Washington that day, alluded to by Cox, which led them to distrust such promises. Gov. John Pettus of Mississippi, fearing steamboat shipments of artillery by the U.S. government downriver from Pittsburgh (shipments already canceled by the Buchanan administration following large public protests in Pittsburgh), on January 12 had stationed batteries of artillery one mile north of Vicksburg to hail southbound steamboats with blank artillery rounds to force the ships to put in at Vicksburg for inspection. The Mississippians threatened to follow any refusal to stop with live fire against the offending vessel. As he finished discussing the subject in his speech, Rep. Cox proclaimed that "rights of transit and outlet are ours by use, by purchase, by possession, and ours they will remain." The views of the northwestern press echoed the sentiments of McClernand and Cox. Gov. Pettus desisted from interference with downriver traffic soon thereafter, having been informed that the Louisiana authorities had taken control of the forts further to the south on the river.

In addition to the above subjects, McClernand and Cox both addressed the "coercion" issue and argued that it was not "coercion" for the federal government to enforce law against those who had seized control of U.S. forts and other installations in the southern states. Southern commentators on the speeches naturally targeted these particular comments in order to label both orations as "coercion" speeches. Both speakers emphasized that disunion, if permitted, would cause the entire government to disintegrate. However, while these northern Democrats seemed to threaten the South on one hand, both McClernand and Cox urged the South to remain in the Union to resolve their grievances and advocated several of the compromise plans. Cox in particular assured the southerners that many northerners would support their rights within the Union, that the Republicans would be powerless to harm them if they remained in the Union, that Lincoln would prove a conservative leader once in office, and that Republicans who had threatened the South would actually take no aggressive action once in power. Cox constantly advised patience on the part of the South, for disunion could only mean war.

Cong. Globe, 36: 2: 367–377; Philadelphia *Press*, January 16, 1861; McClintock, *Lincoln and Decision for War*, 95–96, 144–145, 159; Nichols, *Dis-*

ruption of American Democracy, 394; Richard L. Kiper, *Major General John Alexander McClernand: Politician in Uniform* (Kent, OH: Kent State University Press, 1999), 19; and David Lindsey, "'Sunset' Cox, Ohio's Champion of Compromise in the Secession Crisis of 1860–1861," *Ohio State Archeological and Historical Quarterly* 61 (October 1953): 354–355. For southern views of the two speeches as "coercive," see: *Charleston Mercury,* January 18, 1861; and Richmond *Daily Dispatch,* January 17, 1861. The drift of McClernand, Cox, and some other northern Democrats away from Douglas in the crisis is mentioned by correspondents in : *Cincinnati Daily Commercial,* January 18, 1861; New York *Independent,* January 17, 1861; New York *Evening Post* (semi-weekly), January 19, 1861; and *Springfield* (MA) *Daily Republican,* January 18, 1861. On the situation regarding the Vicksburg batteries and Mississippi River navigation, see: *Chicago Daily Tribune,* January 22, 25, 28, 29, and February 2, 25, 1861; *Cincinnati Daily Commercial,* January 14, 1861, declaring that the Northwest would never submit to "political inquisition at the cannon's mouth"; *New Orleans Daily Crescent,* January 28, 1861; *New York Commercial Advertiser,* January 22, 1861, in which a Washington correspondent wrote that the Mississippians were reacting to a reported movement of artillery from Ft. Leavenworth to Baton Rouge arsenal; *New York Daily Tribune,* January 24, 28, 1861, reprinting detailed article on the batteries from the *Vicksburg Weekly Sun* of January 16; and Springfield *Daily Illinois State Journal,* January 16, 24, 1861.

5. Another appropriate use of analogy by Henry Adams, this time likening President Buchanan to a weary boxer whose supportive friends attempt to keep him going until the end of the fight. The president held his first regular every-two-week reception of the session on January 15, three days after his niece Harriet Lane had begun to hold her weekly Saturday morning receptions at the White House. Republicans were anxious to bolster the new-found firmness of Buchanan in policy, especially since the disunionists had all been purged from his cabinet. Some of the few southern ladies who did attend and who had been particular favorites of President Buchanan in previous times now swept by the president with a cold-shouldered curtsy. However, many Republican politicians braved the elements—snow, sleet, slush, and mud following a period of very pleasant weather—to attend the function. Rep. Charles Francis Adams

at the levee noticed that Sen. Seward then seemed to be taking a "guiding hand" at the helm of Buchanan's administration. Republican friendliness towards him, for a change, along with the aid of General Scott and Holt, Stanton, and Black in his new cabinet, undoubtedly boosted the old president's morale at the end of his administration. C. F. Adams Diary, January 15, 1861, roll 76, part 1, *MAP; Boston Daily Courier,* January 21, 1861; *Boston Morning Journal,* January 23, 1861; *Charleston Daily Courier,* January 17, 19, 1861; *Charleston Mercury,* January 21, 1861; *Cincinnati Daily Commercial,* January 17, 1861; *Louisville Daily Journal,* January 17, 1861; and *New Orleans Daily Crescent,* January 26, 1861.

6. Other than the White House receptions and a few other social gatherings, Washington society lacked its usual social whirl in the Secession Winter. The departure of many southern politicians and their families from Washington as their states seceded partly accounted for the dullness, since southern ladies had traditionally assumed a leading role in organizing social activities. The *Louisville Journal*'s Washington correspondent confirmed Henry Adams's assessment of the social scene, writing on January 14 that there were "no balls, or parties, or soirees, or dinners, and very few operas or concerts. . . ." *Louisville Daily Journal,* January 17, 1861.

LETTER 13

Boston Daily Advertiser, January 22, 1861

Letter from Washington
[FROM OUR OWN CORRESPONDENT]

Washington, Jan. 18, 1861

The debate in the House has been quite interesting this week. The Southern men complained so bitterly of not being allowed to speak that Mr. Sherman gave them four days before putting the army appropriation bill on its passage.[1] In these four days quite a number of speeches have been made on all sides.

The best one from the secessionists was, to my mind, Mr. Garnett's. He brings the whole thing fairly down to what it really is:–"what the minority section wants is *power.*" His strictures on the Massachusetts school of politics are worth reading to one who is accustomed, with Mr. Seward, to consider that school as the best exponent yet known of republican institutions. Mr. Garnett is a Virginian and a gentleman. He is a young man, with a face of a good deal of energy and still more vehemence, good looking, and for a Congressman, of wonderfully polished manners, but he is a warm secessionist, and is doing his worst to drag Virginia after South Carolina.[2]

Mr. Sickles, too, made a speech yesterday. So far as his personal weight goes, Mr. Sickles's opinion would not weigh a straw on one side or the other. Still he is certainly a man of ability, and what is even more, a man of notoriety. As a speaker he does not amount to much. His voice is high and sharp, and he has a disagreeable air and expression. I should call it pertness, but one is not always a fair judge from the galleries of the House. His speech was a great satisfaction to the republican side of the House, not because it came from him, but because it showed how the city of New York is going, for Mr. Sickles is not a man to run in the face of his constituents. At the end of it he took very strong and firm ground, and went for holding on to the Southern forts at any price.[3]

Today has been the most interesting debate of the session. Mr. Sherman made a long speech and a very good one. As the republican leader in the House he carries a good deal of weight. For a wonder nearly all the members were in their seats listening, and the galleries were pretty full, which is rather uncommon now, as since Mr. Seward's speech the interest in the debates seems to have pretty much died out. I don't know whether Mr. Sherman's reputation has fairly reached Massachusetts yet. Here he does not rank as one of the stiff-necked republicans, in spite of the howl that was raised about him when he was candidate for Speaker, but he is republican enough to be a sound anti-slavery man, and his energy, coolness and steadiness have made him a first-rate leader. He is a tall, angular Westerner, not a graceful speaker, but strong in his own way. His speech today seems to have pleased the republicans very much.[4]

When he had finished, Crawford of Georgia asked "a few minutes" to reply, and in spite of Mr. Grow who reminded him several times that he ought not to abuse the courtesy of the House, he took three-quarters of an hour. His speech, or remarks rather, made very little impression. Afterwards, however, his colleague, Hill, got up, and made a Union speech, which was listened to with the deepest attention. It is the first time, I think, this session, that any one of the Southerners has fairly avowed himself for the Union, and has honestly and in good faith tried to help towards an accommodation. He is a hard-featured, rough-looking man, but he spoke gravely and earnestly and was not afraid to tell the democratic secessionists that they were in the wrong, nor to advocate the policy of making Georgia a distinct nation rather than have her join a Southern confederacy.[5]

After this, and a good deal of questioning and talking, the Army bill was taken up again and read. Mr. Dawes tried hard for an extra appropriation for making arms.[6]

In the Senate, the Crittenden resolutions have given some trouble, but it seems settled that they cannot pass, so it is of very little consequence whether they hang on a while longer or not. Mr. Simmons of Rhode Island astonished that body by quite a touching reference to the secession of Georgia and the grave of Gen. Greene. He is almost the last man there, from whom one would expect sentiment, and it had the more effect for that reason.[7] Mr. Seward's speech has certainly done a great deal of good. One feels it at every turn. It is the tone of the speech, not the mere propositions, that gives it such weight, and I have no doubt that by the 4th of March, every one will feel that that speech saved the republican party. Mr. Seward himself is quite satisfied, I believe, with its effect.[8]

NOTES

1. Passage of the regular appropriation bills was a top priority of Republicans in the session, and John Sherman of Ohio, chair of the Ways and Means committee, and his fellow Republicans had made these bills special orders and had stifled southern attempts to interfere with the proceedings. Under House Rule 114 the regular appropriations bills enjoyed a precedence over all others. However, Sherman decided to open up a limited period of speeches by both northern and southern representatives from January 15 through January 18 on the army appropriation bill.

2. Henry Adams interpreted the essence of southern concerns, as expressed in Democrat Muscoe R. H. Garnett's speech, as loss of southern political power. This attitude reflected the basic view held by other Republicans in the crisis, that all southern grievances and rationales for secession added up to nothing more than "rule or ruin." Republicans simply could not fathom the reality of southern white fear of them on the slavery issue, and tended to dismiss discourses such as Garnett's as attempts by an arrogant, slaveholding planter aristocracy to cover their sense of shame at merely losing political power in the election of Lincoln to the presidency. Garnett, well described in Adams's *Advertiser* letter, presented on January 16 one of the better analyses of why southerners feared Republicans in national power and disdained compromise.

Muscoe R. H. Garnett, at age 39, was among the younger members of the House and a nephew of Sen. Robert M. T. Hunter of Virginia. Garnett hailed from the tidewater county of Essex in that state and had emerged in the 1850s as one of the "Young Chivalry" of the South in his stalwart defense of hierarchical structure in southern society and the righteousness of slavery. In his January 16 speech Garnett occupied much of his time in detailing how fanatically antislavery the Republicans were, how those Republicans would use their newly won political power to destroy slavery in the southern states, and how the destruction of slavery there would transform the South ultimately into a society similar to that of Haiti or the British West Indies. At several points in his address, Garnett emphasized Lincoln's anticipated use of federal patronage appointments in southern states, and, through this vehicle, the creation of Republican antislavery parties in the slave states to become the principal means for the abolition of slavery there. For Garnett and southern secessionists the crucial factor was fear of how Republicans would use political power to destroy slavery, not the loss of power itself by southern leaders. Congressman Garnett expressed no faith in compromises, especially those involving amendments to the Constitution, which he believed would require too much time for ratification, even if they did receive approval from two-thirds of both houses in Congress. *Cong. Globe,* 36: 2: 411416; C. F. Adams Diary, January 16, 1861, roll 76, part 1, *MAP;* Link, *Roots of Secession,* 21, 24, 111–112, 114, 128, 140–142; and Simpson, *Good Southerner,* 80, 84, 88–90. The most well-known statement of southern fear of Republican use of federal patronage to destroy southern society is an editorial in the *Charleston Mercury,* October 11, 1860. Numerous southerners and their newspapers voiced the same fear during the secession crisis.

Henry Adams's account of Garnett's speech was one of the few notices it received among Washington correspondents. The one-hour House speeches were often not well attended either by the public or even by House members themselves. Sometimes a member delivered his well-prepared discourse to a nearly empty chamber, especially if the speech took place during an evening session. Reporters and the public generally regarded House oratory as "buncombe" primarily for the edification of the member's district; the term had been in use since 1820 when a member from Buncombe County, North Carolina, had insisted on speaking for his district during the Missouri Compromise debates. A few of the more prominent House members might command wider attention to and attendance at their speeches, but the Senate remained by far the center of oratorical interest for the public and the press. Another factor at this particular time, which diminished the number of correspondents and other auditors for House speeches, was the spate of snowy, slushy, rainy weather Washington was experiencing. *Charleston Daily Courier,* January 19, 1861 ("buncombe" speeches); and Richmond *Daily Dispatch,* January 21, 1861 (weather keeping a reporter from visiting the Capitol). Immediately following Garnett's speech on January 16, stalwart Republican John A. Gurley addressed the House; a New York correspondent noted that no more than ten of his fellow representatives were in the chamber paying attention to his hour's remarks. *New York Evening Express,* January 17, 1861. For one correspondent's lengthy and sarcastic accounts of the session's "buncombe" speeches in general, see *Cincinnati Daily Commercial,* January 2, February 8, 1861.

3. Rep. Daniel Sickles (already discussed in Letter 7, note 6) in his January 17 speech provided an excellent example of a traditionally pro-southern "doughface" Democrat from the North mercurially attempting to shift his views to adjust them to the increasingly anti-southern political barometer in New York City. For much of his address Sickles continued to blame southern secessionism on the Republicans, their antislavery views and refusal to grant equal rights to the South in the territories, and the expected Republican onslaught against slavery once Lincoln assumed the presidency. The New York Democrat urged a compromise settlement and opposed federal coercion of southern states. But in the latter part of his speech Sickles adopted a tough stand against actions taken by southern states in seizing forts and other federal property and in firing on the *Star of the West.* He heartily endorsed the steadfast refusal of Maj. Anderson to evacuate and surrender Ft. Sumter. And while Sickles denied that the federal government could coerce a state, he argued that southern states had been the aggressors in taking over federal positions by force and that those states could not now protest use of federal force to recapture its rightful possessions. This type of federal action, he declared, would not constitute federal coercion of a state. Sickles wanted peace but believed the republic to be "imperishable" and warned that the South was forcing the Union to take action to maintain it. When Sickles had finished, nearly all his fellow northern Democrats came forward to congratulate him. Republicans, as young Adams noted in his letter, enjoyed those parts of his remarks where he condemned

southern seizure of federal property and showed a determination to employ force to reclaim them, even if it meant war. *Cong. Globe*, 36: 2: App., 87–91; Boston *Daily Atlas and Bee*, January 21, 1861; *Cincinnati Daily Commercial*, January 18, 21, 1861; Columbus *Daily Ohio State Journal*, January 23, 1861; *New York Daily Tribune*, January 18, 1861; New York *World*, January 19, 1861; and Swanberg, *Sickles*, 110–112.

4. The speech by Rep. John Sherman (R-OH) represented the official close of debate on the army appropriation bill. Sherman actually drew a considerable gallery crowd, in addition to a goodly number of House members; besides Sherman's own prominence, the fact that the Senate was then engaged in a closed-door executive session on the nomination of Joseph Holt as secretary of war vacated those galleries and brought many of those listeners to the House chamber. As Henry Adams pointed out, Sherman did not possess a "graceful" oratorical style, but he was nonetheless very agile in House debate, with rapid and animated delivery of his logical arguments and quick retorts to those southerners who interrupted him. The Ohio leader delivered most of his address standing beside his desk but, when he wished to emphasize particular points, he would frequently advance down the aisle as he spoke before returning to his desk.

Sherman's speech summarized all the basic Republican positions. It was the southern states which had committed constant aggressions against the property of the United States within the boundaries of those states, and federal coercion to recapture these seized installations would be fully justified, he said. Against southern charges that Ohio's personal liberty law represented open rebellion against the Constitution's fugitive slave clause, Sherman answered that Ohio had only enacted a statute to protect its own black residents from kidnapping. He stated that the Republicans would not agree to a compromise under secessionist threats, especially the Crittenden plan. Sherman derided talk of compromise as useless under circumstances where the cotton states really wanted disunion, not compromise or conciliation, and were committed to the erroneous notion that the secessionist whim of a single state's majority could destroy the Union at their pleasure. Republican views, he averred, had been grossly distorted into abolitionism by southern radicals, when in fact Republicans absolutely disavowed any intention to interfere with slavery in southern states and favored laws to guard states against invasion by armed groups from other states, i.e., other John Brown-type raids. However, Sherman also asserted the free speech rights of northerners to oppose slavery and argued that southerners should permit free discussion of the issue in their states; mob violence against such discussion in the slave states, he declared, was a confession by southerners of the inherent weakness of their social system. On the territories issue Sherman proclaimed that the climax of that struggle had occurred in Kansas, that free soil had won the victory there, and that the South should accept Kansas statehood as the end of the territorial slavery issue. New Mexico, the only remaining territory contiguous to the slave states, would be useless to them as far too barren to support widespread slave labor; with extensive peonage, or servitude to pay off debt, and only a few black house servants of U.S. officials and officers, New Mexico could never become a real slave state. Sherman's very negative comments on the character of the New Mexican population elicited a brief but spirited defense of his territory by delegate Miguel Otero. Sherman concluded his speech with a strong denunciation of the Crittenden Compromise, especially because it would force protection of slavery for the future onto New Mexico and any subsequent U.S. territorial acquisitions to the south. He stated his opposition to any such acquisitions. Sherman urged the South to accept the limitation of slave labor to the states which already recognized it, to accept the legitimacy of Lincoln's election, and to allow the Republicans to assume power in Washington as a road to lasting sectional peace.

Republicans were duly impressed by Sherman's speech. The *Cincinnati Commercial*'s effusive Washington correspondent described the address as "so strong, comprehensive, and convincing, that there was hardly a friend of the Union and the integrity of the Government present but felt that his own sentiments were being expressed by an orator of rare abilities." Diarist Charles Francis Adams wrote that Sherman's speech was "full of fine passages" and "the most effective speech of the session. . . ." The *Charleston Mercury*'s reporter also praised Sherman's effort as honestly adhering to the Republican platform and admitting that party's refusal to compromise. Particularly this correspondent stressed Sherman's open declaration that the U.S. Army, subject of the appropriation bill under debate, should be used to retake federal property seized in southern states. "It gives the South exactly that information which it most desires," the correspondent wrote. "It is an unequivocal declaration of war." *Cong. Globe*, 36: 2: 450–456; C. F. Adams Diary, January 18, 1861, roll 76, part 1, *MAP; Charleston Mercury*, January 23, 1861; *Cincinnati Daily Commercial*, January 19, 22, 1861; Columbus *Daily Ohio State Journal*, January 23, 1861; and John Sherman, *Recollections of Forty Years in the House, Senate, and Cabinet: An Autobiography* (Chicago: Werner Co., 1895), 215–225.

5. While Sherman's speech was officially scheduled to close the debate on the army bill, leave was accorded to Georgia congressmen Martin J. Crawford, Democrat, and Joshua Hill, American, to give brief remarks. All knew that Georgia's convention was in the process of passing a secession ordinance that day and that this would probably be the last time for these two men to address the House before departing for home. Reporters noticed an air of levity permeating the chamber as first Crawford and then Hill spoke; secession seemed to have lost its shock value by mid-January. Crawford, probably the most fanatical disunionist in the Georgia delegation, spent his time accusing the Republicans of aggressions on southern rights and portraying their talk of coercion as a declaration of war. He attacked Sherman's defense of freedom of speech as an indicator of his support for printing and circulating antislavery propaganda in the South, and declared that the Republicans intended to invade the South in defense of that "freedom." Crawford argued that the only safety for the slave states depended upon their being able to withdraw peaceably from their union with the North. Hill's shorter statement was quite different in character. While he asserted Georgia's willingness to fight if need be and deplored Republican talk of coercion, this Bell-Everett moderate proclaimed even then that the door to settlement was not closed. However, Hill stated that prospects for reconciliation depended upon Republicans in government power being willing to offer the South a reasonable compromise close to the provisions proposed by Crittenden. Disagree with Hill though they did, Republicans were sad when moderate southern Unionists like Joshua Hill left Washington. Republicans, Democrat Isaac Morris of Illinois, and Hill himself wept as they shook hands before he departed. *Cong. Globe*, 36: 2: 456–459; *Cincinnati Daily*

Commercial, January 19, 22, 1861; and St. Louis *Daily Missouri Democrat*, January 25, 1861, copying articles from *Cincinnati Gazette* and *Cincinnati Commercial*. Crawford's fanaticism can be judged from letters by a Georgia newspaperman in Washington and one of his own letters. J. Henley Smith to Alexander H. Stephens, December 9, 20, 26, 1860, and Crawford to Stephens, January 7, 1861, roll 6, A. H. Stephens Papers, Manuscripts Division, Library of Congress.

6. Henry Adams appears to have made an error here. After the Crawford-Hill remarks, members offered various amendments to the army bill, but none of them directly involved an increased appropriation for arms production. Henry L. Dawes of Massachusetts was a staunch Republican and did participate in this debate. Kentucky disunionist Democrat Henry Burnett offered an amendment to the bill which would have prohibited any of the army appropriation from being used by the federal government to make war against or to coerce any of the seceding states. Following some debate on Burnett's proposal, Dawes moved an amendment as a substitute for Burnett's. It read: "That it is the duty of the President to so use the appropriations herein made as to protect the flag of the country, and regain and defend the possession of the forts, arsenals, and other property of the United States." Dawes's amendment was ruled out of order at that stage of proceedings on the bill. The Committee of the Whole on the State of the Union then reported the army appropriation bill to the House. *Cong. Globe*, 2: 36: 462–463.

7. Sen. James F. Simmons (R-RI) was one of the moderate Republicans who supported William Seward's proposals for a compromise. On January 16 Simmons denied that southern secession was warranted by either the Constitution or circumstances. Though he vigorously opposed the Crittenden Compromise, with its unrepealable constitutional amendments, he made clear his desire for a more reasonable settlement along the lines suggested by Seward in his speech four days earlier. Simmons defended the Republicans against southern charges of abolitionism or advocacy of black racial equality with whites. He urged the southern states to remain in the Union and to trust that the Republicans in power would fully protect southern rights under the Constitution. The passage to which Henry Adams referred in his letter occurred in the last paragraph of Simmons's speech. Simmons attempted to use the memory

of Gen. Nathaniel Greene, born in Rhode Island, who became a great hero of the American Revolution in the southern theater of the conflict and who died and was buried in Georgia in 1786, to symbolize the ties of Union between North and South. This emotional appeal from the usually taciturn Simmons wrung down applause from the galleries. *Cong. Globe,* 36: 2: 404–408; New York *Independent,* January 24, 1861; and New York *World,* January 18, 1861.

The Rhode Islander's speech took place during Senate debate on the Crittenden Compromise, and more specifically on a proposed substitute for the Crittenden resolutions by Sen. Daniel Clark (R-NH). This substitute, offered on January 15, was the Republican answer to Crittenden's plan and its supporters. Clark's amendment declared that the Constitution as it stood was already sufficient to preserve the Union, that it needed to be obeyed rather than amended, that public property needed to be protected and laws enforced rather than new guarantees or concessions granted to satisfy unreasonable demands, that all attempts to dissolve and then reconstruct the Union were "dangerous, illusory, and destructive," and that all efforts must be made by both government and citizens to maintain the Union and the Constitution. Subsequent to Simmons's speech and a shorter one by his Rhode Island Republican colleague Henry B. Anthony on the 16th, the Senate adopted the Clark substitute by a roll call vote of 25-23. Republican votes passed it, but six southern Democrats who were present at the time refused to vote against it to block it. They wanted to use the Clark amendment in the southern states as representative of Republican opposition to any compromise. Even moderate Republicans like Simmons voted for the Clark substitute as an alternative to Crittenden's. The Crittenden resolutions, as amended by Clark, were then tabled. Crittenden's plan remained essentially what most pro-compromise members of Congress desired, but the Clark substitute had dealt it a devastating blow, with some southern Democratic connivance. *Cong. Globe,* 36: 2: 379, 408–409; Johannsen, *Douglas,* 825–826; and Kirwan, *Crittenden,* 399–401.

8. See Letter 11, note 11, on Henry Adams's growing appreciation for Seward's speech.

LETTER 14

Boston Daily Advertiser, January 24, 1861

Letter from Washington
[FROM OUR OWN CORRESPONDENT]

Washington, Jan. 21, 1861

The tide is certainly turning. The excitement is wearing itself out. It is not so very easy to show how or where, but one feels in the atmosphere that the disunionists are checked and wavering, and it would not take much to turn the scale against them. People have not the air of war that one would expect. They do not believe in war at the bottom of their hearts, and even Jefferson Davis is thought to be no enemy of conciliation.[1]

The debates in the House are encouraging. There is a decided tone of good nature and moderation about them that promises better things. Mr. Corwin's and Mr. Millson's speeches today will both have a good influence on Virginia, and though it is possible that they will not prevent her going out, they will build up the Union party there and make it strong and active. Mr. Corwin did not, I must say, come up to my expectations. Like most of our other legislators, he carries the stump oratory into Congress, and speaks there as he would at a mass meeting in his district. What he said may have been excellent, but his manner of saying it prevents anyone from hearing enough to judge by. He begins his sentences with the greatest energy of voice and action, and ends them in a whisper and without a gesture on the most emphatic part, and yet he fills the hall and the galleries. Today he was listened to with great attention; members drew their chairs out into the area before the Speaker's desk, and sat still through the whole; it seemed like an echo of old times.[2]

Mr. Millson of Virginia, who followed, is, or is said to be, the ablest of the whole Virginia delegation. His speech was very good, of considerable ability, and of still more ingenuity. His idea of slavery, that it is a mere personal relation like that of man and wife, is a specimen. His speech was evidently intended more for effect on his State than on Congress, but he was quite effective in delivery and seemed to exasperate the secessionists, for, when his hour was out they made a dead set at him to choke him off. Burnett of Kentucky, who has a voice like a bull and a face not very unlike his voice, was particularly active, but it was of no use, and after a sharp skirmish Mr. Millson continued. When he had finished, the House adjourned.[3]

Meanwhile the Senate has admitted Kanzas, which a not unusual but quite objectionable prevalence of whisky had more than anything else prevented from coming in last Saturday. Georgia has seceded, but as the occasion was a pressing one and votes were of value, Mr. Iverson assisted in making a majority of one to tack on an amendment by which it is hoped to saddle this already too hardly used territory with a certain Pettit of Indiana for a Judge.[4] If the virtue of the young State can stand this trial, she is impregnable. Still it is to be hoped that the nomination, if made, will be rejected. In addition to this, Mr. Jefferson Davis made another last speech;[5] this time positively the last; and so, like Cataline and his friends, these men are vanishing from the capitol to find their own ruin, I hope, without the need of an army or civil war, in some obscure village in the South.

It is rather hard just now to find out what the real plans of these men are. The truth is, their original plan has crumbled to pieces. Their hope that the shock of secession would shatter the whole government, has been utterly crushed. They find themselves now face to face with a power greater than themselves, and at whose absolute mercy they lie. I believe that Mr. Hill of Georgia knew what he said, when he declared that even South Carolina would return if a reasonable advance were made to her.[6]—These men do not want to go and they will yet make another effort. Virginia will act as mediator; will try to unite all the southern States on some ultimatum;[7] and my belief is that if the price is not outrageous they will be back in the Union before six months are over. Still, this is only conjecture founded on general indications and talk, and there may happen a thousand things to change the course of events.

There are already between thirty and forty names on the list to speak in the House on the Report of the Committee of Thirty-three. Mr. Lovejoy speaks this week. Mr. Adams will probably speak next week.

NOTES

1. Henry Adams wrote a similarly hopeful statement to his brother Charles on January 24. Levenson et al., eds., *Henry Adams Letters,* 1: 225.

2. Thomas Corwin, who had chaired the House's special Committee of Thirty-three, drew a large gallery audience, but by all accounts this moderate Republican leader's speech on January 21 was, as young Adams indicated, not very impressive in content or style. Congressman Adams referred to Corwin's effort as "a sort of mixed warp of silver and brass wire." Corwin spoke for an hour and a half (House members were usually willing to extend a speaker's time beyond his allotted one hour under their chamber's rule), urging adoption of his committee's plan to resolve the crisis. He particularly touted statehood for New Mexico as a reasonable compromise to finally settle the old territorial slavery issue, although he professed belief that slavery would never really take hold there. Corwin supported repeal of any unconstitutional personal liberty laws and suppression of any publications aimed at stirring up slave insurrections, and denied that the Republicans possessed either the will or the authority or the power to abolish slavery in southern states; but he also defended the right of Congress to coerce individual citizens to obey the laws and refuted the idea that this would amount to coercion of states. Reporters generally considered the speech able, conservative in tone, and probably helpful to southern Unionists in the upcoming elections for seats in Virginia's special convention. However, more radical Republicans opposed to any compromise, especially some of Corwin's colleagues in the Ohio delegation, displayed their disdain as Corwin spoke by pointedly ignoring him, writing letters, and reading newspapers. *Cong. Globe,* 36: 2: App., 72–76; C. F. Adams Diary, January 21, 1861, roll 76, part 1, *MAP; Cincinnati Daily Commercial,* January 22, 1861; *Cincinnati Daily Enquirer,* January 22, 1861; *New York Commercial Advertiser,* January 22, 23, 1861; *Morning Courier and New York Enquirer,* January 23, 1861; *New York Evening Express,* January 22, 23, 1861; and Letter 12, note 1.

3. John S. Millson, Democratic congressman from the Norfolk district in Virginia, was one of the southern Unionists most feared by the Virginia secessionists; he was a Democrat rather than one of the more traditionally Unionist Americans and he represented a tidewater con-

stituency rather than one of the more mountainous, nonslaveholding areas in the western part of the state. Noted much more for the logic and intelligence of his remarks than for oratorical dynamism and gesticulation, Millson in his January 21 address argued that none of the South's grievances against past northern actions justified secession. He considered that the free states had won the struggle for the national territories and that slavery expansion was not the issue most essential to southerners. The basis for the South's fear of Lincoln and the Republicans, he said, was their concern about future Republican interference with slavery in the slave states. To remedy that southern concern, Millson insisted that further constitutional guarantees be afforded to the South to render their slave property secure from federal government interference, no matter who was in power. He discussed the issue of slavery's ambiguous status under the Constitution in some detail. Of the propositions from Corwin's special committee, the plan for a constitutional amendment to protect slave property from federal intervention was the only measure of the committee which Millson endorsed as useful in calming southern fears. He declared that stronger constitutional guarantees than that were required to secure southern rights and he strongly recommended the calling of a constitutional convention. Henry C. Burnett, Kentucky Democrat and ardent disunionist, was the member who in vain attempted to prevent the House from hearing the conclusion of his speech once Millson's hour was up. Secessionists naturally condemned Millson's speech as traitorous to the South but Union men of all parties North and South lavishly praised it and hoped that its sentiments would prove efficacious in the Virginia convention elections. *Cong. Globe*, 36: 2: App., 76–80; C. F. Adams Diary, January 21, 1861, roll 76, part 1, *MAP; Charleston Mercury*, January 26, 1861; *Cincinnati Daily Commercial*, January 22, 1861; *New York Commercial Advertiser*, January 23, 1861; New York *World*, January 24, 1861; *Philadelphia Inquirer*, January 22, 1861; Philadelphia *North American and United States Gazette*, January 23, 1861; St. Louis *Daily Missouri Democrat*, January 26, 1861; *Springfield* (MA) *Daily Republican*, January 25, 1861; Cox, *Union–Disunion–Reunion*, 73–74; and Crofts, *Reluctant Confederates*, 124–126.

Millson's speech can be considered the beginning of a Unionist counterattack against the southern secessionists in preparation for the crucial Virginia election scheduled for February 4. The fate of Virginia, Maryland, the District of Columbia, and possibly the entire border slave state area seemed to hang on the outcome of those elections. Should the Unionists gain a majority of the convention seats, Virginia and the border states would almost certainly remain attached to the Union until after Lincoln's inauguration; should the secessionists win those elections, however, no one could be sure that Washington, D.C., would even be available for Lincoln to assume the presidency on March 4. The Unionist campaign of late January became multifaceted. Partly this consisted of House speeches by the southern Unionists: Millson on January 21, Sherrard Clemens (D-VA) on January 22, Emerson Etheridge (A-TN) on January 23, Thomas A. R. Nelson (A-TN) on January 25, John A. Gilmer (A-NC) on January 26, and J. Morrison Harris (A-MD) on January 29. Not only were they sincerely devoted to the Union as the most beneficial arrangement for all, but they were also conscious of the fact that the border area would likely become a major battleground in any civil war between North and South. As the *New York Commercial Advertiser*'s Washington correspondent "Raconteur" colorfully portrayed the underlying fear of southern conservatives, they had "a chaos of armed force, fears, doubts and popular phrenzy dancing past their eyes like the strange dissolving views of a phantasmagoria, leaving on the retina a bewildering specimen of the grotesque and hideous." *Cong. Globe,* 36: 2: 580–583 (Gilmer); and App., 103–106 (Clemens), 106–111 (Nelson), 111116 (Etheridge), 116–118 (Harris); *New York Commercial Advertiser,* January 23, 1861; and Letter 15, notes 2, 5. Newspaper journalists often praised two or more speeches together in their commentaries and expressed the belief that they would positively influence opinion in both North and South. Baltimore *American and Commercial Advertiser,* January 30, 1861; *Cincinnati Daily Commercial,* February 4, 1861; *Louisville Daily Journal,* January 29, 31, 1861; *New York Commercial Advertiser,* January 28, 1861; New York *World,* January 22, 1861; Philadelphia *North American and United States Gazette,* January 26, 1861; Philadelphia *Press,* January 29, 1861; and Springfield *Daily Illinois State Journal,* January 28, 1861.

Union men in Congress helped distribute printed copies of these speeches by Millson and Clemens as widely as possible in Virginia. Democrat "Sunset" Cox of Ohio claimed later to have had a major role in disseminating Millson's address. So fearful were secessionists of the impact of these speeches on Virginia public opinion that ten disunionist members of Virginia's congressional delegation on January 22 telegraphed their opinion to the state that all hope for meaningful compromise in Washington had ended due to Republican intransigence. Not to be outdone in the dispatch competition, on January 28 Senators Douglas and Crittenden and Virginia Representatives Alexander R. Boteler (American) and John T. Harris (Democrat) responded with a message to John Barbour of the Virginia state legislature that the prospects for a settlement had never been brighter than they were at that time. Congressman Millson added, in a separate dispatch, his strong confidence that the Peace Conference, called for by the Virginia legislature and to assemble beginning on February 4 in the large meeting hall of Willard's Hotel in Washington, would arrange a satisfactory compromise to save the Union. The ubiquitous Sen. Seward, who had insinuated himself into the deliberations of Douglas and Crittenden though opposing their compromise proposals, probably had some agency in the Virginia Unionist dispatch, but Seward's hand in the process cannot be proven. *Charleston Daily Courier,* January 28, 1861 (the Virginia disunionist dispatch); *Cincinnati Daily Commercial,* January 28, 1861; *Cincinnati Daily Enquirer,* January 30, 1861; *New York Commercial Advertiser,* January 23, 1861; *New York Evening Express,* January 28, 1861; *New York Daily News,* January 28, 1861; New York *World,* January 24, 30, 1861; Philadelphia *North American and United States Gazette,* January 26, 1861; Philadelphia *Press,* January 28, 1861; Richmond *Daily Dispatch,* January 29, 1861; Springfield *Daily Illinois State Journal,* January 29, 1861; Washington *Evening Star,* January 26, 1861; and Cox, *Union–Disunion–Reunion,* 73.

While the main object of these efforts was to influence Virginia to remain in the Union, one must never forget that this was only part of the continuing attempt by southern Unionists to influence the Republicans to support a compromise at least acceptable to the border slave states. Certainly the House speeches of the southern conservatives increased the appreciation of northerners in and out of Congress for Unionist southerners willing to stiffen their backs against the disunion tide. Added pressure on Republicans in Washington arrived in the person of Kentucky Republican Cassius M. Clay, there on behalf of Gov.

Beriah Magoffin and others favorable to compromise in that state; Clay mainly spent his time in Washington trying to convince congressional Republicans of the merits of Rep. Charles Francis Adams's constitutional amendment and New Mexico statehood bill. Pro-compromise delegations of business leaders from several northern cities also descended on Washington in the last week of January in their efforts to cajole Republicans into compromise. A group of five prominent Boston leaders also came, escorting a "monster" petition from that area in favor of compromise. It is a testament to how firmly committed most Republicans in Congress remained against compromises they considered a surrender of principles that they did not succumb to the enormous pressure to which they were subjected in late January. Schuyler Colfax to Robert Carter, January 27, 1861, Carter Correspondence; *Cincinnati Daily Enquirer,* January 30, 1861; *Louisville Daily Journal,* January 29, 1861; *New York Herald,* January 25, 26, 28, 1861; Springfield *Daily Illinois State Journal,* January 28, 1861; Stegmaier, "An Imaginary Negro," 278–279; and Letter 16.

4. Kansas (often spelled Kanzas in the mid-nineteenth century), subject to such bitter strife since 1854 over the issue of slavery in national territories, had witnessed a victory for the free-soilers there. They had devised the Wyandotte Constitution and submitted it to Congress in their quest to be admitted to the Union as a free state. The House of Representatives had passed the bill during the first session of the 36th Congress, but the Senate, with stronger southern opposition to Kansas's adding two more free state members to the northern majority already in the upper chamber, had delayed its consideration of the bill until the short second session. By mid-January the southerners realized they could delay the bill no longer. Only one chance remained for them to block the bill. If the southern senators and their dwindling number of northern Democratic friends could amend the House bill in some way obnoxious to the House's Republican majority, then the House might not concur in the Senate amendment and the whole bill-passing procedure would have to be restarted. Sen. James S. Green (D-MO), chairman of the Committee on Territories, prepared several amendments which became the focus of Senate debate on Saturday, January 19, but the Senate rejected all of them. Also on the agenda was an amendment offered the day before by Sen. Graham Fitch (D-IN), longtime friend to

southern interests, to establish a U.S. District Court in the new state. Everyone seemed to realize that, if this amendment became part of the final statehood act, President Buchanan would quickly nominate John Pettit for the position. Pettit was an old friend of Buchanan's, had served as a Democrat from Indiana in both houses of Congress, and was then serving as federal judge for Kansas Territory. Kansas free-soilers did not consider him a friend to their cause. After a long day of wrangling on the 19th, over Fitch's amendment at first but mainly over various of Green's proposals, senators were hungry, worn out, and bored to death–or to drink as the case may have been. Henry Adams was the only correspondent to mention liquor as a factor that day, but the consumption of liquor by senators in such a session would have surprised no one at that time. As the senators grew hungrier in the late afternoon, Sen. Green let it be known that he was going to deliver a four-hour speech. That was too much for Republican Sen. John P. Hale of New Hampshire to bear; the fat, lazy Hale had a difficult time sitting for long periods as it was, and the prospect of another four hours was unendurable for him. To the rescue came a move to adjourn, and the Republican votes of Hale and Sen. Simon Cameron of Pennsylvania aided its passage. Thus Kansas statehood had to wait at least two more days.

On Monday the 21st the battle resumed. But a non-Republican majority of one, on a roll call vote of 29-28, managed to pass the Fitch amendment for a federal judicial district in Kansas; the majority were all non-Republicans, the minority all Republicans, except for Douglas and Crittenden. The Senate then passed the amended bill, and the House took it up a week later on January 28. The Fitch amendment actually provided no impediment to the House Republicans. With little debate the House simply concurred in the Senate's amendment, and Kansas was admitted to statehood. As for the prospect of President Buchanan appointing Judge Pettit to the life tenure of a federal judgeship in the new judicial district, Republicans understood that they held the trump cards. President Buchanan might nominate Pettit for the judgeship, but Republicans knew that they could block his confirmation by the Senate during the few remaining weeks of the session. Their desire was that President Lincoln have the opportunity to appoint a Republican to the new judgeship. President Buchanan did indeed nominate his friend Pettit anyway, and Pettit even traveled to Springfield to discuss the judgeship in a long interview with President-elect Lincoln on January 30. Pettit then headed to Washington in hope that the Senate would confirm him, but to no avail as the Senate Republicans thwarted action on Buchanan's later appointments. *Cong. Globe,* 36: 2: 447–448, 465–476, 487–489, 603–604; *Cincinnati Daily Commercial,* January 25, 31, 1861; *New York Herald,* January 22 and February 7, 1861; New York *Evening Post* (semi-weekly), January 23, 1861; and *Springfield* (MA) *Daily Republican,* January 25, 1861.

5. Sen. Davis withdrew on January 21, along with several other senators whose states had seceded. In his brief remarks, Jeff Davis defended the South's right to secede, and stated that the South did so out of fear of the Republicans, whom he said had perverted the Declaration of Independence into a document which assumed the racial equality of blacks and whites. *Cong. Globe,* 36: 2: 487; Crist, ed., *J. Davis Papers,* 7: 18–23; Poore, *Perley's Reminiscences,* 2: 55–56; and Chalfant, *Both Sides of the Ocean,* 217.

6. *Cong. Globe,* 36: 2: 458; and Letter 13, note 5.

7. Virginia's legislature, in calling for the Peace Conference at Washington, desired for that meeting to endorse the Crittenden Compromise or something very similar. Neither northern nor southern radicals appreciated the idea. The Washington correspondent "Alpha" of the *Evening Traveller,* one of Boston's Republican presses, wrote that, while Virginia's move had the appearance of compromise, it made "safety pivot upon an impossible contingency" for Republicans, i.e., the Crittenden Compromise. From the southern radical side also came rejection of the Peace Conference plan. According to the *Charleston Mercury*'s Washington correspondent, the convention had been cooked up as a gimmick by Gov. John Letcher and Unionist state senator Alexander H. H. "Sandy" Stuart of Virginia to keep Virginia within the "Abolition Confederacy" until after March 4. So sure was this writer that Virginia's move would fool the border slave states into remaining in the Union that he decided to change his pseudonym. During the earlier part of the session, believing that all the slave states might secede, this reporter had signed himself "Fifteen" on his letters. Following his letter attacking the Peace Conference, however, he signed his name "Seven." Boston *Daily Evening Traveller,* January 24, 1861; and *Charleston Mercury,* January 24, 1861.

LETTER 15

Boston Daily Advertiser, January 26, 1861

Letter from Washington
[FROM OUR OWN CORRESPONDENT]

Washington, Jan. 23, 1861

Yesterday and today there has been good speaking in the House; speaking of really marked ability. Mr. Bingham, who spoke first yesterday, did not make so much impression as some of the others, but his speech was a good one nevertheless.[1] Mr. Clemens, who comes from the Panhandle district of Virginia, made what people call here a heroic speech. You who are all Union men off in Massachusetts where the worst chance could hardly bring either war from without or a reign of terror within, are hardly likely to appreciate the moral courage it needs for a Virginian to make a speech like this. To be sure Mr. Clemens comes from a firm Union district, but that does not take away the credit of his course.[2]

The people of Virginia and the other border States have been and are being seduced into this secession movement by a back road, as it were. They do not call themselves precisely disunionists. There is too much odium in that word. They are "reconstructionists." They want all the States to secede until they can "reconstruct" a new Union without New England and the other most obnoxious parts of the confederacy, and in this way they can claim to be for and against the Union at the same time.[3] Nearly all the Virginia delegation are either strong disunionists or reconstructionists, and Mr. Clemens has to defy his old friends and subject himself to the charge of being friendly to New England and against Virginia, when he comes out so boldly as he did yesterday. If Virginia goes out, he will have to emigrate or submit to the worst sort of oppression. He speaks with the rope round his neck, and it is in this way that his course is really heroic. Two years ago, I think, he was forced against his will, for he is said to be quite a religious and non-duelling [*sic*] man, into a duel with Mr. Wise, and after exchanging shots twice, he was wounded, the third time, so badly, that he has not yet wholly recovered, and probably never will.[4] He has every reason, therefore, not to make himself obnoxious, and yet he was not afraid yesterday to speak out in the very way that would be most likely to bring a dozen such affairs of honor on his head.

It is not quite so with Mr. Etheridge of Tennessee, who spoke today. His opinions are well known. He belongs to the South Americans and ranks with Winter Davis and several others, whose course has long since made them as obnoxious to the democrats as they can be. Still, it is a very bold and honorable thing for him to declare himself so openly. I never listened to anything more interesting than his speech this morning, which "brought down" the crowded galleries several times, and evidently told very hard on the secessionists. He declared himself willing to accept anything he could get as a compromise, and if necessary, go home and resist disunion sword in hand. He is an amusing speaker and a hard-hitter; managing to keep the House in a good humor and yet say the roughest things. When his hour was out the southerners tried to choke him off, and succeeded in stopping him long before his audience was tired of listening to him.[5]

When he finished, Mr. Lovejoy took the floor. Before he began, the letter of the Georgian members was read, withdrawing from the House, and one from Mr. Hill of Georgia resigning his seat. Mr. Hill is a popular member, and his way of doing things is at least straightforward and honorable. He was in the House and a crowd of members flocked round him to shake hands and bid him good bye.[6]

Mr. Lovejoy then set to work. His manner is violent to the last degree, and before long he took off his cravat, and opened his shirt collar, and roared so that he might almost have been heard at Baltimore. Some ingenious member on the other side, set the House in a titter by mildly suggesting "Louder!" I confess to liking Mr. Lovejoy. He is no such fanatic as people call him, and fanatic or no, he is bold, honest, good-natured and straight-forward. A broad-shouldered, massive man, with a rather coarse and animal face, but Cromwellian in expression, he says what he thinks right and says it well. Republicans may think his speech injudicious, but after all he said little that any republican would not theoretically endorse. With all his violence of manner, he was very good-natured and kept the House in a roar all through; for now that the violent men are mostly gone, no more of those blackguard scenes of last winter take place. His speech will probably do no harm, and may do good as coming from him.[7]

NOTES

1. Rep. John A. Bingham of Ohio was one of the most uncompromising, antislavery Republican radicals in the House. On January 22, 1861, he delivered an address brimming with all the elemental points of radical northern orthodoxy. Bingham argued that no justification existed for southern secession under the Constitution, that there should be no compromise with rebels who seized U.S. property, and that the duty of the federal government was to maintain the Constitution and Union as they were and to suppress rebellion by military force. Any southern grievances could be resolved within the court system, he said, not by the revolution of disunion. The worst of all grievances in the country, Bingham declared, was slavery, which crushed the hopes of four million people and their posterity, people who might one day engage in revolution themselves. He opposed every concession designed to further safeguard this evil system; even the Corwin Amendment from the Committee of Thirty-three, Bingham asserted, would deny Congress the right to assist in the future emancipation of slaves. In an implied threat to the South, Bingham alluded to the belief expressed years before by John Quincy Adams that slavery might be abolished under the war powers of the federal government if a civil war occurred. Bingham denounced all the other measures from Corwin's committee before concluding his speech with a final plea for the maintenance of the Constitution and the Union and for the enforcement of the laws. Charles Francis Adams described the speech as "eloquent and vigorous," but the speech received little attention. Everyone expected a radical antislavery, anti-disunion, pro-coercion speech, and Bingham delivered one. Bingham himself was disappointed by the northern newspaper reporters who either attacked or ignored his

speech in their columns, while they lavished high praise on every southern Unionist speech for compromise. He overheard one northern correspondent refer to his address as "a d–d abolition speech." So strong was the public passion for compromise at the time that Republicans themselves did not rush up to congratulate Bingham at the end of his hour. They themselves might oppose compromise as much as Bingham, but they refrained from making an obvious show of their feelings. Instead, as Bingham wrote in a letter, a number of his Republican colleagues came to his room afterward to thank him for his speech. *Cong. Globe,* 36: 2: App., 80–84; John A. Bingham to Joshua R. Giddings, January 25 and 28, 1861, roll 4, Giddings Papers; C. F. Adams Diary, January 22, 1861, roll 76, part 1, *MAP; Cincinnati Daily Commercial,* January 28, 1861; and New York *Evening Post* (semi-weekly), February 2, 1861.

2. Sherrard Clemens represented the Wheeling area of far northwestern Virginia (at that time) west of Pittsburgh, a mountainous region of "white" counties with small farms and few slaves. Clemens had been crippled in an 1858 duel [see note 4 below]. Z. K. Pangborn ("P") of the Boston *Atlas and Bee* described him on January 22 during his speech as a handsome-looking man of short stature, very energetic in his delivery but not a fiery speaker, and possessed of a fine voice and dramatic manner. During his hour he kept the House spellbound and attacked southern secessionists on those aspects of slavery and disunion where they were most sensitive. Southern Unionist orators generally praised Union, supported compromise, denied that circumstances justified secession, and urged the North to make concessions and the South to delay any disunion impulse. Clemens adopted a different approach, directly refuting all the basic assumptions of the seceders about the advantages of separating from the Union. He began with an assault on the essential premise which underlay disunion, that it would provide the South with greater security for slavery. Instead, Clemens proclaimed, dissolution of the Union would destroy the slavery system, and he described how radical abolitionists William Lloyd Garrison and Wendell Phillips delighted in the crisis as they anticipated just such an outcome to secession. Clemens ridiculed the southern radicals who utilized every northern antislavery speech to stir up the southern populace; it was they, he said, who really circulated the dreaded abolitionist propaganda throughout

the South. The western Virginia congressman denounced any secessionist ideas that disunion would facilitate the fulfillment of slavery expansionist dreams; such would be impossible, Clemens argued, given his expectation that Mexico would probably fall into the grasp of the United States and that Central America would be protected from southern designs by Great Britain. He also portrayed the diversified economy of the Upper South as very distinct from the cotton economy of the Gulf states, and asserted that Lower South efforts to build a slave empire in Latin America would totally alienate the border slave states from the Deep South. Clemens did criticize northern extremists and did urge the North to grant greater constitutional guarantees to protect southern slavery, but the bulk of his address consisted of "merciless invective" against the disunionists, as Ben Perley Poore ("Sigma") described it for the *Cincinnati Commercial.* While several correspondents noted how uneasy the southern radicals appeared under Clemens's relentless attacks, Poore provided the most detailed description of the scene. Senator Mason of Virginia came into the House during the speech, and immediately left the chamber. Disunionists Muscoe Garnett of Virginia and Henry Burnet of Kentucky, both Democrats, "were especially conspicuous in their spasmodic efforts to conceal the rage and mortification" they experienced. "They filibustered about the hall, in a fidgety and uncertain mood–now laughing or talking loudly, now beckoning somebody into the cloak room, and now turning their back on the speaker, and in short trying every means to hide their real intense interest and chagrin." Disunion presses naturally attacked Clemens's speech as traitorous to the South, while Republican and southern Unionist newspapers praised it. Charles Francis Adams waxed positively ecstatic about it in his diary as the first positive repudiation by a southerner of "the spread of this pestilence [slavery]" in Congress. As with Millson's speech, Unionists were reported to have had 200,000 copies of Clemens's speech printed for distribution, especially in Virginia to help the Unionist campaign in the approaching convention delegate elections. At least twelve Republican House members, both radicals and moderates, contributed $5 or $10 each toward the effort to spread copies of Clemens's address. For this list, dated January 23, 1861, see roll 5, container 5, Justin S. Morrill Papers, Mss. Division, LC. See also: *Cong. Globe,* 36: 2: 103–106; C. F. Adams Diary, January 22, 1861, roll 76, part 1, *MAP;* Boston *Daily Atlas and Bee,* January 25, 28, 1861; *Charleston Mercury,* January 28, 29, 1861; *Chicago Daily Tribune,* January 28, 1861; *Cincinnati Daily Commercial,* January 23, 28, 1861 (for "Sigma"'s identification as Poore, see note 7 below); *New Orleans Daily Crescent,* February 1, 1861; *New York Commercial Advertiser,* January 23, 1861; *Morning Courier and New York Enquirer,* January 25, 1861; *New York Evening Express,* January 24, 1861; *New York Daily Tribune,* January 23, 1861; Philadelphia *Press,* January 31, 1861; Richmond *Daily Dispatch,* January 29, 1861; and Cox, *Union-Disunion-Reunion,* 73. The distribution of the hundreds of thousands of copies of southern Unionist speeches throughout the border slave states was handled mostly by volunteers in a rented office under the direction of Joseph C. G. Kennedy, whose official government position was that of chief superintending clerk of the census. Southern radicals complained about this propaganda effort to influence the Upper South but it continued. *New York Herald,* February 13, 1861.

3. On "reconstruction" schemes, see Letter 7, note 5.

4. Clemens had been severely wounded and left crippled in a duel with O. Jennings Wise, editor of the *Richmond Enquirer* and son of Henry Wise. The duel had originated in Virginia political rivalries and had occurred in September 1858. Simpson, *Good Southerner,* 178–179.

5. Emerson Etheridge was a conservative American representative from northwest Tennessee, 41 years old, a lawyer tall in physical stature and noted for his intellect, firm-minded attachment to the Union, and ability in debate. His speeches were well organized and logically argued. Benjamin Perley Poore ("Sigma") described his "intense earnestness of manner" and bursts of "genuine eloquence" during his address of January 23 but also remarked that Etheridge made his points effectively without dramatic gestures. As a southern Unionist he denounced any right of secession and saw no justification for disunion in any northern action so far. Etheridge believed the North had dutifully surrendered all but a few fugitive slaves and that disunion would only hurt the border slave states by relieving the North of that duty. Disunion, he said, was largely based on imagined future Republican aggressions against slavery, not on existing realities. Secession would do nothing to increase security for slavery, Etheridge declared, but the South could help block any Re-

publican antislavery moves if the slave states stayed in the Union and their members remained in Congress. He expressed his own support for any of the major compromise plans and urged the Republicans to do the same. The most dramatic moments came toward the end of his hour. After Etheridge ridiculed the southern extremist delusion that Lincoln planned to stir the slaves into revolution against their white masters and denounced the "reign of terror" in those southern areas where secessionism predominated, there arose "a thin piping voice, proceeding from a weazened-face little man, in a shrill tone," as Poore described it. The voice was that of Virginia Democrat and disunionist Shelton F. Leake, who sarcastically inquired of Etheridge whether he was speaking on the side of the North or the South. The Tennessee unconditional Unionist quickly retorted: "I am speaking on a side that has few Representatives upon this floor. I am speaking on the side of my country." The galleries erupted in thunderous applause. Etheridge's hour was up soon thereafter, and southern radicals objected to any extension of his time so that he could finish his address. The speaker pro tem did allow him a few extra minutes, at the end of which enthusiastic applause again rained down from the galleries. On Etheridge's speech and reactions to it, see: *Cong. Globe,* 36: 2: App., 111–116; C. F. Adams Diary, January 23, 1861, roll 76, part 1, *MAP;* Boston *Daily Atlas and Bee,* January 26, 1861; *Charleston Mercury,* January 28, 29, 1861; *Cincinnati Daily Commercial,* January 24, 26, 1861; *New Orleans Daily Crescent,* February 1, 1861; New York *Independent,* January 31, 1861; *New York Times,* January 25, 1861; New York *World,* January 25, 1861; Philadelphia *North American and United States Gazette,* January 24, 1861; Richmond *Daily Dispatch,* January 26, 1861; and Washington (DC) *Constitution,* January 24, 1861.

6. See Letter 13, note 5, for Hill's earlier withdrawal speech.

7. Republican Owen Lovejoy of Illinois was an abolitionist radical and among that contingent of his party in Congress who were absolutely opposed to compromise. His brother Elijah Lovejoy had become a martyr for the abolition cause in 1837 in Alton, Illinois, when a mob destroyed his newspaper press and murdered him. Owen Lovejoy was a short, stout man with a large head and coarse facial features, as a New York *World* reporter described him. But what impressed people most when he gave an address was the ferocity of his manner of delivery. No one else in Con-

gress could match this Yankee fire-eater in vehemence, loudness, and dramatic gesture. His contortions frightened some and moved others to laughter. The *Charleston Courier*'s correspondent wrote" "He pounds the desks, kicks over the chairs, and makes the dust fly from the floor, in his violent gesticulations." Mr. Poore, though, in one of his "Sigma" letters to the *Cincinnati Commercial,* outdid all his fellow journalists in portraying Lovejoy on January 23. Poore wrote:

> He is a man of considerable brains, and a good deal of body; and his style of utterance . . . was of the hyper-intense school. He began his speech at the top of a voice of most prodigious compass, and kept on in the same key, which it were a mild description to characterize as a roar. When some waggish member on the Southern side cried "Louder," the effect upon the audience was convulsing. There stood Lovejoy, with his coat off and his collar open, his big bushy head thrown back like a lion at bay, and brandishing his arms aloft, while his whole body rocked and quivered with excitement, hurling his denunciations, not at the slave power this time, but at the secessionists. His tremendous voice rang through the hall like the peal of a trumpet, and when he arose, as he sometimes did, to a strain of eloquence, in describing the insult to our flag, it was truly fine to hear.

The content of Lovejoy's speech was, for the most part, hard-core anticompromise radical Republicanism. He denied any right by a state to secede from the Union, held that the federal government could coerce citizens of states to obey U.S. law, and absolutely opposed any compromise with rebels who had fired upon the U.S. flag-bearing *Star of the West* on January 7. The Illinois abolitionist particularly condemned the Crittenden Compromise's guarantee of unlimited expansion and perpetuity to slavery, an "outrage" to Christian civilization. Compromise, he vividly proclaimed, was the slaveholder's collar placed upon the necks of the northern populace. Lovejoy pledged that Republicans would never retreat from their platform of slave restriction, recently given a popular mandate in the national election. However, after delivering such fiery oratory, toward the end of his speech Lovejoy surprised everyone by striking a more moderate tone. He denied that any power in the Constitution would permit the federal government to abolish slavery in southern states and promised that Republicans favored no congressional interference in the slave states. Though he admitted his personal desire for abolition, he also avowed that Republicans did not profess belief in the political, social, or intellectual equality of blacks to whites. He urged southern Unionists to continue to stand by the Constitution and argued that southerners should migrate on an equal basis with northerners to the western territories, i.e., without slaves. Lovejoy concluded by stating his belief that slavery was only temporary and would ultimately end by the acts of southern states themselves. Despite all the violence of Lovejoy's manner of oratory and the antislavery radicalism of much of it, even the southern radicals seemed to feel that Lovejoy presented his views in an open and good-natured fashion, as Adams pointed out, rather than an abusive one, and they did not object to an extension of his time. Southern Unionists, desperate for any sign of Republican moderation, derived some comfort and hope from the moderate sentiments near the end of the address. *Cong. Globe,* 36: 2: App., 84–87; Boston *Daily Atlas and Bee,* January 26, 1861; *Charleston Daily Courier,* January 26, 1861; *Cincinnati Daily Commercial,* January 24, 26 (the latter issue having the long description of Lovejoy), 1861; *Louisville Daily Journal,* January 29, 1861; *National Anti-Slavery Standard* (New York), February 2, 1861; *New York Evening Express,* January 25, 1861; New York *World,* January 25, 1861; Philadelphia *Press,* January 25, 1861; Poore, *Perley's Reminiscences* 2: 50–51; and Edward Magdol, *Owen Lovejoy: Abolitionist in Congress* (New Brunswick, NJ: Rutgers University Press, 1967), 265–269.

On the identification of Poore as the *Cincinnati Commercial*'s "Sigma," one need only compare the description of Lovejoy by "Sigma" quoted in this note from the January 26 issue with the description in *Perley's Reminiscences,* 2: 50–51. With some minor variations in wording the two passages are virtually identical. Poore apparently liked this piece of his journalism enough to copy it into his memoirs nearly verbatim. Benjamin Perley Poore was one of the best-known members of the correspondent corps in Washington in the mid-nineteenth century, but as "Perley" in the *Boston Journal* rather than as a correspondent for any other paper. His first letter as "Sigma" for the *Cincinnati Commercial* did not appear until the January 19 issue and was dated the 16th. Telegraphic dispatches from him, also dated the 16th, had appeared in the issue of the 17th. His best, most informative articles from that time until the end of the session appeared in the *Commercial;* meanwhile his dispatches to the *Journal* became rather lackluster. Henry Adams himself provided a clue in one of his letters to his brother as to what may have motivated Poore to start writing his best reports for another paper. Besides complaining about his own letters to the *Advertiser* having been cut, Adams related on February 5 that Poore had gotten so disgusted with the *Journal*'s chopping of his correspondence that he pretty much quit writing to that paper for a time. Apparently the *Commercial* allowed Poore to express himself in journalism as fully as he wished. He still continued to write for his normal employer, the *Boston Journal,* and even disguised his identity as the *Commercial*'s new reporter from Washington. In his first letter to the *Commercial,* in the January 19 issue, "Sigma" reported his arrival in Washington–a city of "mud, blacklegs [crooks], and politicians"–after a long train trip to make it appear that he was a newcomer to the capital. Levenson et al., eds., *Henry Adams Letters,* 1: 227; *Cincinnati Daily Commercial,* January 17, 19, 26, 1861; and Poore, *Perley's Reminiscences,* 2: 50–51.

LETTER 16

Henry Adams's "Five Wise Men of Boston"—A Suppressed Letter

Probably on January 27 or 28, Henry Adams wrote a letter to the *Boston Advertiser,* which he mentioned in a letter of January 28 to his brother Charles. He told Charles: "I have written a letter to the *Advertiser* chaffing the five wise men of Boston which [editor Charles] Hale will not publish I suppose. As he always cuts out the spicy parts of my letters, I don't expect it. Still, I thought I would make the attempt." A few days later on February 5, the young correspondent groused to his brother again about Hale expunging anything of "an unfavorable personal character" from his letters. Adams also stated in the same letter that all the Boston papers did the same thing to their reporters' letters and particularly cited Poore's problems with the *Boston Journal.* As Henry Adams had predicted, Hale did not print his letter on the "five wise men." Adams's biographer Edward Chalfant wrote that Adams was targeting Boston's extreme abolitionists such as William Lloyd Garrison and Wendell Phillips in his never-published and no-longer-existent letter. But in fact the "five wise men" he criticized were staunch Massachusetts conservatives who had arrived in Washington in late January to lobby for the adoption of compromise measures in Congress and who brought with them a huge petition signed by over 14, 000 people in the Boston area. The five-man committee escorting the pro-compromise petition to the nation's capital included two former Whig U.S. senators, 66-year-old Edward Everett and 51-year-old Robert C. Winthrop. Everett had been the Constitutional Union Party's vice-presidential candidate in the recent election, and his good friend Winthrop was descended from the original Puritan founder of Massachusetts. Joining them were two significant leaders of the Massachusetts business community, merchant-industrialist-philanthropist Amos A. Lawrence, 46 years old, and shipping magnate-banker-president of the board of trade Edward S. Tobey, 47 years old. The youngest member of the group was 40-year-old Charles Levi Woodbury, U.S. district attorney for Massachusetts and the only Democrat among this lot of northern Americans. Lemuel Shaw, famous chief justice of the Massachusetts supreme court and just recently retired, was prominently named on the petition with the five who traveled to Washington, but the 80-year-old, infirm jurist did not accompany them. Joining the five committee members and acting as secretary to the group was Oliver H. Spurr, a Boston city government official.[1]

The "monster" petition from Boston in favor of compromise was one of many either sent to or brought to Washington during the Secession Winter. The petitions and memorials reflected the avid interest of the public in the outcome of the crisis. Some of the petitions favored compromise in general, such as that brought by the "five wise men" from Boston; it prayed "that such measures may be speedily adopted . . . to restore tranquillity and peace to our now distracted country." The very vagueness of the petition's wording may have helped to secure some signatures to it, and Winthrop himself wrote that he believed the petition would serve New England and the country well because it was "rather indefinite & feeble." The Democratic *Boston Courier*'s Washington correspondent, however, argued that the memorial's failure to endorse any definite compromise plan rendered it "the weakest kind of a weak bread-pill." Many of the pro-compromise memorials indeed did favor one or the other of several compromise plans; by far these supported the Crittenden Compromise more than any other set of proposals. The petitions and memorials opposed to compromise, sent to Congress mainly by Republican groups from the North, emphasized "The Union, the Constitution, and the Enforcement of the Laws" and argued that no changes in the Constitution and no compromises were necessary in the crisis. Some senators and congressmen grew tired of the inundation of Congress by the petitions, believing that they changed no one's mind but wasted a lot of time in the two houses as members introduced and read them. Sen. Robert W. Johnson, a secessionist Democrat from Arkansas, protested on two occasions in February in the Senate that these memorials consumed the whole morning sometimes and carried "not one particle of force on the face of God's earth"; he declared a few days later that "You might as well sing psalms to a dead horse as to get up and read these petitions . . ." which consumed so much time.[2]

As for the Boston committee, after the Union petition organizers had succeeded in assembling the five prominent Bostonians under the chairmanship of Everett, the group left Boston by train at 11 a.m. on January 23. Staying that night in New York, the five boarded a train at 8 the following morning and, after an all-day journey via Philadelphia and Baltimore, they arrived in Washington at 6:30 that evening. While Everett went off to stay with his daughter who lived in the area, the other four took up residence in a comfortable suite at the big, fashionable Willard's Hotel. Everett came to the hotel to discuss strategy with his colleagues at 8 that evening.[3]

Initial indications at the hotel were that the committee's path in Washington would be anything but smooth. Both radical Republican senators from Massachusetts, Charles Sumner and Henry Wilson, showed up at Willard's and immediately began chastising Amos Lawrence and Edward Tobey about the petition. Where Wilson expressed his disapproval of the Boston petition and the committee, Sumner became downright sarcastic, saying variously that the petition was nothing but a lot of "wind" and likening it to a penny-whistle in a storm or to attempting to hold a man up in a tempest with a little anchor from Jamaica Pond (a popular boating and recreation area in the Jamaica Plain section of Boston). Sumner entirely turned away from and refused to recognize the presence of Winthrop, his longtime conservative political enemy in the state. Amos Lawrence did register a sharp reply to Sumner's "wind" comment, telling him that the committee came there to prick a bag of wind (Sumner) and cause it to collapse for the good of the country. The committee would find over the next few days that the hostility and ridicule of Sumner and Wilson toward them was more widespread in Washington than they had originally expected. Correspondent Z. K. Pangborn ("P") of the Boston *Atlas and Bee* labeled them the "Boston Fossil Committee," and a southern congressman called them "an old ladies Commission" whose influence extended only to "Boston gentlemen who worship at the shrine of cotton," according to a *New York Times* dispatch. These attitudes were probably very similar to those expressed by Henry Adams in his suppressed *Advertiser* letter. Of the eleven members of the Massachusetts House delegation, all but five—Reps. Alexander Rice, Eli Thayer, T. Dawes Eliot, Charles Francis Adams, and John B. Alley—

would studiously ignore the committee while they were in Washington. And among those five only the lame duck Thayer sympathized at all with their mission.[4]

Congressman Rice, though he viewed compromise and northern concessions as needless, nonetheless came over to Willard's on the evening the committee arrived and consulted with its members in a cordial and friendly manner. He agreed to cooperate with them in whatever way he could, probably because the Boston petition was worded so generally that Rice believed he could work with the group without compromising his principles. The Boston committee requested that Rice be the Massachusetts delegation member to introduce the Boston memorial in the House on the following Monday, the 28th, which he agreed to do. Actually the agenda of the five "wise men" was much more specific than the prayer of their petition; every one of them intended to press the Crittenden Compromise as their preferred mode of settling the crisis. Although Everett and Winthrop both held strong reservations about the greater constitutional protection and great potential for slavery expansion which Crittenden's plan would guarantee for slavery, they were willing to swallow their objections. Both men considered this set of proposals as the most viable alternative to the horrors and bloodshed of civil war. Lawrence, also well aware of northern objections to the Crittenden Compromise, held the same view as Everett and Winthrop, and was actively engaged in organizing petition drives for the Crittenden plan itself. On one major point Everett and Lawrence strongly differed, however; where the elderly Everett was willing to endure the division of the Union into two confederacies if compromise efforts failed, the younger Lawrence adamantly opposed secession or the idea of peaceable separation. The members of the Massachusetts congressional delegation, not so downright hostile as Sumner acted toward the Boston committee, realized that they should handle the visitors with the politeness due to prominent citizens from their state. But the delegation knew that no prominent Republican leaders in Massachusetts had endorsed the petition, though the committee claimed that the signers came from every party persuasion. And as Charles Francis Adams stated in his diary, he realized that the Boston committee were "evidently for a good deal more concession" than he could ever support. Further diminishing Republican respect in Washington for the memorial as representative of Boston public opinion on compromise were the accumulating reports that many of the petition signatures were fraudulent–minors, names copied from directories, people pressured by Boston police to sign, and so forth.[5]

The Boston committee began their serious work of lobbying for compromise on Friday, January 25. They sent their calling cards to the Massachusetts congressional delegation and addressed their formal request to Rep. Rice to present the petition. The five men then visited with Sen. Crittenden, whose courage and stamina they all admired; he indicated a willingness to adjust his compromise in phrase and substance if it would help. Elderly ex-president John Tyler of Virginia, in Washington for the beginning of the Virginia-called Peace Conference on February 4, gave the Boston visitors a warm reception; Tyler declared to them that slavery extension to the southward must be opened to the southern states, given the rapid multiplication of the slave population. If the North refused to allow this outlet, Tyler said, then he would favor peaceful separation of the Union. During their visit with Tyler, Virginia disunionist Sen. James M. Mason walked in and began a good-natured banter with Winthrop; Winthrop wondered when Mason might come up to Bunker Hill and Mason replied that if he came, it would be as an ambassador from Virginia. Unfortunately, someone who overheard the exchange entirely missed the humor of it and telegraphed a report around the country that Winthrop and Mason had engaged in a serious confrontation. Only several days later was this dispatch corrected. Next the group traveled to the White House, where President Buchanan, still clad in his dressing gown and slippers, received them cordially. They found him discouraged that the Union was dissolving over a "mere abstraction" and that the North was blocking slavery from an area where God had prohibited it by adverse climate and geography. The Boston committee concluded their first busy morning in Washington with a visit to Sen. William Seward of New York. Seward tried to entertain them with his usual repartee about his having no fear that any more slave states would be added, about Union feeling reviving in the country except among ultra-Republicans like Sumner, and about his confidence that the crisis would be settled. He gave a self-serving "spin" to his own compromise efforts for these Crittenden Compromise supporters from Boston, stating that he would have moved a lot further and faster on compromise if Lincoln had given more support to these efforts. Actually Seward and Lincoln did not seriously differ on what type of compromise measures Republicans could support. Seward's pleasantness changed, however, when Edward Tobey badgered him to provide specifics of a settlement. At that point, Seward, who had maintained his equanimity during the crisis despite pressures from all sides, lost his temper–the only time Winthrop could remember his doing so. Seward responded to Tobey "with great harshness of tone and expression," Winthrop reported. The New York senator obviously wished to remain flexible as to adjustment plans and did not wish to tie himself to any particular proposal. That afternoon, the Boston group split up, with Everett and Winthrop calling on General Winfield Scott and the British ambassador, Lord Richard Lyons. Reps. Thayer and Eliot visited with the Boston committee that evening.[6]

On Saturday the 26th, the committee received various callers at their hotel, including House Speaker William Pennington (R-NJ), but the Massachusetts congressional delegation generally contrived to rebuff them. Their state's members were unhappy that the Boston petition committee had sent their cards rather than calling on them personally, and so they merely answered by sending their own cards to the committee–except Sumner, who refused to do even that. Everett and Winthrop both believed that the proper protocol in previous times would have been for the state's delegation to call upon them first. Thus the committee played a frustrating game of one-upmanship with the Massachusetts senators and representatives. At least Everett and Winthrop were able to attend Miss Harriet Lane's White House reception and one at the home of Sen. Stephen Douglas and his wife. The committee members already were clearly promoting the Crittenden Compromise in their conversations with others and indicating their conviction that the people of Massachusetts would favor that plan of settlement by a wide margin; but they made no inroads on the Republican leaders with whom they talked. On Sunday Robert Winthrop paid a visit to the home of Rep. and Mrs. Charles Francis Adams. He found the congressman a gracious host and revealing conversationalist. When Winthrop expressed praise for Adams's compromise effort in the Committee of Thirty-three, which Adams had finally voted against due to lack of southern support for it,

Adams responded by indicating that the Unionist House speeches of Millson, Etheridge, and other border state southerners were causing him to reassess his earlier disavowal of his plan. Kentucky Republican Cassius M. Clay had also urged Adams on January 23 to renew support for his propositions. Winthrop added his encouragement, and particularly emphasized that Adams should publicly re-embrace those proposals in the coming week in order to positively influence the upcoming Virginia convention elections. Adams stated that he might deliver a House speech in a few days. (Adams had already written most of it and he finished it that night.)[7]

Monday, January 28, was to include the climactic event of the Boston committee's sojourn in Washington–Congressman Rice's presentation of the Boston "monster" petition in the House of Representatives. Before journeying to the Capitol, the group received a call from reconstructionist Sen. Robert M. T. Hunter (D-VA) and "pure, simple & final" secessionist Sen. John Slidell (D-LA). When the five committee members arrived at the House, they were sequestered in Speaker Pennington's room for a half-hour and then were escorted to the diplomats' box on the House floor. After the day's session came to order and some preliminary business was dispensed, the "wise men" witnessed Rep. Rice bringing forward the Boston petition "gift," draped in the American flag, and placing it upon the speaker's table to considerable applause from a few thousand spectators gathered for the event in the chamber and galleries. Rice introduced the petition with only brief remarks and moved that it be read and printed. Only the abolitionist Republican Owen Lovejoy of Illinois objected. The petition was ordered laid on the table and printed. Some noted the presence of old John Tyler on the floor, with his 12-year-old son Alex in tow; the white-haired former president was dressed in the garb of a Virginia farmer, "wearing a well-worn snuff-colored overcoat and thick buckskin gloves." Tyler's purpose in being there that day was probably to listen a bit later in the proceedings to President Buchanan's message praising Tyler and the Virginia Legislature for calling the Washington Peace Conference which would begin on February 4. Despite all the fanfare surrounding the Boston memorial for compromise, the House did nothing further to it for the remaining weeks of the session.[8]

For the rest of that day and on through Friday, Everett and Winthrop continued their lobbying efforts, mainly in the Senate chamber from a sofa there for the use of honored guests. Receptions, parties, dinners, and visits occupied their evenings. Lawrence and Tobey conversed with Sen. Douglas and then Sen. Sumner for several hours on Tuesday the 29th. Amos Lawrence found Sumner obsessed with the slavery issue and unwilling to do anything to prevent secession by the slave states, even if they were all to leave the Union, as Sumner himself thought they would. The recalcitrant Sumner also refused to reconcile with Winthrop; each blamed the other as the offending party in their long-standing rift. Lawrence left Washington for Boston on the next day, probably together with Tobey. Before leaving town, Lawrence sent the American flag in which the Boston petition had been wrapped to the editor of the *Richmond Whig*, that city's most Unionist paper. In an accompanying note he described the gesture as one of good will from Massachusetts to Virginia, a state about to hold its election for state convention delegates. Charles L. Woodbury agreed to stay on with Everett and Winthrop for a few days longer. Woodbury's activities during the Washington trip are given little mention in any sources, but, being the only Democrat among the group, he probably spent most of his time working the Democratic sides of the Senate and House for compromise. Robert Winthrop left Washington on Saturday, February 2, to spend the next few days visiting his close friend John Pendleton Kennedy, novelist, essayist, and political activist, in Baltimore before leaving there for Boston on the 5th. Edward Everett did not depart from Washington until the 8th. The members of the Boston petition committee entertained no illusions about the impact of their persuasiveness on members of Congress; those in favor of a compromise settlement still favored it, but the committee had not budged any of their main target group–the Republicans–toward support of the Crittenden Compromise. A frustrated Winthrop had written to Kennedy on the 29th that everything appeared to be in "confusion & chaos." Everett had written on January 30 to ex-president Millard Fillmore that there was no prospect of a satisfactory solution to the crisis. Amos Lawrence, on his return to Boston, continued doggedly to organize petition drives and spoke on February 5 at a Crittenden Compromise rally in Faneuil Hall, but even such an enthusiast as Lawrence had to inform those who asked him that realistically the prospects in Washington looked "very dark at present." And, while these conservative leaders had been in Washington proclaiming that the Boston petition reflected the will of the popular majority there and that they would also endorse the Crittenden Compromise if it passed Congress, Republican stalwarts in Boston such as John Murray Forbes were organizing their own memorial drives disavowing the petition of the conservative compromisers.[9]

The five emissaries from Boston were neither the first nor the last group representing northern business interests to descend on Washington during that last week of January to pressure congressmen and senators to support compromise. Such activity was especially acute because this appeared to be a most crucial period in the Secession Winter. The Virginia convention delegate elections, the opening of the Peace Conference in Washington, and the assembly of delegates from already-seceded states to form a southern Confederacy were all slated to occur in the first week of February; northern business leaders knew that, if they were to effectively influence events and exercise a positive influence in favor of compromise, this particular period of time represented their best opportunity. A convention of some fifty railroad presidents, thirty-three representatives of a Philadelphia workingmen's meeting, delegations from the Chicago and Milwaukee boards of trade, and twenty-five leading New York merchants arrived in Washington at that time to lobby for compromise, principally the Crittenden plan. Despite kind words from Seward, who introduced a petition of the New York businessmen in the Senate for the border state compromise, and from other moderates, all of these delegations left Washington without converting the Republicans to their views.[10]

The departures of the New York commercial leaders and the Boston committee ended this late-January flurry of pro-compromise delegations from northern boards of trade and chambers of commerce. The assembly of the Peace Conference in Washington and the Unionist victory in Virginia's convention elections during the first week in February encouraged much of the public to believe that the Union–except for the Cotton South states preparing to form their own confederacy at Montgomery, Alabama, at that time–might be saved. With compromise efforts apparently stalemated in Congress, the public's attention shifted for the next few weeks to the Peace Conference and what ideas for a settlement those delegates might produce. The Republicans, especially, were probably glad to see the northern business committees leave town. They could not entirely ignore these influential and wealthy citizens while they visited the capital, but neither could they submit to their pressure, suasion, and blandishments to support the Crittenden Compromise or the border state plan without surrendering the strongly held principles which they had consistently maintained so far during the session. This was certainly what Henry Adams had in mind when he penned his letter to the *Boston Advertiser* "chaffing the five wise men of Boston," a letter which editor Charles Hale refused to print. If Hale had published it, the five targets of Adams's mockery might well have undertaken a strong effort to uncover the identity of their satirist, something young Henry Adams would not have wanted. Adams especially disliked Everett, whom he described to his brother on January 28 as an "old villain, . . . gadding about" Washington, "making love to women, and breaking their hearts."[11]

NOTES

1. Levenson et al., eds., *Henry Adams Letters,* 1: 226, 227; and Chalfant, *Both Sides of the Ocean,* 217–218. A printed copy of the petition, "Memorial of Edward Everett, Lemuel Shaw, Robert C. Winthrop, Amos A. Lawrence, Edward S. Tobey, Charles L. Woodbury and fourteen thousand one hundred and twenty-seven others, citizens of Boston . . ." is in the broadside collection of the Massachusetts Historical Society. On Spurr's role with the group, see *New York Herald,* January 26, 1861.

2. Winthrop's view is in a letter to Everett, January 21, 1861, roll 18, Allis, ed., *Microfilm Ed.–Everett Papers.* The *Courier* correspondent's opinion is in *Boston Daily Courier,* January 30, 1861. The "bread pill" referred to was an old form of placebo, often composed of bread crumbs. A printed version of a typical Republican anti-compromise memorial is in *New York Daily Tribune,* February 5, 1861. For Sen. R. W. Johnson's comments, see *Cong. Globe,* 36: 2: 895, 1011.

3. James C. Converse to Amos A. Lawrence, January 22, 1861, box 15, A. A. Lawrence Papers, and A. A. Lawrence Diary, Sep. 23, 1858–Jan. 5,

1868, p. 115, Massachusetts Historical Society; Winthrop to Everett, January 21, 1861, roll 18, and Everett Diary, January 21–23, 1861, roll 40, Allis, ed., *Microfilm Ed.–Everett Papers;* and Winthrop to Laura Winthrop, January 24, 1861, and Winthrop's January trip journal, pp. 1–3, roll 29, Gutheim, ed., *Microfilm Ed.–Winthrop Papers.*

4. Charles Sumner to John A. Andrew, January 26, 1861, roll 2, Andrew Papers; Winthrop to L. Winthrop, January 25, 1861, and Winthrop trip journal, pp. 3–5, 11–12, 14–15, 22, roll 29, Gutheim, ed., *Microfilm Ed.–Winthrop Papers;* Boston *Daily Atlas and Bee,* January 28, 1861; and *New York Times,* January 25, 26, 1861.

5. A. B. Ely to A. A. Lawrence, January 22, 1861, box 15, A. A. Lawrence Papers; C. F. Adams Diary, January 26, 27, 1861, roll 76, part 1, *MAP;* Everett to John J. Crittenden, December 23, 1860, to William Everett, January 21, to Sir Henry Holland, January 21, and to Rep. A. H. Rice, January 25, 1861, Everett Letterbooks, roll 31, Allis, ed., *Microfilm Ed.–Everett Papers;* Winthrop to Kennedy, January 7, 1861, roll 18, vol. 16, Boles, ed., *J. P. Kennedy Papers Microform; Boston Morning Journal,* January 28, 1861; and McClintock, *Lincoln and Decision for War,* 152–154. For numerous letters describing the alleged fraudulency in some of the petition signatures, see roll 21, Charles Sumner Papers.

6. Winthrop to L. Winthrop, Jan. 25, 1861, and Winthrop trip journal, pp. 5–11, 27, roll 29, Gutheim, ed., *Microfilm Ed.–Winthrop Papers;* A. A. Lawrence Diary, pp. 115–116; C. F. Adams Diary, February 5, 1861, part 1, roll 76, *MAP;* and *Cincinnati Daily Commercial,* January 28, 1861. Seward had regained his composure and calmness by that evening when he dined with the Adamses. Charles Francis Adams recorded that he was "bright and hopeful" and "still believes in a peaceful issue to the difficulty, and a restoration of the Union." C. F. Adams Diary, January 25, 1861, roll 76, part 1, *MAP.*

7. Winthrop trip journal, pp. 11–16, roll 29, Gutheim, ed., *Microfilm Ed.–Winthrop Papers;* F. Adams Diary, January 27, 1861, roll 76, part 1, *MAP; Charleston Daily Courier,* January 30, 1861; St. Louis *Daily Missouri Republican,* January 30, 1861; and Stegmaier, "An Imaginary Negro," 278.

8. Winthrop trip journal, pp. 16–17, roll 29, Gutheim, ed., *Microfilm Ed.–Winthrop Papers;* Everett Diary, January 28, 1861, roll 40, Allis, ed., *Microfilm Ed.–Everett Papers;* A. A. Lawrence Diary, pp. 116–117; *Cong. Globe,* 36: 2: 597, 600–601; *Charleston Daily Courier,* February 4, 1861; *Phil-*

adelphia Inquirer, January 29, 1861; and *Springfield* (MA) *Daily Republican,* February 8, 1861 (Tyler's overcoat, gloves).

9. Winthrop to L. Winthrop, January 29, 1861, and Winthrop trip journal, pp. 17–26, roll 29, Gutheim, ed., *Microfilm Ed.–Winthrop Papers;* Everett Diary, January 29–February 8, 1861, roll 40, Allis, ed., *Microfilm Ed.–Everett Papers;* A. A. Lawrence Diary, pp. 117–118; Lawrence's Faneuil Hall speech, February 5, box 15, Lawrence Papers; Kennedy Journal, February 2, 4, 5, 1861, roll 3, vol. 12, Everett to Kennedy, February 6, 1861, roll 14, vol. 5, and Winthrop to Kennedy, January 29, 1861, roll 18, vol. 16, Boles, ed., *J. P. Kennedy Papers Microform;* Everett to Fillmore, January 30, 1861, roll 49, Smith, ed., *Microfilm Ed.–Fillmore Papers;* John M. Forbes to C. F. Adams, February 2, 1861, "Letters Received, etc.," roll 551, part 4, *MAP; New York Evening Express,* January 30, 1861; and *New York Herald,* February 6, 1861. On Lawrence's sending the flag to Richmond, see *Richmond Daily Whig,* January 31, 1861.

10. On the Railroad Convention, see *New York Herald,* January 22, 25, 26, 1861; and *New York Times,* January 25, 1861. For accounts of the Philadelphia workingmen's meeting, resolutions, and journey, see: *Cincinnati Daily Commercial,* January 31, 1861; and *New York Times,* January 28, 1861. For the Chicago and Milwaukee committees, see Boston *Daily Atlas and Bee,* February 2, 1861; and *New York Herald,* January 29 and February 3, 1861. On the New York merchants and their efforts see: *Cong. Globe,* 36: 2: 657; *Boston Morning Journal,* January 28, 1861; *Charleston Daily Courier,* February 4, 5, 1861; *Cincinnati Daily Commercial,* January 31, 1861; *New York Herald,* January 26, 30, and February 2, 1861; New York *Evening Post* (semi-weekly), February 2, 6, 1861; Philadelphia *North American and U.S. Gazette,* February 1, 1861; and Philadelphia *Press,* February 4, 1861.

11. For Henry Adams's critiques of the Crittenden Compromise in the *Advertiser,* see Letters 5 and 9. His comment on Everett is in Levenson et al., eds., *Henry Adams Letters,* 1: 226; it is doubtful that he included such a personally insulting statement in his suppressed *Advertiser* letter.

LETTER 17

Boston Daily Advertiser, February 2, 1861

Letter from Washington
[FROM OUR OWN CORRESPONDENT]

Washington, Jan. 31, 1861

Another spasm of fear has come over this city lately, and we have again brought ourselves up to the point where we could look forward with more or less philosophy to the chance of a *coup d'ètat.* We are at its mercy, if a well organized attack should be made now, and nothing short of several thousand soldiers quartered in the city will give people confidence. It is, or is said to be, more than probable, that some attempt or other will be made to prevent the counting of votes and declaration of Lincoln's election. As the day comes near, the city is getting a little nervous, not so much from fear of an attack from without as from treachery within. All confidence in the honesty of any one coming from the Southern States seems to have been destroyed.[1]

In spite of this, we are gayer here than for some time past. The President's reception last night was a jam of the orthodox sort.[2] Then we are to have a ball, the first one this winter, and dinners have become quite the fashion again. Secession has done its worst, unless war comes, for, as it is now fairly understood that the Southern States will go, and are not to be kept, people are getting tired of crying about it, and have made up their minds for whatever may happen.

The talking goes on as usual. Yesterday Mr. Conkling made a good speech in the House.[3] He is one of the New York members and has a high reputation as a young member. He accepts substantially the report of the Committee of Thirty-three. Indeed the feeling in favor of the measures offered by the committee seems to me to be very decided, at least, if it can be shown that their passage will do any good.

The pressure has been very strong on the republicans to yield to something like Mr. Crittenden's measures, but it is of no use.[4] When people press Gov. Seward to yield to this, in order to save the country, he replies: "Gentlemen, you think I can save the country by sacrificing myself. Suppose I were to save the country as you wish, I should have put an end to my power for good or evil forever. I should have to go back to Auburn and amuse myself with writing history for the rest of my life. I am not so blind to experience as to suppose that I can both sacrifice myself and remain leader at the same time. Now, do you want me to retire from public life?" The answer is of course, "No, Governor; we can't do without you.["] "Then," returns he, "you must let me save the Union in my own way."[5]

This way is, as I understand it, to shift the present, or rather the past issue. The measures which Mr. Adams proposed in committee, and which are now under discussion; the speech of Gov. Seward,[6] which evidently looks at those measures as the only middle ground; and the course of the South Americans, Mr. Clemens, Andrew Johnson, and others,[7] who seem willing to accept those measures as a settlement, all tend to show that the effort of the republican leaders now is to change the front of battle; to settle the slavery question in a way that all honorable men can acquiesce in, and with a united North behind them, and a strong and able minority party in the South with them, to stand up as the *Union* party,[8] and maintain as their one great and all important object, the Union, the Constitution, and the enforcement of the laws. If this can be effected; if the Union men of the South can find some fair ground on which they and the republicans can act energetically together, then there is some hope of saving the Union and ending forever this whole matter of secession. But the North need not suppose that the South is going to yield easily. If the contest can once be fairly arranged on this ground, it will only be the beginning of the fight. If this effort fails, then we shall either have the Crittenden measures on us, or the whole South will go, which will shake the country through and through.

The movement is a bold one, only justified by the greatness of the danger. Those who do not believe in the danger, will not be apt to acquiesce in the motion. Being in Washington, and seeing what the feeling all over the South really is, I believe that this is a wise and far-sighted policy; the only one that great statesmen could follow. We shall be anxious to learn what you in New England say to it.

NOTES

1. Letter 8, note 10; Winthrop trip journal, p. 25, roll 29, Gutheim, ed., *Microfilm Ed.–Winthrop Papers;* and Potter, *Lincoln and His Party*, 256. The electoral vote count in Congress on February 13 went off without disruption.

2. The president's reception actually took place on the evening of January 29, not the 30th as implied in Adams's letter. Winthrop trip journal, p. 20, roll 29, Gutheim, ed., *Microfilm Ed.–Winthrop Papers.* Adams may have written this part of his *Advertiser* letter on the 30th, which would account for the apparent error of misdating the president's reception.

3. Roscoe Conkling represented the Oneida district of upstate New York in the House. Young, about 6 feet, 3 inches, in height, Conkling was handsome looking, blond haired, and with a full pointed beard. His most noted physical feature then and later was the golden curl of hair which fell across the center of his forehead. Besides the care he took in preening, his vanity was also apparent in the colorful clothing he usually wore to make himself stand out amidst the drab black and gray attire favored by most congressmen. He cultivated a lordly, dignified demeanor when speaking. Conkling addressed the House on January 30 in a speech which ranged all over the Republican spectrum. He argued that the South misunderstood Republican intentions towards them and that the Republicans would and could do the South no harm if the South remained in the Union. Conkling declared southern complaints against the North frivolous, but directly admitted that the North hated slavery as "an iron-heeled, marble-hearted oppressor" which the government under Republican control would never allow to spread by further conquest into Latin America. He favored enforcement of the federal laws, denied any right to secede, and declared that the government could not negotiate with anyone unless they first submitted to the laws. Conkling's remarks here were definitely aimed at the seceding Deep South states. But he also favored reasonable concessions to demonstrate the good will

of the North toward the southern Unionists of the border slave states. In this regard the New York congressman expressed support for several of the Committee of Thirty-three measures, especially C. F. Adams's constitutional amendment and his New Mexico statehood bill. Conkling stated that he did not believe the climate and geography of New Mexico would support the existence of slavery there for long and noted that the territory had only an estimated twelve slaves under its slave code. Henry Adams certainly appreciated Conkling's support for his father's propositions. *Cong. Globe,* 36: 2: 649652; David M. Jordan, *Roscoe Conkling of New York: Voice in the Senate* (Ithaca, NY: Cornell University Press, 1971), 30, 35–36; and McClintock, *Lincoln and Decision for War,* 159.

4. This pressure on the Republicans is best illustrated in the essay in Letter 16.

5. This quote from Seward appears to be a summary of what Henry Adams heard Seward say in response to queries on several occasions. This view of Seward's handling of pressure is given only in this account by young Adams, and it displays Seward's general hopefulness that he could still achieve a settlement to salvage the Union–but not at the price of the Crittenden Compromise.

6. See *Cong. Globe,* 36: 2: 343–344 and Letter 11, note 3, on Seward's proposals in his January 12 speech.

7. Among the notables in this group Henry Adams would probably have included, besides Rep. Sherrard Clemens (D-VA) and Sen. Andrew Johnson (D-TN), Reps. John S. Millson (D-VA), Henry Winter Davis (A-MD), Emerson Etheridge and Thomas A. R. Nelson (A-TN), and John A. Gilmer (A-NC).

8. The Union party to which Henry Adams here refers was not intended to be an organization separate from the Republican Party but an alliance of southern Unionists–Democrats and Americans–with the Republicans in defense of Union, Constitution, and laws. This was what Seward had in mind also, and the purpose of this alliance was to maintain the adherence of the border slave states to the Union. Adams's biographer Edward Chalfant wrote of this "Union party" idea as if it was to be ultimately "something greater and better" to replace the Republican Party with a different organization. Chalfant here misinterprets Seward, the Adamses, and others who spoke of a "Union party." Advocates of

this idea always saw it as a coalition developing within the then-existing party structure. Seward, political intriguer that he sometimes could be, was not trying to subvert the Republican Party or the incoming Lincoln administration, in which he had already agreed to become secretary of state, by fostering a separate party organization from the Republicans. Sen. Seward envisioned a coalition of Republicans, northern Democrats, and southern Unionists committed to the common theme of "the Union, the Constitution, and the enforcement of the laws," as Henry Adams's letter and most Republicans phrased it, not a new partisan entity. For Chalfant's view, see *Both Sides of the Ocean,* 218–219. See also Letter 12, note 4, on the adherence of prominent northwestern Democrats in the House to the same theme. Seward discussed the idea of building a national party with the Boston petition committee; what he wanted was for his fellow Republicans to be conciliatory enough to the Upper South leaders that they could transform the theretofore strictly sectional Republican Party into an organization broad enough in appeal to include significant border slave state elements within it. A. A. Lawrence Diary, January 25, 1861, pp. 115–116. For a recent commentary on the Union Party idea, see Daniel W. Crofts, *A Secession Crisis Enigma: William Henry Hurlbert and "The Diary of a Public Man"* (Baton Rouge: Louisiana State University Press, 2010), 96.

LETTER 18

Boston Daily Advertiser, February 6, 1861

Letter from Washington
[FROM OUR OWN CORRESPONDENT]

Washington, Feb. 4, 1861

If the news comes to the North some fine morning that the telegraph wires are down, and the railroad interrupted between here and Baltimore, you may take it for granted that the war has begun and that we are shut up here like so many rats in a trap, to work our own salvation. If this does really happen, you can have the consolation of knowing that Gen. Scott can hold out against any ordinary force. My own belief is that he expects an attack of some sort. At any rate, all his troops are arranged for one; at a minute and a half of notice any hour, day or night, a battery of artillery will be at the White House, another at the Capitol, and so on, ready to open fire on any enemy. We see the troops parading and hear the bugles morning and evening. Houses here and there are turned into barracks, with, at night, a sentry before them, bayonet and all. I should almost think it was some European town, though in point of fact there are not a thousand men in all, and the General wants ten thousand.[1] The change would not strike a stranger much, however, for there is purposely as little noise and show as possible.

The republicans here and the northerners generally have felt pretty gloomy for the last few days. They are very anxious about Virginia, and do not like the prospect. Accounts from there are very contradictory, and some of them look very badly.[2]

It has been quite an eventful week, and matters have advanced a good deal. History is being made very rapidly. New combinations are coming up so fast that outsiders no longer know where they stand. Mr. Garrison and Mr. Phillips[3] may scold as much as they like, but no power on earth can prevent a greater evil from swallowing up a lesser; and disunion has just now swallowed up everything. It is forcing all parties to a common ground.

Last Thursday both Gov. Seward[4] and Mr. Adams spoke, as I understand them, pretty much to that effect. I heard Mr. Adams's speech. It was listened to by the House with an attention that old members called most extraordinary, and which not many members can command at all. It has received great applause here from all the intermediate men, and even the stiff-necked are willing to take one-half and keep it, even though they have to let the rest go.[5]

It must have been a great triumph for Mr. Adams, for his course has made him a mark for most violent and unreasonable attacks,[6] as any bold step always must, and the reception his speech has met sustains him completely. By the way, I see various rumors about a quarrel between him and Mr. Sumner. According to the telegraph, Mr. Sumner would be made out quite a dangerous character. First he was reported to have had "high words" with the Boston committee,[7] and now to have had more with Mr. Adams. The whole story and both stories are very unfair to Mr. Sumner indeed, and are only one more example of the evils of "*sensation* reports." There has been no quarrel between these two gentlemen, though no doubt there will be men enough who will do their worst to make one. They disagree in their ideas of treating present affairs. So they have done many times before; but nothing but newspaper reporters could have made it a quarrel.[8]

The truth is, there is no time to quarrel in these days. If Virginia goes out, the whole North will be in one box, and the whole mass of party lines rubbed out, to begin all over again. People only lose their breath in scolding or swearing.

The attacks on Mr. Alley's speech, which have been rather more bitter than usual, show that it has made an impression. The Massachusetts delegation are no great talkers, but when they do speak they command the respect and attention of the House. Mr. Alley is a working member, always in his seat, and in his very quiet way, a valuable member. It's about as useless to attack him as it would be to pound at a marble statue. Every one here respects him and he is strong enough to fight his own battles.[9]

The Virginia election takes place today. If it goes wrong, you may expect immediate trouble in Maryland, where there have lately been indications that the secession spirit was stronger than was believed. Mr. Winter Davis was to have spoken last Thursday, after Mr. Adams, but could not get the floor, so that I suppose if he speaks at all he will do it this week, as the debate will soon be closed. His speech is expected with a great deal of interest?[.]

NOTES

1. Henry Adams also mentioned General Scott's demand for ten thousand men to guard Washington in his letter to his brother on January 28. Levenson et al., eds., *Henry Adams Letters,* 1: 226. Scott was constantly fearful of an attack on the District by groups from Maryland or Virginia or by subversives within the District. Rumors constantly added to these fears. Gen. Scott never amassed anywhere near the number of troops he desired to protect the capital, but he effectively utilized the ones he had to guard strategic points and paraded his men around enough to make Unionists feel secure and to dissuade any local secession sympathizers from attempting to challenge his forces. Fanciful threats from Maryland and Virginia were unlikely to materialize as long as neither of those states passed secession ordinances. See also Letter 7, note 7; and Chalfant, *Both Sides of the Ocean,* 221.

2. The Virginia convention delegate elections took place on February 4, the same date Adams penned this *Advertiser* letter. Immediate secessionists, conditional Unionists, and unconditional Unionists contested for delegate seats in what was considered, especially for those in Washington, a crucial election for that state and the nation. H. Adams to C. F. Adams, Jr., February 5, 1861, Levenson et al., eds., *Henry Adams Letters,* 1: 228.

3. Extreme Massachusetts abolitionist William Lloyd Garrison and his close associate Wendell Phillips had for a long time desired disunion so that the northern states could disassociate themselves from the moral evil of slavery. The very motto of Garrison's famous Boston abolitionist newspaper, *The Liberator,* at this time was "No Union With Slaveholders!" which was also the title of an editorial therein on February 15, 1861. This very radical position, held by these two men and many of their fol-

lowers, was a view supported by only a small minority of abolitionists. Henry Adams certainly had no liking for it, and neither did Republican politicians.

4. Twenty-five New York business leaders brought a generally pro-compromise petition from that city with 38,000 signatures. The businessmen themselves wanted to lobby for the Crittenden Compromise, but, when they encountered the fierceness of Republican opposition to it, these merchants instead drew up resolutions supporting the border state plan (Letter 9, note 8). It was in that form that Sen. William Seward of New York introduced the New York committee's report and the gigantic petition from New York citizenry on Thursday, January 31. Seward delivered a nice short speech in presenting the petition, generally praising the effort of the business leaders for compromise without specifically endorsing the border state plan. He pressed the idea that peace and Union could still be preserved if leaders would place the national interest over those of party and section. The New York senator dismissed the territories issue as no longer practical, asserting that, under the operation of the 1857 Supreme Court decision in the *Dred Scott* case, which opened all national territories to slavery, only twenty-four slaves were now reported to be in those territories. Though Seward pointed out that the South had not yet presented any compromise plan which the Republicans could support, he expressed his general willingness for conciliation and recommended that, if the present session of Congress failed to resolve the issues satisfactorily, then he would support the calling of a national constitutional convention for the purpose. His speech impressed most who heard it, including Robert Winthrop of the Boston committee, as appropriate, sincere, and even eloquent at times. Secessionist Sen. James M. Mason (D-VA) immediately rose after Seward had finished to attack his conciliatory remarks as fraudulently inconsistent with the refusal of Seward and other Republicans to support the Crittenden Compromise and the vote by those same Republicans for the Clark resolution as a substitute for Crittenden's on January 16, a resolution which declared the Constitution sufficient as it was without need of amendment and urging enforcement of the laws (Letter 13, note 7). Despite Seward's protests that Mason's implications were unjust, Mason managed to characterize Seward for his southern listeners as a Republican

coercionist at heart who was ready to make war on seceding states. This touched off a debate for the rest of that day's session involving primarily the pro-compromise Douglas (D-IL), the sarcastically anti-compromise Hale (R-NH), and the bibulous disunionist Wigfall (D-TX). *Cong. Globe,* 36: 2: 657–670; Winthrop trip journal, p. 22, roll 29, Gutheim, ed., *Microfilm Ed.–Winthrop Papers;* Bragg Diary, January 31, 1861; *Charleston Daily Courier,* February 4, 1861; *Chicago Daily Tribune,* February 5, 1861; *New York Herald,* February 2, 10, 1861; New York *Evening Post* (semi-weekly), February 6, 1861; New York *World,* February 2, 1861; *Philadelphia Inquirer,* February 1, 1861; Philadelphia *North American and U.S. Gazette,* February 1, 1861; and Springfield *Daily Illinois State Journal,* February 6, 1861.

5. Henry Adams's brief account of his father's speech in the *Advertiser* letter displayed his enthusiastic approval of the address and its reception, but in the subdued manner of a son anxious not to give clues to his identity as the *Advertiser* correspondent by writing an excessively laudatory description of the elder Adams's performance. Charles Francis Adams had completed writing his speech four days before he delivered it and Henry, as his secretary, had already dispatched copies to some newspapers. Unfortunately the congressman had also contracted a cold and fever, and he did not sleep well the night before his speech. Despite feeling unwell, Rep. Adams presented his views to the House and a large crowd in the galleries on January 31. Some of the Washington press corps were there but most of the reporters appear to have been in attendance in the Senate to watch as Seward presented the New York pro-compromise petition. Charles Francis Adams had no reputation for oratory; his voice was "slight," as D. W. Bartlett of the New York *Independent* wrote. But he commanded attention, not only because of his famous family history but also as a spokesman for the more moderate wing of the Republican Party and their firmly Unionist but conciliatory views. Even the southerners were eager to hear Adams and many of them hovered over on the Republican side of the chamber to better listen as the Massachusetts congressman spoke. It was the first time in his House career that the flamboyant Democratic secessionist Roger Pryor of Virginia had taken a seat on the Republican side of the main aisle. Adams declaimed for an hour and twenty minutes in a chamber where the silence was so complete, even in the sometimes tumultuous galleries, that even Adams's voice could be heard in every part of the hall.

The 53-year-old, thinly built Adams, with his short beard stretching from ear to ear below his jaw and chin, embodied the part of a pleasant-looking scholar as he spoke. After opening his address with a defense of the validity of Lincoln's election and a condemnation of secession as rebellion, Adams expressed a willingness to hear and consider southern complaints. He then stated that the three major southern grievances of which he was aware concerned northern states' laws interfering with the South's recovery of fugitive slaves, northern denial of a southerner's claimed right to hold slaves as property in national territories, and southern fear of northern political power increasing to a point where the North might be tempted to abolish slavery even in southern states. Adams dismissed the fugitive slave topic quickly, arguing that a softening of the harsher provisions of the 1850 fugitive slave law would encourage greater northern enforcement of it. The Massachusetts congressman then tackled the territorial slavery issue at some length, asserting that southern economic interests had restricted their slave labor to the fertile lands of the southern states. Slavery had proven unsuited to New Mexico territory; despite its slave code, the huge area stretching from Texas to California had fewer than twenty-five slaves and would ultimately become a free state.

While he was still discussing the territory issue, Charles Francis Adams ridiculed the preferred southern formula in the Crittenden Compromise of a constitutional guarantee for slavery in territory "hereafter acquired" below 36°30' N. Lat. The South, he said, threatened disunion unless the national government pledged to impose slavery on foreign countries before we acquired them, a "dogma of slavery propagandism" which he would refuse to disgrace himself by supporting. Adams, however, leveled his greatest sarcasm when he attacked the South's grievance about fears for the future of slavery in the southern states. He cited the supposed threats of Seward's "irrepressible conflict" and Lincoln's "house divided" comments, but argued that the South only invited conflict and northern invasion by seceding from the Union instead of trying to repress the conflict within the Union. When he likened disunionsts' panic to children frightened by imaginary terrors, Pryor of Virginia indignantly stood up and went back to the Democratic side of the chamber. Southern paranoia that Republicans in power would move to abolish slavery in the South was without foundation; not only did Republicans absolutely disavow any such purpose but, Adams stated, there would never be enough northern states to force slavery's abolition through constitutional amendment.

Having denied the legitimacy of southern complaints and fears, Charles Francis Adams expressed his desire to resume support for the settlement put forward from the Committee of Thirty-three. He declared that the New Mexico statehood bill would finally resolve the territorial slavery issue, although he believed that New Mexico would soon become a free state. Republicans could never support, Adams said, the Crittenden Compromise and its "hereafter acquired" slavery guarantee for future territories. He labeled this a scheme devised by secessionists to render any reconciliation of North and South impossible. The Massachusetts Republican concluded by asserting that, in his view, secession would be a failure and that he would oppose any coercion of seceding states unless they themselves committed the initial aggression. His Republican colleagues crowded around Adams after he finished to offer their congratulations, as did some of the most Unionist southerners. Most of the latter group liked Adams's conciliatory spirit in the speech but desired greater concessions than he or his fellow Republicans were willing to offer. Everett and Winthrop were both in the audience for the speech and both were very positively impressed by Adams's effort.

Most of the reaction in the northern press was very adulatory. Those correspondents who heard the speech and editors who read it mostly praised Adams's effort as the most logically organized and forcefully argued explication of the moderate Republican position on the crisis. Adam's ideas were not much different from those of Seward or Conkling, as expressed in their speeches at the time. But Adams probably increased popular hope for a settlement more than the other Republican moderates, for he put himself on record on January 31 in favor of a plan which he had done much to author in the Committee of Thirty-three and which he had then repudiated. But, encouraged by southern moderate addresses recently in the House and the strong lobbying of Cassius Clay of Kentucky, Charles Francis Adams had chosen to reinvigorate popular hopes for a reasonable settlement and to bolster the efforts of southern Unionists in the border slave states. Adams derived great satisfaction from the outpouring of supportive letters he received after his speech.

Northern antislavery radicals, of course, continued to express their displeasure with the Adams-Seward position, especially Adams's willingness to potentially allow New Mexico to enter the Union as a slave state. For the speech itself, see: *Cong. Globe,* 36: 2: App., 124–127; C. F. Adams Diary, January 31 and February 1, 1861, roll 76, part 1, *MAP;* Adams to C. F. Adams, Jr., January 31, 1861, Levenson et al., eds., *Henry Adams Letters,* 1: 226–227; Duberman, *C. F. Adams,* 248–250; and McClintock, *Lincoln and Decision for War,* 159–160. For good descriptions of Pryor of Virginia, see: *Boston Herald,* January 30, 1861; and St. Louis *Daily Missouri Democrat,* February 2, 1861. For positive northern comment on Adams's speech, see: many letters to Adams in "Letters Received, etc.," roll 552, part 4, *MAP;* F. Adams to R. H. Dana, Jr., February 9, 1861, box 16, Dana Family Papers; Everett Diary, January 31, 1861, roll 40, Allis, Jr., ed., *Microfilm Ed.–Everett Papers;* Winthrop trip journal, pp. 22–23, roll 29, Gutheim, ed., *Microfilm Ed.–Winthrop Papers;* Boston *Daily Atlas and Bee,* February 4, 1861; *Boston Post,* February 7, 1861; Boston *Daily Evening Traveller,* February 1, 1861; New Haven *Daily Palladium,* February 2, 1861; *Morning Courier and New York Enquirer,* February 2, 1861; *New York Herald,* February 1, 2, 1861; New York *Independent,* February 7, 1861; *New York Times,* February 1, 1861; *New York Daily Tribune,* February 1, 1861; New York *World,* February 2, 1861; *Philadelphia Inquirer,* February 1, 1861; Philadelphia *North American and U.S. Gazette,* February 2, 1861; and *Springfield* (MA) *Daily Republican,* February 2, 1861. For negative commentary on Adams's speech and position, see the February letters to Charles Sumner from antislavery Republicans and abolitionists John Jay, William Harlow, Edward L. Pierce, Samuel Cabot, Jr., Francis W. Bird, and William Lloyd Garrison, roll 21, Sumner Papers.

6. The most notorious and comprehensive attack on Adams and his New Mexico statehood bill had been written by Massachusetts Republican leader Edward L. Pierce and covered much of the front page of the January 9 issue of the Boston *Daily Atlas and Bee.* See also Stegmaier, "Imaginary Negro," 275–276.

7. See Letter 16, p. 167; and *New York Times,* January 26, 1861.

8. Henry Adams here tried to minimize the increasingly bad rupture in relations between his father and his old friend Sen. Sumner. Young Adams at that point certainly hoped that the rift could be mended, al-

though it proved otherwise. Sumner's alienation from the Adams family greatly disheartened Henry Adams, for Sumner had been a friend and inspiration to him during his formative years. The radically antislavery, anti-compromise, and personally touchy Sumner had disapproved of Adams's conciliatory stance toward the South since Adams had adopted it in late December. Sumner believed that any compromise gesture, no matter how slight, which Republicans like Seward and Adams were willing to offer the South, would split the party and betray Republican principles, thus showing weakness which could only benefit their enemies. Despite their differences on policy, Adams had managed to maintain his friendship with the testy Sumner and Sumner was a regular weekly dinner guest at the Adamses.

The surface cordiality, however, ended on January 28 as Adams and Sumner vehemently disagreed on whether or not Massachusetts should send a delegation to the Peace Conference in Washington. The eccentric Charles Sumner believed that the meeting was not organized to devise a Union-saving compromise but was secretly designed to be a staging ground for a disunionist seizure of the nation's capital. Sen. Sumner had therefore written privately to Gov. John Andrew opposing any dispatch of delegates by Massachusetts to the convention. It turned out that the other members of the Massachusetts congressional delegation did not share Sumner's conference-as-conspiracy view. On January 28 Sen. John P. Hale of New Hampshire came to Rep. Adams's desk in the House and asked him to write a letter to Gov. Andrew urging that Massachusetts send delegates. Adams, aware of the importance of the Peace Conference to border slave state Unionists, agreed and wrote a letter to Andrew. He then secured the signatures of the other Massachusetts members to the letter, including Sen. Henry Wilson. But Sumner refused, having already taken his stand against the meeting. Sumner explained his conspiratorial fears to Adams; Adams told him these fears were unreasonable, he thought, but that, even if the convention was part of a secessionist plot, it was important for Massachusetts to have a delegation in attendance to expose such a plot. Sumner, hurt, angry, and feeling isolated among the delegation, could not leave the matter alone. He soon came over to the House and began berating Congressman John B. Alley, the Republican representative from Lynn, Massachusetts, who sat next to Adams. Sumner's brow-beating of Alley proved unendurable for Adams, who realized that he was also the target of Sumner's invective. Charles Francis Adams descended on Sumner heatedly; "Sumner, I won't submit to this dictation," he began and pointedly informed Sumner that his policy was "insulating" Massachusetts from having a role in possibly resolving the crisis. Adams refused to play Sumner's game. After Alley had left and the House had adjourned, Adams and Sumner continued their argument at length until the cleaning crew finally convinced them to leave the chamber. Adams, ordinarily a paragon of sedate politeness, must have stunned Sumner with his "warm" remarks. According to Adams's son John Quincy II, who had arrived in Washington from Boston and learned of the incident from his father, Charles Francis Adams gave Charles Sumner "a tremendous wigging" of a tongue-lashing.

Although Adams apologized to Sumner the next day "for all undue warmth of manner," Sumner was still "pained" by Adams's "strictures" and defended the purity of his own motives. Adams attempted to gloss over the dispute with Sumner, but he must have realized that his previously close relations with the senator were at an end. Sumner quit coming to dinner at the Adamses, except once on February 17 for a pleasant visit. Sumner was conspicuously absent when Adams delivered his House address on January 31 and continued thereafter to denounce the Republican moderate position of Adams, Seward, and their like-minded colleagues. C. F. Adams Diary, January 28, 29, 31, February 2, 3, 10, 14, 17, 1861, roll 76, part 1; C. F. Adams to R. H. Dana, Jr., February 9 and to F. W. Bird, February 11, 1861, C. F. Adams Letterbook, roll 164, part 2; C. F. Adams to C. F. Adams, Jr., February 10 and J. Q. Adams II to C. F. Adams, Jr., February 16, 1861, "Letters Received, etc.," roll 552, part 4, *MAP;* and H. Adams, *Education,* 79–80, 83–84. See also: Winthrop trip journal, p. 24, roll 29, Gutheim, ed., *Microfilm Ed.–Winthrop Papers;* Chalfant, *Both Sides of the Ocean,* 222; Donald, *Sumner,* 372–381; Duberman, *C. F. Adams,* 250–251; McClintock, *Lincoln and Decision for War,* 179; and Samuels, *Young Henry Adams,* 87.

9. John B. Alley, just turned 44 years old, had addressed the House on January 26. The speech was unremarkable in content and typical of those Republican speakers who opposed any compromise with the South. Alley defended Republican antislavery convictions and attacked any moves

to extend slavery, but, like all Republicans, he pledged no interference with slavery in southern states and northern obedience to all its constitutional obligations to the South. Instead of recognizing any validity to supposed southern grievances, Alley spent much of his hour cataloging the southern aggressions against the North, from the Negro seamen laws of southern states and southern censorship of U.S. mails to southern efforts to expand slavery into Kansas. He declared that the North would never surrender its antislavery principles and that the North possessed more than ample power to fight the weaker South if the latter started a civil war. Charles Francis Adams noted the speech as "very sound, sensible" but of not much use in defusing the crisis. The press paid no particular attention to Alley's speech. Henry Adams's letter mentioned bitter attacks on it, but no one in the House or Senate speeches up to the time Adams wrote his letter to the *Advertiser* made any direct reference to or attacks on Alley's speech. Adams may have been referring to personal criticisms of Rep. Alley's remarks which he had heard bandied about in conversation. The uncompromising nature of Alley's speech may explain why Sen. Charles Sumner singled out this particular Massachusetts congressman as the target of his wrath after all the state's delegation but Sumner signed Adams's letter to Gov. Andrew. After Alley's extremely anti-southern speech of January 26, Sumner probably thought of Alley as one of his closest anti-compromise allies among the delegation. All the greater sense of betrayal Sumner probably felt when Alley signed the Adams letter, and Sumner reproached him for doing so. What Sumner could not understand was that Alley might not interpret the conference itself as having a nefarious foundation. Neither Alley nor the other Massachusetts members who endorsed the letter to the governor understood the meeting as in conflict with Republican principles the way Sumner did. *Cong. Globe,* 36: 2: 583–586; and C. F. Adams Diary, January 26, 1861, roll 76, part 1, *MAP.*

LETTER 19

Boston Daily Advertiser, February 8, 1861

Letter from Washington
[FROM OUR OWN CORRESPONDENT]

Washington, Feb. 5, 1861

A gasp of relief went through our whole community this morning on the receipt of the news from Virginia. For more than two months the Seward republicans have been watching, hoping, praying for the signs of a break in the storm. Governor Seward's reputation as a political prophet, his influence as a statesman, perhaps even his life, depended and was pledged on this result. He has gone on the principle that this was only a temporary fever, and now it has reached the climax and favorably passed it, so that the patient is no longer in danger, with proper care and low diet. He says that it[']s all right, and we can work along again into deep water.

Still, this is not the only opinion advanced here on the subject. Some people think this to be only the beginning of troubles. They foresee a convention; a united South under the lead of Virginia; a compromise, and another battle. The stiff-necked republicans are very hard to please. They talk as though they would have preferred the direct secession of Virginia with all its consequences. This is of course only because they fear worse troubles behind the present delay; and perhaps they may be right; but for my part I prefer the "pleasant optimism" of Governor Seward, who hopes that this step will so strengthen the Union men in the border States that a month hence secession will be one of the nightmares of the past. At any rate, it is our first beam of light, and we enjoy it. On all sides it seems conceded that the capital is now safe, and war no longer to be feared.[1]

Yesterday the Louisiana Senators took their leave,—Mr. Slidell gravely. Mr. Benjamin impertinently.[2] Secession is making a social revolution in

Washington. The old land-marks are disappearing. General Cass's gallery of works of art,[3] one of the attractions of the city, is packed up and sent off; his house dismantled, and his family preparing to leave for Detroit. Mr. Slidell's house will soon be closed, as Mr. Benjamin's has been for some time. Nearly all the Southerners who were socially important have disappeared. The new administration will bring such a revolution with it as has not been since Jackson came in,[4] and people are at their wit's ends to know who is to do the entertaining when all the old set are gone.

We have had a number of distinguished characters here lately. Some are no doubt on cabinet business, but what they have to tell is kept from the world. Others look more suspiciously. The course of Governor Seward has not met with the approbation of all his friends. The strong anti-slavery men do not like it and have never pretended to do so. Mr. Adams's speech and the evident impending consolidation of the North on the Union issue, seems to have forced the radical branch of the republicans to consider the possible necessity of some counter-agent, and from what is said here, it seems very likely that some step in this direction will be taken. It is universally known that formal consultation on the matter has been had; with what success I cannot say. I do not know what the strength of this branch is likely to be in Congress. The line is not yet clear. Nor does it make much difference what its strength is, provided only Mr. Lincoln is once quietly and successfully inaugurated and can put the government in motion.

NOTES

1. Virginia elected 152 delegates on February 4 to its state convention. Only about a third of them were in favor of the state's immediate secession. Some of the rest were unconditional Unionists, especially delegates from the westernmost, mountainous, generally nonslaveholding counties destined to become the new state of West Virginia during the Civil War. Many of the Unionists elected, however, were of the conditional variety whose continued loyalty to the Union depended on the passage of a satisfactory compromise settlement, particularly Crittenden's plan. The *Richmond Whig* listed the 1860 presidential preferences

of those elected as: Bell, 85; Douglas, 37; and Breckinridge, 30. On the results of the election, see: *Richmond Daily Whig*, February 13, 1861; and Link, *Roots of Secession*, 226–227.

While moderate Republicans understood the contingent nature of much of Virginia's Unionism, the February 4 election did represent to them a "first beam of light," as Henry Adams termed it. The Seward wing realized that, even though Virginia might still secede, it would not now happen until after Lincoln had assumed the presidency. Virginia's Unionists, unconditional and conditional, would force the Virginia convention, set to begin on February 13 at Richmond, to wait and see what actions Congress or the Washington Peace Conference might take in relation to compromise before the convention made any decisive move. Since there were only a few weeks left in the congressional session, Lincoln's inauguration on March 4 was now certain to take place without interference from Virginia. Thus the great sense of relief experienced at Washington when news of the Unionist victory in the Virginia elections arrived. Seward and his friends could be cautiously optimistic about the Unionist surge, no matter how qualified, in border slave states like Virginia. C. F. Adams Diary, roll 76, part 1, *MAP;* H. Adams to C. F. Adams, Jr., February 5, 1861, Levenson et al., eds., *Henry Adams Letters,* 1: 228; H. Adams, "Great Secession Winter," 24, and *Education,* 82; and Samuels, *Young Henry Adams,* 22. The Republican *Chicago Tribune* displayed a decidedly skeptical view of the "conditional Unionism" of most of the Virginia delegates who were elected, describing them as "conditional disunionists" instead. *Chicago Daily Tribune,* February 9, 19, 27, 1861.

2. Louisiana's convention passed its secession ordinance on January 26. After official word of this reached Washington, Louisiana's U.S. senators, as had become the custom for members of seceding states' delegations in previous weeks, delivered short withdrawal speeches in the Senate on February 4. John Slidell had been a major figure in Democratic political maneuvering for years and would soon become the Confederate regime's minister to France; the suave and brilliant orator Judah Benjamin had formerly been a Whig, had become a Democratic secessionist by the later 1850s, and would soon serve the Confederacy as secretary of war and then secretary of state.

A man in his late sixties, of medium height and proportions, very red-faced and white-haired, the agitated Slidell spoke with his hand trembling and in a tone of voice nearly inaudible to anyone but those near him on the Senate floor. House clerk John Forney, correspondent "Occasional" of the Philadelphia *Press,* described what he heard as a shrewish "tirade." John Slidell opened his address by pledging that Louisiana would join the Confederate States but would guarantee free access to the Mississippi River through its territory to those in the northern states who depended upon it. He stated his desire for amicable relations with the North and eventual reconstruction of the old Union, but also warned that the South would fight against any northern attempt to militarily coerce the seceding states. Slidell described the South's revolution, not as the culmination of some long conspiracy, but as a vast popular uprising against the anticipated effort of Lincoln and the Republicans to destroy slavery. While he declared that he did not fear slave revolt, he did believe that the slaves would interpret southern acquiescence in Lincoln's inauguration as an indication that they would soon be emancipated. Slidell expressed regret at separating from northern colleagues who had stood courageously with the South in defense of its claimed rights.

Described by the St. Louis *Missouri Democrat*'s correspondent as a "low, broad shouldered, short limbed, fat bodied little man" with black eyes and hair, Sen. Benjamin was nearly 50 years old and, since the earlier leave-taking by Florida's Sen. David L. Yulee when that state seceded, the Senate's only member of Jewish descent. Forney referred to him as a "dapper little agitator," and he had a reputation for delivering very analytical, lawyer-like speeches in a mellifluous voice. Judah Benjamin spent much of his farewell speech defending his state's right to secede against the Republican threat to destroy property in slaves and to establish an unlimited despotism over the degraded southern states as "provincial dependencies." The South, he said, faced "absolute extermination" under Republican rule, and he denied that northern coercion could maintain the Union. Benjamin asserted that, if the Republicans had acknowledged the right of secession, their fanatical course would have been arrested because they would not have risked causing the southern states to exercise that right. He also praised those northern senators who had defended southern rights. *Cong. Globe,* 36: 2: 720–722; Philadelphia *Press,* February 7, 1861; and St. Louis *Daily Missouri Democrat,* February 8, 1861.

3. At least some of Lewis Cass's art collection appears to have become part of the collection in the University of Michigan's Museum of Art. Lewis Cass's daughter Matilda had married Henry B. Ledyard in 1839 while her father was serving as U.S. minister to France. Mr. Ledyard was Cass's private secretary there. The Ledyard's three children–sons Henry and Hugh and daughter Matilda (who often used the diminutive Maud), who by marriage in 1897 became Baroness von Ketteler–later donated a few late-nineteenth-century items to the Detroit Institute of Art. But the baroness herself bequeathed nearly forty items to the UMMA, many of which could have been collected by Lewis Cass while in France from 1836 to 1842. These include two ornate crosses, several large sixteenth-century Flemish tapestries, other fine examples of beautifully decorated seventeenth- and eighteenth-century textiles, and a few paintings and other items. How much of this was part of Lewis Cass's collection to which Henry Adams refers in his *Advertiser* letter will have to await further research, but the likelihood is that Baroness von Ketteler, Cass's granddaughter, bequeathed some items to UMMA originally collected by Lewis Cass. Carole McNamara of UMMA provided a detailed list of Baroness von Ketteler's bequest and Iva Lisikewycz of DIA provided information on the Ledyards' donations to that institution, and this note is based on that information. See also Willard C. Klunder, *Lewis Cass and the Politics of Moderation* (Kent, OH: Kent State University Press, 1996), 7, 43–44, 94, 97, 102.

4. A reference to the uproarious celebration of President Andrew Jackson's inauguration in March 1829, when a huge mob of "common" citizens ended up trashing many White House furnishings.

LETTER 20

Boston Daily Advertiser, February 11, 1861

Letter from Washington
[FROM OUR OWN CORRESPONDENT]

Washington, Feb. 7th, 1861

A grand field day in the House. The morning's paper announced that Mr. Winter Davis would speak today; "the champion of the light weights"; the head of the South Americans; the handsomest man in the House; the traitor, the renegade; the demagogue; the Plug-Ugly, as the Maryland democrats call him, who have no words with sting sharp enough to express their hatred; the clear sighted, astute, ambitious young politician as he is known on the republican side. He was to speak, and the galleries were packed and jammed a half hour before he began, and the floor was crowded with Senators, strangers, and members of our Union-saving Convention.

When the history of our great secession comes to be written, a century or two hence, the historian ought to make a parenthesis to describe Mr. Winter Davis. He ought to describe him as he rose in his seat today, and stood with his arms folded, in rather a studied attitude, waiting for the House to come to order. The democrats call Mr. Davis a demagogue, but no man ever had less the appearance of a demagogue than he. Rather short than tall; with a graceful figure; a finely-cut expressive face; crispy hair, close-cut, so as to show a finely-shaped head to the best advantage; remarkably neat and well dressed in his round-cut English clothes, Mr. Davis gives one the idea of rather an aristocratic person, and forms a very striking contrast to most of his associates. His manners too, are very quiet and refined; not in the least those of a demagogue; far less of a Plug-Ugly, whom one associates with the ideas of bar-rooms and street fights, of blustering manners and coarse conversation, nothing of which belongs to Mr. Davis as one sees him here.[1]

He speaks remarkably well. His voice is not very strong nor altogether pleasant, but his manner is fine, and it is a relief for once to be spared the rude and ungraceful stump-oratory of most of our politicians. His speech seemed to me wanting in compactness and logical conclusion, but his points were remarkably well made, and the whole effect was moving and exciting.[2] If Mr. Crittenden had allowed himself to be guided by Mr. Davis rather than by Humphrey Marshall,[3] our troubles would now be in a fair way to settlement. With a really practical and reasoning statesmanship, Mr. Davis has done his best to settle the question, and if the good Massachusetts people who are agitating for the passage of the Crittenden measures, would read his speech, they might perhaps form some sort of an idea of what an unpatriotic and unreasonable course they are taking.

The scene was quite striking when Mr. Davis, with an earnestness that carried his whole audience with him, declared that on this question he represented Maryland and would meet his opponents anywhere on that issue. Kunkle [Kunkel] of Maryland sprang to his feet in a violent passion and tried to interrupt him. Mr. Davis refused to yield, and continued in a still bolder style. Mr. Kunkle [Kunkel] again broke in, and under a perfect storm of calls to order, shouted something of which we could only hear the word "Plug-Ugly." Mr. Davis took no notice of him, and kept on in the coolest and pluckiest way.[4]

The galleries broke in twice with actual cheering. They seem to look on Congress as a sort of a mass-meeting where they can applaud or hiss as they like. In the Senate this behavior has several times gone so far that the men's side has been cleared, but in the House the Speaker is good natured and is satisfied with threatening.

When Mr. Davis finished, the House was for some time in confusion and it was only with a good deal of trouble that Mr. Sedgwick of New York, who next got the floor, was able to begin. Mr. Sedgwick is a man of weight and ability. He is, I believe, at the head of the bar in his (Syracuse) district. He is probably the most extreme man in the House on the slavery question, and would have done well for a member of the Long Parliament;[5] some quiet and rigid Puritan, who believed himself to be the instrument of God's will, and saw salvation only in the utter destruction of his enemies. As a representative of the party opposed to conciliation, his speech was well worth hearing, for he took broad disunion ground and was not afraid to say fairly that he wished disunion, and believed it the only way of settling our difficulties. If all the stiff-necked republicans will take that ground, it will be the best defence of those who follow the other lead. But I know of no one who has yet ventured to declare himself so strongly as Mr. Sedgwick.[6]

NOTES

1.Given this letter's lengthy praise of Davis and Adams's later extended description of him in his "Great Secession Winter" essay, it is obvious that the congressional leader Henry Adams most admired at this time, outside his own father and Sen. Seward, was Rep. Henry Winter Davis of Maryland. See H. Adams, "Great Secession Winter," 15–19; and Letter 5, note 7. Besides Adams's portrayal of Davis in his *Advertiser* letter, another good physical description of Davis during his speech was provided by Benjamin Perley Poore ("Sigma") in *Cincinnati Daily Commercial,* February 11, 1861, in which he described Davis as "a slight, pale-faced, intellectual looking man, and a little below the medium height, with a mobile and good-humored countenance. His manner of speaking is graceful, quiet, and free from all clap-trap of vociferation." To another correspondent, Davis appeared "boyish in looks and dress." *Boston Herald,* February 9, 1861.

2. The 43-year-old Henry Winter Davis was one of the House members sure to draw a crowd when he gave a speech, and the weather conditions outside the building only enhanced the sense of excitement in the chamber that day. Wind and rain the night before had turned Washington's streets into a sea of mud, and it was a tribute to their stamina that so many people braved the continuing windy conditions to hear Davis's speech on February 7. After the Maryland unconditional Unionist began his address, a big storm broke over the city and the noisiness of the tempest and wind outside not only drowned out Davis's voice sometimes but seemed at times ready to blow the roof off the House chamber. The storm caused an eerie daytime darkness to settle on the proceedings, and the gas lights were lit as in an evening session. At one point a huge

crash panicked the gallery denizens and many scurried out from what they thought might be the roof falling in upon them; the alarm proved false—one of the derricks being used in construction of the Capitol dome had blown over.

Amidst these natural effects which any Old Testament prophet would have appreciated in support of his warnings, Davis forcefully presented his arguments. The Baltimore congressman began by placing the blame for the crisis squarely on the Democratic Party and the demoralized, inept President Buchanan for turning the country from pursuit of its great interests in the 1850s to a disastrous revival of the slavery issue. Following the election of 1860, six southern states had taken advantage of Buchanan's weakness to secede, set up their own government, seize federal government forts and installations, and prepare to make war on the United States. Only two choices were now possible, Davis said—either the federal government had to recognize the right of states to secede and thus condemn itself to ignominy in the eyes of the world, or the federal government must enforce the Constitution and the laws in the southern states and collect the federal revenues on ships off southern ports. He accused southern political leaders of distorting Republican intentions on slavery in their propaganda, thus poisoning the minds of southern whites against the North and the incoming administration. In opposition to this perverted view of Republicans as abolitionists, Davis cited, supported, and defended the plan offered by the Committee of Thirty-three, particularly the measures devised by Charles Francis Adams of Massachusetts. Davis referred to and praised Adams several times during the course of his speech. He declared the Crittenden Compromise, favored by most southerners, impossible to get. Congressman Davis proclaimed his confidence that Maryland would remain loyal to the Union and did not recognize a right to secede. The gallery crowd broke into extended applause on at least two occasions—first, when Davis strongly advocated the enforcement of federal laws in the seceded states, and second, when he declared that Maryland would adhere firmly to the Union.

Despite occasional hisses from the southern sympathizers in the chamber, Davis's Unionist oratory pleased the great majority of auditors. Even the admiring Henry Adams recognized that it was not a great speech, noting its lack of "compactness and logical conclusion." Charles

Francis Adams explained in his diary that, despite the speaker's effectiveness, Davis had tried to cover too much for a one-hour speech and thus it seemed "truncated" toward the end. The elder Adams also felt that Davis had been too confrontational toward the Democrats—"he is too much in antagonisms to rise above the partisan." Even the generally laudatory correspondent of the *Boston Herald* asserted that Davis emphasized federal coercion of the South too much. The *Cincinnati Enquirer*'s Democratic correspondent made the same point. Both the disunionist Baltimore *Sun* and the Washington correspondent for the American *New York Express* likened Davis's speech to those of extremist Republicans. The speech, however, received strong support from reporters for Republican newspapers—Boston *Atlas and Bee, Cincinnati Commercial,* New York *Evening Post,* New York *World,* and Philadelphia *North American*—as the most eloquent and strong defense of the Union by a border slave state congressman in the session. The crash of the derrick during Davis's speech was not the first time in the session that a derrick on the Capitol roof had broken from its moorings and crashed. The same thing had occurred on January 22. *New York Herald,* January 23, 1861.

For the speech itself, see *Cong. Globe,* 36: 2: App., 181–185. For various reactions to it, see: C. F. Adams Diary, February 7, 1861, roll 76, part 1, *MAP; Baltimore American and Commercial Advertiser,* February 9, 1861; *Baltimore Clipper,* February 8, 1861; Baltimore *Sun,* February 11, 1861; *Boston Daily Atlas and Bee,* February 11, 1861; *Boston Herald,* February 9, 1861; *Cincinnati Daily Commercial,* February 9, 11, 1861; *Cincinnati Daily Enquirer,* February 13, 1861; *New York Evening Express,* February 9, 1861; New York *Evening Post* (semi-weekly), February 13, 1861; New York *World,* February 9, 1861; and Philadelphia *North American and U.S. Gazette,* February 8, 1861.

3. Humphrey Marshall was a former Whig and American congressman from Kentucky who was practicing law in Washington during the Secession Winter of 1860–1861. Other than the inference provided by Henry Adams in his *Advertiser* letter, there is no record that Marshall influenced or even consulted with Sen. Crittenden in regard to his compromise plans during the session. Maybe Adams had learned of a Crittenden-Marshall connection since lost to historians. Two existing letters of Marshall's during this period, however, indicate no input by him in the

Crittenden Compromise. One of these in January was written by Marshall to a friend in Kentucky; that person published a lengthy excerpt from the letter in a local newspaper, and it was then reprinted in other papers. Humphrey Marshall's letter expressed his and Kentucky's firm adherence to the Union unless absolutely pushed out of it. A few weeks later Marshall's attitude had changed. In a personal letter on February 2, Marshall desponded of hope for the Union and believed that at least two new confederacies would form from the old Union, with only Maryland and Delaware of the slave states not seceding. Like the earlier excerpt, this letter made no mention of the Crittenden Compromise. *Philadelphia Inquirer*, January 16, 1861, reprinting letter from Maysville (KY) *Eagle;* and Marshall to __Hunter, February 2, 1861, box 2, folder 13, Humphrey Marshall Papers, Filson Historical Society, Louisville.

Assuming that Marshall had no direct influence on Crittenden, why then might Adams have mentioned him in this context? Adams simply may have wanted to cite Marshall as a contrast to Henry Winter Davis because of the notoriously anomalous position which Marshall had assumed in the recent presidential election. Like Davis and Crittenden, Humphrey Marshall had been a Whig and then an American. But, where Davis and Crittenden had supported the Constitutional Unionist candidate, John Bell of Tennessee, Marshall had deserted the American ranks to publicly support the southern Democratic states-rights candidate John C. Breckinridge of Kentucky, a former rival of Marshall's in Kentucky politics. Marshall thus stood out in the campaign by his exceptional position, speaking in favor of a candidate whom the southern disunionists championed. Adams thus may have used Marshall as a foil for Davis in the secession crisis, and may have felt that Marshall's stance in the campaign had generally influenced Crittenden to adopt the Breckinridge platform's plank of federal protection for slavery in national territories as the essential ingredient in his Secession Winter compromise proposals. Just as Marshall had deserted the Constitutional Unionist presidential ticket in the recent election in order to support the southern Democrats and their platform, so now did Crittenden appear to be following in Marshall's footsteps in the secession crisis. Humphrey Marshall, once the Civil War began, did join the Confederacy and became a general in their army. On Humphrey Marshall in the 1860 election and generally, see: *Speeches of Hon. Humphrey Marshall & B. F. Hallett, in the City of Washington on the Nomination of Breckinridge and Lane* (Washington: McGill & Witherow, Printers, 1860); Charles Messmer, "Louisville on the Eve of the Civil War," *Filson Club History Quarterly* 50 (July 1976): 278–279; and E. Merton Coulter, "Humphrey Marshall," in Malone and Johnson, eds., *Dict. of Am. Biog.*, 6: 310–311.

4. Jacob M. Kunkel (D-MD) usually took little part in debates, but was a states-rights Democrat, who, along with other members of his party in the state, loathed Davis and the voter intimidation engaged in by "Plug-Ugly" thugs of the American Party in Baltimore. Kunkel challenged Davis's right to represent his views as those of Maryland itself. The reporters of the debates of the *Congressional Globe* apparently did not hear or chose not to include in the official record Kunkel's hurling of the epithet "Plug-Ugly" at Davis. *Cong. Globe*, 36: 2: App., 184.

5. The Long Parliament, dominated by Puritans opposed to the policies of King Charles I, was the British legislative body during the English Civil War and the first part of Oliver Cromwell's Interregnum, 1640–1653. This parliament was also in session 1659–1660, until the Restoration brought King Charles II to the throne.

6. Rep. Charles B. Sedgwick (R-NY), as indicated by Henry Adams, was about the closest to a radical Garrisonian abolitionist among the House members, although even he would admit in his speech that Republicans claimed no power to interfere with slavery in southern states. Evaluating compromises as useless or worse, Sedgwick attacked the Committee of Thirty-three propositions as worthless in persuading any seceded state to return to the Union. Amending the Constitution was a dangerous response to the "imaginary fear for the future" in the South, and disunionists demanded ironclad guarantees for slavery in future territories rather than the "barren gift" of New Mexico offered in the committee bill. He labeled slave state complaints groundless. What lay at the root of the crisis, Sedgwick declaimed, was the "black pall" of slavery, "a perpetual weakness, a disgrace, a calamity." The South, he said, wanted constitutional recognition and protection of slavery's "rightfulness," and, if granted, the slave states would then demand the reopening of the African slave trade, the silencing of any criticism of slavery in speech or press, and the seizure of adjacent lands to the south. Sedgwick pro-

claimed his belief that free and slave labor were "irreconcilable" within the same Union. After arguing that the federal government must first force the South to obey the Constitution and laws and must recapture federal property seized by the disunionists, Sedgwick then posited that those states desiring to keep slavery could then be allowed to set up their own confederacy while a policy of compensated gradual emancipation and colonization might be adopted for those slave states choosing to remain aligned with the North. Sedgwick's ideas were not exactly in accord with Garrison's on some issues—Garrison opposed compensated gradual emancipation and colonization of freed slaves—but Garrison and other abolitionist radicals did advocate a separation by the North from a Union with slave states. Outside of Henry Adams's *Advertiser* letter, Sedgwick's radical speech received little attention in the press. Though Sedgwick was not considered to be an effective speaker, Charles Francis Adams found some parts of his extreme address very impressive. *Cong. Globe,* 36: 2: 795–798; C. F. Adams Diary, February 7, 1861, roll 76, part 1, *MAP; New York Evening Express,* February 9, 1861; and New York *World,* February 9, 1861. The best source of information on Sedgwick, although it contains no information on this speech, is Field, "Sedgwick's Letters," 129–139.

A Hiatus in Henry Adams's *Advertiser Letters*, February 7–March 3, 1861

The *Advertiser* letter which Henry Adams penned on February 7 proved to be his last regular correspondence for that paper. What occasioned this cessation of letter-writing was the arrival of the *Advertiser*'s publisher, Charles Hale, in Washington. It seems that when he learned that Hale planned to remain there until after the inauguration on March 4, Adams asked Hale to take over the correspondent's duties for his paper. Adams indicated in a letter to his brother Charles on February 13 that he himself instigated this change of correspondents; he wrote in the letter that Hale "evidently had no objection." The publisher generally complimented young Adams for the letters he had written for the paper since early December, but Adams now saw in Hale's arrival an opportunity to get "out of the traces" and apparently requested Hale to take over.[1]

For various reasons Adams had decided to discontinue his newspaper letter-writing. While he was pleased with his contribution to the correspondents' profession, the job had also worn him down. Acting as private secretary for his father, making the obligatory social calls, and writing personal letters to his brother and public ones to the *Advertiser* sapped the young man's time and energy. He was not the sort of correspondent who telegraphed short dispatches each day nor a practiced journalist who could quickly write letters to his paper every day. Adams's letters display some care in composition and he wanted those who read them to find them not only good analyses of the sectional crisis in Washington but also pleasant to read. Given his input into his *Advertiser* letters, all the more frustrated was Adams when Hale rearranged his material or eliminated his "spicy" comments of "an unfavorable personal character." Still, it seems that Hale must have printed Adams's letters pretty much the way Adams wrote them, or Adams would have given up the task in disgust long before he did. In only one case, the piece criticizing "the five wise men of Boston," did Hale totally suppress an Adams letter.[2]

Another factor which may have led Henry Adams to relinquish his *Advertiser* work was the growing inconvenience of doing it. The labor he endured to get out his letters to the *Advertiser* was probably compounded by the fact that by mid-February Henry was no longer living in his parents' house. So many members of the family were coming to Washington to attend the inauguration that the younger son was crowded out and had to take lodging at Jost's boardinghouse on Pennsylvania Avenue. When Charles Francis Jr. arrived from Boston on February 19, he moved in to share these rooms with his brother. Given the crush of family and social obligations and his continuing duties as his father's secretary, the added strain of boardinghouse living would not have been conducive to production of thoughtful newspaper correspondence.[3]

The course of events in Washington also diminished Henry's interest in writing further *Advertiser* letters. Lincoln's inauguration lay only a few short weeks away. The Buchanan administration and the second session of the 36th Congress were rapidly approaching their end. A few things seemed certain at that point: none of the Upper South states, especially after Tennessee voters on February 9 soundly rejected a call for a state convention, would secede and join the seven states of the Confederacy before March 4th; Washington, D.C., would neither be attacked from without nor subverted from within; and no compromise of a substantive nature was likely to pass Congress. The measures accorded the best chance of approval were those of the Committee of Thirty-three, and out of deference to the Peace Conference dragging on behind closed doors at Willard's, Corwin of Ohio refused to press the proposals from his committee to a final vote. Most Republicans, even the moderate minority in the party who supported them, probably enjoyed not having to vote on the propositions just yet. With the Peace Conference occupying center stage and the difficulty he would have in learning much from their closed-door proceedings, Henry confessed to his brother Charles in the aforementioned February 13 letter (the last before Charles came to Washington) that he had lost interest and was confident that the crisis was "going to simmer down." He told Charles, however, that he planned to write an essay on "The great Secession Winter" (the first known use of that phrase) for the *Atlantic Monthly*.[4]

Charles Hale became rather prolific in his correspondence to the *Advertiser,* writing fourteen letters from February 12 to March 6 under the pseudonym "Carolus." They varied in length from short missives to more elaborate reports. An early letter describing the counting of the electoral vote in Congress on February 13 was particularly detailed. But Hale proved inconsistent and unfocused in his correspondence. Taken together, his letters do not contain much that would interest a modern reader or researcher. They include some comment on the sectional crisis and the Peace Conference, but often these letters become bogged down in discussions of the Morrill Tariff bill and various other topics outside the sectional crisis. Hale's self-effacing young predecessor expressed his belief to his brother that Hale could do a better job than he at writing the *Advertiser* correspondence, but Henry Adams's letters were better written and never strayed from Adams's essential concentration on the fate of the Union in the Secession Winter. Hale turned out to be much more the mere journalistic reporter of the *Advertiser*'s two Washington correspondents in 1860–1861.[5]

Of course, as Henry Adams correctly surmised, there was not that much to write about as Washington awaited the arrival of Lincoln and the inauguration. The president-elect left Springfield, IL, on February 11 for a twelve-day train trip to the nation's capital. Stopping at various towns and cities in Indiana, Ohio, Pennsylvania, and New York, Lincoln gave numerous speeches, which reporters eagerly analyzed for glimpses of his intended policies toward the South. After creating a public furor by appearing to take a coercive stance toward the seceded states in his Indianapolis speech, Lincoln realized his misstep and gave no hints on policy in his many speeches during the remainder of the journey. With his advisors worried about a rumored plot against Lincoln's life when he came through Baltimore, the president-elect traversed that city in the middle of the night on a special train, arriving in Washington at 6 a.m. on February 23 to take up a suite of rooms at Willard's. Social gatherings, cabinet selection, and other patronage matters then occupied much of his time prior to March 4.[6]

A few days after Lincoln's arrival in Washington, the Peace Conference lumbered to its conclusion on February 27. The Republican and southern state delegates who opposed compromise, from different viewpoints, had delayed the production of a settlement plan, and the seven-part constitutional amendment finally proposed by the convention at the end of February satisfied neither group of radicals. For the most part the proposal was similar to the Crittenden Compromise, but its territorial division at 36°30' N.Lat. would not apply to future acquisitions. Also, the last clause of section 7 would require Congress to pass laws to enforce the "privileges and immunities" clause of the Constitution (Art. 4, sect. 2, clause 1) for citizens. Southerners rightly interpreted this provision as an attempt to protect northern citizens in southern states from violence by mobs who assumed that virtually all northern travelers there were abolition agents. Congress gave the Peace Conference proposals little heed during the session's last few days. The House did not provide enough votes to even bring the Peace Conference amendment up for consideration. Sen. Crittenden, seeing his own compromise as unattainable now, substituted the Peace Conference plan for his own and at least got the Senate to consider it, but the proposition was voted down by a wide margin as the Senate concluded its proceedings in the early morning of March 4.[7]

The second session of the 36th Congress could boast of the passage of some practical measures during its course—the admission of Kansas as a free state; the new Morrill Tariff, which was more protective of domestic production against foreign competition; and the organization of territorial governments in Colorado, Nevada, and Dakota without any provisions in relation to the slavery question. But neither house proved able to pass a comprehensive compromise which might have influenced some of the seceded states to hesitate in joining a southern Confederacy. Especially with so many southern members having resigned from Congress and so many Republicans opposed to the proffered compromises, none of the most heralded plans—Crittenden's, the border state compromise, the Peace Conference proposals—came close to passage in the last frantic days of the session at the beginning of March. Among the Committee of Thirty-three proposals, the New Mexico statehood bill was tabled in the House. The committee's proposed amendment to the Constitution to prevent federal interference with slavery in southern states did succeed in securing a two-thirds vote in both houses, but not in the form given to it by Charles Francis Adams in the committee. Even though the amendment became known as the Corwin Amendment, Rep. Corwin on February 26 got the House to agree to substitute the less cumbersome wording originally offered by Sen. Seward in the Committee of Thirteen, to prevent Congress from ever interfering with the institution of "persons held to labor or service" in southern states [Letter 6, note 11]. Lincoln had discussed the matter with Corwin and did not object to the amendment, and Seward undoubtedly had had a hand in the substitution of his wording for that of Adams. Seward's version squeaked through both houses with just enough votes for approval of a constitutional amendment. Two states, Ohio and Maryland, would actually ratify this amendment after the Civil War had begun.[8]

The activities of Henry Adams during those last weeks of the session are obscure. In his February 13 letter to his brother, Henry provided a detailed description of a ball held at the home of Sen. and Mrs. Douglas. He seemed to pity the young, beautiful, and charming Adele Cutts Douglas, but had nothing but negative comments about her "little beast of a husband," Sen. Stephen A. Douglas. He also criticized the devotion of participants at the ball to Sen. John J. Crittenden and former president John Tyler, neither of whom Henry thought worthy of such admiration. A few days after Charles Jr. arrived, Henry and he traveled to nearby Arlington, Virginia, on February 22 to dine with the Lee family. Col. Robert E. Lee was not present but his son William Henry Fitzhugh Lee, with whom Henry had been a classmate at Harvard, was amidst the pleasant gathering. Other than these recorded social occasions, Henry Adams appears to have confined himself to his duties as his father's private secretary.[9]

Henry would not be the only Adams to engage in newspaper letter-writing during this period. Charles Jr. penned a few letters to the *Boston Evening Transcript* in March, one of which provided a lengthy account of Lincoln's inauguration as president. It is very probable that Rep. Charles Francis Adams himself wrote a letter published in the *Boston Advertiser* on March 5. This letter, written on March 1, bore the signature "A," and the newspaper differentiated it from the letters from "Carolus' by labeling it simply as "From Another Correspondent." The letter presented a substantial analysis of the situation in Congress as the session neared its end. It was strongly critical of the shortsightedness and petty bickering which had blocked the Corwin Amendment's approval up to that time, and the letter appears obviously written by someone very involved in the situation. The writer went on to praise Sen. Seward as "the Northern hero of this struggle" as he attempted to guide the country through the crisis despite being attacked by radicals of both North and South. The letter also expressed belief that the New Mexico bill would fail due to the fear of border slave state Unionists that New Mexico would become a free state. The author of the letter finished by praising Lincoln's choice of Gideon Welles of Connecticut to be New England's representative in his cabinet as secretary of the navy. Evidence definitely points to Rep. Adams as the author. His diary entries for February 26–28 contain the same criticism of Congress's dilatory refusal to pass the Corwin amendment. The laudatory view of Seward in the letter was very similar to Adams's description of his co-worker for a moderate compromise in a February 9 letter where he referred to his friend as the one man who understood the crisis and how to deal with it. The New Mexico section of the March *Advertiser* letter is very similar to Charles Francis Adams's discussion of the topic in the February 28 entry of his diary.[10]

On March 7, two days after the publication of the above letter in the *Advertiser,* that paper printed a letter almost certainly written by Henry Adams on March 3, the final day of the congressional session. Although Charles Hale was still writing his "Carolus" correspondence to the paper, young Adams apparently decided to write one last newspaper commentary on the session and the crisis.

NOTES

1. Levenson et al., eds., *Henry Adams Letters,* 1: 230; and Chalfant, *Both Sides of the Ocean,* 225.

2. Levenson et al., eds., *Henry Adams Letters,* 1: 204, 205, 212, 216, 218, 219, 224, 225, 226, 227, 230 for various comments by Henry Adams during these months in letters to his brother Charles about his frustrations with Hale, the late nights he spent trying to keep up with his correspondence, and his general satisfaction with his *Advertiser* letters.

3. *C. F. Adams, Jr., Autobiography,* 76; Levenson et al., eds., *Henry Adams Letters,* 1: 230, 231; and Chalfant, *Both Sides of the Ocean,* 228.

4. Levenson et al., eds., *Henry Adams Letters,* 1: 231.

5. For Hale's letters as "Carolus," see *Boston Daily Advertiser,* February 14, 15, 16, 21, 23, 25, 27, 28, March 4, 5, 6, 8, 1861.

6. For comprehensive accounts of Lincoln's journey from Springfield to Washington, see Harold Holzer, *Lincoln President-Elect: Abraham Lincoln and the Great Secession Winter, 1860–1861* (New York: Simon & Schuster, 2008), 295–407; and Burlingame, *Lincoln,* 2: 1–37.

7. The best account of the Peace Conference is Robert G. Gunderson, *Old Gentlemen's Convention: The Washington Peace Conference of 1861* (Madison: University of Wisconsin Press, 1961).

8. For congressional proceedings from February 26 to the early morning of March 4, see *Cong. Globe,* 36: 2: 1202–1433. On final passage of the Corwin Amendment, see: Nichols, *Disruption of American Democracy,* 484–491; and Lee, "Corwin Amendment," 22–26.

9. Levenson, et al., eds., *Henry Adams Letters,* 1: 231–232; and *C. F. Adams, Jr., Autobiography,* 90–91.

10. C. F. Adams Diary, February 26–28, 1861, roll 76, part 1 and Adams to R. H. Dana, Jr., February 9, 1861, C. F. Adams Letterbook, roll 164, part 2, *MAP; C. F. Adams, Jr., Autobiography,* 96, 105–106; and *Boston Daily Advertiser,* March 5, 1861.

LETTER 21

Boston Daily Advertiser, March 7, 1861

Letter from Washington
[FROM OUR REGULAR CORRESPONDENT]

Washington, March 3, 1861[1]

The long play is at an end. The struggles and trials of these three months are fairly over. They have left many men ruined and disgraced whom they found honored and powerful, and have given their power and honor to others. The battle has been long and hard, but it is over, and we breathe free again.

Events have been too much crowded in the last few days for a fair account to be possible, but the main interest has centred on two, which belong together; one was the formation of the Cabinet; the other the action of Congress on the Corwin report.

It has been clear ever since Mr. Seward's speech that the republicans are divided. Two distinct lines of policy are fighting for control, and the end is not yet all that clear.

The National or Seward republicans have marked out a distinct course. It is to adapt the party to the new issues; to enlarge its basis; to make it the one Union party, and on that issue to take into the Cabinet Union men from the slave States, who had never been republicans, but who would strengthen the Administration. To bring this about, they brought forward some propositions which were very harmless and yet were satisfactory. With them Messrs. Andrew Johnson and Etheridge guaranteed Tennessee, and other good authorities including Winter Davis and Gov. Hicks undertook to manage Maryland and Virginia. These once adopted by Congress, it was expected that the old democratic disunionist leaders could be annihilated at the next election in the border States. This done, the rest was plain sailing.

The other wing of the republicans refused to have anything to do with this movement. They would not consent to meet their new enemy on any but the old ground. They were not willing to let strangers into the party. Practically their course looked to the secession of all the slave States, a blockage and non-intercourse, famine and a slave insurrection and civil war. Many of them asserted this boldly; others used softer words.[2]

The strength of this party lies in the democratic wing of the republicans, which is and always has been restive under the lead of Gov. Seward, and in New York still keeps its distinct organization for the benefit of its leaders, after the usual style of New York politics and politicians. If Gov. Seward had taken coercion ground, these men would have conciliated. And over the low intrigue and factiousness of this movement, an appearance of dignity and principle was thrown by the pure and great names of men like Charles Sumner and Preston King,[3] whose motives no one ever found fault with, whatever one's opinion of their sagacity may be.

The last ten days has [*sic*] brought out the strength of these two sides in the battle over the Cabinet. Mr. Seward had the start and has kept it. His opponents pressed Mr. Chase[4] into the cabinet, though I have yet to learn what the conciliatory policy is to suffer from him. Mr. Blair,[5] a Maryland republican and of the anti-Seward stamp, goes into the cabinet much against the will of Maryland, because Mr. Gilmer[6] of North Carolina declined. There is nothing very bad in this that I have heard of, though there has been a good deal of feeling because Winter Davis was not put in. Altogether, so far as I can learn, the cabinet is conservative and strong as any reasonable man would ask.

With this excitement, the discussion and battle over the Corwin report has chimed in. The national republicans thought it very important to pass something, no matter how little, in order to hold back Virginia, since they had to refuse the Peace Convention report. To vote against these measures was a very grave responsibility. Every one knows here how much weight these measures have had. They have won ground every day since they were first proposed in the Committee of Thirty-three. They are at one time abused as gross concessions; at another as no concessions at all. To vote against them was to divide the party on a secondary question. It was to repudiate the lead of Gov. Seward. It was to run a very grave risk of destroying the influence which is just bending Virginia towards the side of Union. On these measures Mr. Seward had fought secession all winter. At one time he had fought it almost single-handed. I remember very well in what despair this city was two months ago, and I know how the strongest of the straight republicans hardly dared to hope then to weather these sixty days, and went to Gov. Seward in despair to say that something must be done. He must save us. And he did save us. For two months he has swayed the whole nation. Not only the republicans of the North; not only the Union men of the South; not only all men who have wanted advice and encouragement, have come to him for it; but even the administration, even James Buchanan himself, has for two months leaned on his great arm as the last hope and salvation. And for a single member or for a body of members of Congress to assume the responsibility of breaking down all that he had done, was a bold thing; for them to raise a factious opposition, was a thing for which, if successful, they might fairly be ranked by Southern Union men, as enemies of the Union.[7]

Now, that Congress has adjourned, the party will be able to pick itself up again and go on. Meanwhile, Mr. Lincoln's inaugural will do much to unite everything again, and these little family quarrels will have time to subside.

NOTES

1. No previous writers on Henry Adams, including biographers Ernest Samuels and Edward Chalfant and chief editor of Adams's letters J. C. Levenson, have recognized this as a letter by young Adams. One problem is that they assumed that Adams had quit writing entirely to the *Advertiser* once Hale took over the correspondence. If they had read further in the *Advertiser,* they would have probably found this letter and identified it as one of Henry Adams's. Its lively style is certainly that of Adams. The newspaper itself also indicated that the letter came from Adams. As a heading for the previous letters by Adams and the later ones from Hale as "Carolus," the *Advertiser* had printed "FROM OUR OWN CORRESPONDENT." But the heading for this one read uniquely "FROM OUR REGULAR CORRESPONDENT" as if to identify this unsigned let-

ter as written by Adams rather than Hale, who always signed his name "Carolus." Adams was the only other "regular" correspondent the *Advertiser* had had from Washington in that session. The content of the letter also harmonized perfectly with the political views expressed by Henry Adams in his earlier *Advertiser* letters, and the content makes clear that the writer was someone who had been in Washington throughout the months of the session.

2. These two paragraphs summarize the division between moderate and radical Republicans quite succinctly and clearly. Adams also leaves no doubt that Seward envisioned the Republican Party as the Union party, a political body broad enough in its appeal to attract loyalists from the Upper South into its ranks; Seward was not thinking in terms of establishing a party organization separate from the Republicans. See Letter 17, note 8.

3. Seward's U.S. Senate colleague from upstate New York, a fat and amiable former Democrat and Free-Soiler.

4. Salmon P. Chase of Ohio, former antislavery Democrat and Free-Soiler, former governor and U.S. senator, became secretary of the treasury in Lincoln's cabinet. Lincoln's offer of a cabinet post to his intraparty rival Chase led Seward for a short while to seriously consider giving up the seat he himself had already accepted as secretary of state. Seward finally decided to remain in Lincoln's cabinet.

5. Montgomery Blair of Maryland, former Democrat and son of President Andrew Jackson's famous advisor Francis Preston Blair, became President Lincoln's postmaster general. He was definitely opposed to compromise and to Seward.

6. The popular, likable Rep. John A. Gilmer of Greensboro, NC, was a former southern Whig, then a member of the American/Opposition group, and a strong Unionist. Seward certainly urged Lincoln to invite Gilmer into his cabinet as a representative of southern Unionists. Lincoln did so but Gilmer turned down the offer after Republicans refused to make what Gilmer considered appropriate concessions to the South on the slavery issue. Lincoln then turned to Montgomery Blair, who accepted a cabinet post. On Gilmer and the cabinet, see Crofts, *Reluctant Confederates,* 222–229, 245–247.

7. As exaggerated as Henry Adams's laudation of Seward sounds in this letter, it was only a prelude to his even more elaborate praise of the

New York senator in his "Great Secession Winter" essay, which he wrote after the session. In the latter work, Adams wrote:

> But by common consent all eyes were turned on him, and he was overwhelmed by entreaties from men in all sections of the country to do something to save the Union. Utterly panic-stricken they came to him with prayers and tears. The people of Washington came to him on the 1st of January in numbers, with positive assertions that they and the whole city would be in the hands of traitors within a month unless he did something to save them. To such appeals his answer was: "Save yourselves; you alone can do it; organize; form military companies; watch your suspected men." Members of the Cabinet came to him in absolute despair and called on him for counsel. The advice that he gave was not thrown away. Letters on letters came to him from the Union men in the border slave States urging immediate action and asking help and advice. He extended his connections far into the slave States, everywhere striving to guide the Union policy and to raise up and unite the Union sentiment. He became virtually the ruler of the country. With that cool wisdom and philosophical self-control, so peculiar to his character, he comprehended at once the true nature of his position and gave all his energies to carrying on the struggle. Foreseeing that the battle was to be fought in the border States, and that they must at all hazards be held back, at least till the 4th of March, he cleared his eyes, without an effort, of the cobwebs that blinded other men, and devoted himself to the labor of effecting a firm alliance with the Unionists of Virginia and Maryland, to check the evil while there was yet time.
>
> Those who saw and followed Mr. Seward during all the anxieties and cares of this long struggle, are little likely to forget the lessons he then taught them. Cheerful where everyone else was in despair; cool and steady where everyone else was panic-struck; clear-sighted where other men were blind; grand in resource where every resource seemed exhausted; guiding by quiet and unseen influences those who seemed to act independently on their own ground; holding the great threads of public policy in his hand without parade or display, and, with his vast power of combination, touching them all with reference only to one clear and definite end; avoiding harsh contact with all

> men, and steering with a firm and steady grasp between his friends who were ready to denounce him, and his enemies who were eager to destroy him, the ultras of the North and South alike; yielding without obstinacy where resistance was too great, yet striking with fresh energy wherever resistance seemed weak; pertinacious in his attack, and inexhaustible in his armory of weapons, he fought, during these three months of chaos, a fight which might go down to history as one of the wonders of statesmanship. . . .
>
> Through all the chaos of anxiety and contest which marked Mr. Seward's reign of two months, it was evident that he at least felt the highest confidence in the course he pursued. He declared himself bent on weathering the storm without the loss of a single life. Under all the dangers and trials, the cares and the triumphs of his dictatorship, he maintained always the same self-control and calmness, never parading his importance and never losing his self-command.

Adams, "Great Secession Winter," 22–23, 28.

AFTERWORD

All the hyperbole and hero-worship aside, Henry Adams was probably not that inaccurate in his portrayal of the pivotal role which Sen. William Seward had played during the Secession Winter in Congress. His version of a proposed amendment to the Constitution was the only major compromise measure to pass both the House and the Senate. He had worked assiduously for moderate concessions to satisfy the southerners of the border states and to retain their loyalty to the Union. Many others, of course, had also been active participants in this effort, including Henry Adams's father. The border state men themselves eagerly sought some excuse to remain in the Union and away from the clutches of the Cotton South. Seward's soft words and calmness did encourage them to feel that the incoming administration would treat the South fairly. Even though they would have liked more concessions than the amendment which passed, many border state Unionists saw even that measure as satisfactory enough. If Seward at times led southerners to believe that he might get his fellow Republicans to deliver more than he ever really intended, one must understand the bluff as part of his overall strategy to delay as much as he could and to make as few concessions as necessary to hold most of the slave states in the Union until Lincoln took office, without compromising any essential Republican Party principles. Seward had had to walk a tightrope, and he had performed this feat quite well under the circumstances. Henry Adams showed his understanding of and appreciation for Seward's role in the crisis.

And yet, young Adams also seems to have been bluffed by Seward's mask of tranquility. Henry Adams apparently never learned that the underlying tensions of the crisis had led Seward into a vocal outburst against Mr. Tobey when the Boston committee had conversed with the New Yorker. In several of Adams's *Advertiser* letters the novice correspondent reflected the upbeat attitudes about settlement prospects nearly always exhibited by Sen. Seward—the importance of moderation, the tide of the crisis gradually turning in favor of the Union, and the conviction that the excitement would die down once Lincoln became president. Lincoln and other Republicans had constantly reiterated the theme that they had no intention of interfering with slavery in the southern states and that they believed the federal government possessed no constitutional authority for such interference. All but the most radically antislavery Republicans preached that doctrine, and it logically followed in the thinking of most Republicans that, once Lincoln had taken power, the Republican chief magistrate would quiet the fears of southern whites about an impending St. Domingue-type bloodbath and race war by fulfilling his noninterference pledges. Then, once the southern states experienced the reality of Lincoln's good will towards them, they would, even the cotton-growing Gulf states, understand the groundlessness of radical anti-Republican propaganda and return to the Union fold. Such were the hopes of the majority of Republicans, and Henry Adams's letters to the *Boston Advertiser* asserted this positive interpretation regarding the course of secession crisis.

Sen. William Seward, however, was too savvy and experienced a Washington politician not to have realized that the much more dangerous alternative outcome of civil war still lurked and that any act of violence might touch off the fuse on that powder-keg. He knew that much depended on the South's actions rather than his calm words. The possibility, maybe even the probability, loomed that southern radical disunionists, who refused to believe that Lincoln and the Republicans were anything but abolitionists, would move to precipitate a military confrontation with the North and forestall Lincoln from displaying any moderation or forbearance towards them. But whatever fears Seward may have harbored that this much bleaker outcome might take place, the senator did not communicate those darker thoughts to young Mr. Adams until mid-February, following Lincoln's unfortunate remarks about "coercion" at Indianapolis. News of that speech brought gloom to the countenances of Seward and the Adamses, for they realized the negative impact which a statement like that could have on Upper South Unionists fearful of "coercion" by the incoming Republican president.[1] Henry Adams, who had up to that time given a hopeful portrayal of Washington events for his *Advertiser* readers, did not pen any newspaper letters during the latter parts of February and therefore never mentioned the change in Seward's attitude by mid-February. Adams also chose not to relate this in his March 3 *Advertiser* letter or his "Great Secession Winter" essay. Instead he concentrated in both of those writings on the ultimate success of Seward, whether mostly bluff or not, in retaining the loyalty of the border slave states to the Union until March 4.

Adams wrote no more letters to the Boston paper after March 3. He did attend the inaugural ball for President Abraham Lincoln on March 4. In his autobiography he confessed that, in this only encounter with Lincoln, he mistakenly did not form a very favorable impression of the new chief executive.[2] He left Washington to return to Boston to study law, despite his lack of enthusiasm for law as his life's profession. Again his father rescued him from this unhappy prospect. President Lincoln, at the advice of Secretary of State Seward and others, appointed Charles Francis Adams in mid-March as U.S. minister to Great Britain, and the elder Adams called upon Henry to be his private secretary in London.

Southern secessionist leaders, as it turned out, did not share the sense of restraint and forbearance of Seward and the Adamses, but instead adopted an opposite agenda. With Unionists, conditional or not, recently triumphant in border slave state elections, legislatures, and conventions, moderation by the new Republican administration and further delay in secession by the border states were the last things for which the Deep South Confederates wanted to allow time. A separate nation of only seven states would simply be too weak to last by itself. If the situation remained unchanged for much longer, and Lincoln undertook no "coercion" against the seven, southern radicals feared that a Unionist reaction, exactly what Republicans had predicted, might begin in the states of the recently crafted Confederacy itself. That such a movement could then lead any of the original seven seceding states to rejoin the Union would cause others to follow, and the Confederacy would quickly collapse. Thus, southern disunionists became convinced that they needed to undertake some polarizing action in order to wean some or all of the border slave states from their Unionist attachments. If President Lincoln had so far refrained from committing an "overt act" of aggression against the Confederacy, then the Confederate radicals would do something to force his hand. Their opportunity came when Lincoln attempted to resupply the federal garrison at Ft. Sumter in April 1861. Rather than permit the Republican administration to maintain this shadow of federal sovereignty in their midst, the Confederates bombarded the Charleston harbor fort into surrender. In response, President Lincoln called for volunteers to put down the rebellion. Four more states—Virginia, North Carolina, Tennessee, and Arkansas—chose to consider Lincoln's move to be "coercion" and declared themselves seceded from the Union, and the four joined the Southern Confederacy. The American Civil War began.[3]

A few weeks later, on May 1, Charles Francis Adams departed for Great Britain aboard a steamship, along with Mrs. Adams and three of their children, including Henry. Ambassador Adams won lasting fame during the Civil War as a supremely talented diplomat. Using a mixture of politeness and forcefulness, Adams played a major role in preventing serious British intervention in the conflict, intervention which could have only aided the Confederacy. Henry Adams served his father dutifully as his private secretary, but would have preferred the chance to do military service in the Union Army. His brother Charles Jr., who had remained behind in Massachusetts, did join the army and proved himself a worthy officer on the battlefield.

Henry Adams read a lot and socialized with British literati and others while serving as his father's secretary, but, outside of a few newspaper reports, he did not resume serious writing until after the war. He began writing historical articles for journals in 1867, and taught history at Harvard for seven years after returning from Europe in 1868. Adams also produced two novels, *Democracy* (1880) and *Esther* (1884), but he seemed much more adept at and comfortable with writing history—biographical works on Albert Gallatin (1879) and John Randolph (1882), and an edited collection of documents on New England Federalism (1877). Following a sojourn in Asia after the untimely death of his wife, Marian, in 1885, Henry Adams returned to the United States and immersed himself in writing his famous nine-volume history of the administrations of presidents Jefferson and Madison (1889–1891). After completion of this monumental historical work, Adams spent the next several years traveling with friends in various parts of the world. While in France he became fascinated with architecture, cathedrals, and the thirteenth century, which led to the publication in 1904 of *Mont-Saint-Michel and*

Chartres, a pioneering work by an American in the field of medieval studies. His autobiographical *The Education of Henry Adams* was printed in 1906. Typically underestimating the value of his contributions, Henry Adams published these latter two works—today probably considered his most important—originally in small privately circulated editions for his friends. Adams died in 1918 at the age of 80.

The letters which Henry Adams wrote for the *Boston Advertiser* during the Secession Winter were part of his preparation for his later work. The letters reveal a young man, who, even in his early twenties, was a keen observer of events and a talented writer. Unfortunately, the newspaper correspondence he wrote as he observed the day-to-day unfolding of the secession crisis has been largely neglected. But, like the observations and commentaries of the other Washington correspondents, Adams's letters to the *Advertiser* were an important contribution to the record of the great sectional conflict between North and South. Historians attempting to understand more fully the events leading to the Civil War would do well to examine the letters written by Adams and other Washington correspondents for the newspapers of the time, just as they examine and analyze any other historical evidence from the press and other sources in their research. One prescient northern editor in the secession crisis recognized the significant contribution which newspapers were making for future generations of historians:[4]

> We are living history in these exciting times, and the historians are the newspaper writers, reporters and correspondents. To be sure, some of them make mistakes at times, and each day's paper is not always an exactly accurate record of each day's events. But the future historian will be able to winnow the solid grains of fact from the chaff of fancy and rumor, and the very sheet which we print today, may at a future time be closely scanned by some patient student, in his search for the actual facts concerning the mad attempt at revolution got up by some of the Southern States of the American Union in the year 1861.

The newspaper letters of the young Washington correspondent Henry Adams, presented together in this book for the first time since their original publication, constitute a part of that contemporary newspaper record, and the modern researcher can now evaluate the contribution of these letters to the study of those last fateful months prior to the Civil War.

NOTES

1. Crofts, *Reluctant Confederates,* 243–244.

2. H. Adams, *Education,* 83. In his "Great Secession Winter" essay, Henry Adams adopted a somewhat ambivalent attitude toward Lincoln, on the one hand seeming to fault him for not coordinating policy with the Republicans in Washington better and on the other hand showing an appreciation for the Herculean task Lincoln faced when he finally arrived in Washington. To Adams, it was Seward who filled the leadership vacuum for the Republicans during the crisis. H. Adams, "Great Secession Winter," 25–26.

3. See Richard N. Current's 1961 essay "The Confederates and the First Shot" in his *Speaking of Abraham Lincoln: The Man and His Meaning for Our Times* (Urbana: University of Illinois Press, 1983), 61–78.

4. Philadelphia *Daily Evening Bulletin,* January 9, 1861.

INDEX